The **Radio**
H A N D B O O K

....

The Radio Handbook is a comprehensive guide to the theory, histor practice of radio broadcasting. Pete Wilby and Andy Conroy conside rationale behind radio production, the organisation of the radio sta and the scope of its technology, and the ways in which the radio text nects with the cultural experience of its listeners.

The Radio Handbook offers in-depth practical advice on every aspec radio, with different sections on learning about radio; radio styles; ad on setting up a radio station; the tools of radio broadcasting; the im tance of the voice in broadcasting; production techniques; and finally programme itself, including tips on covering events such as electio sport and outside broadcasts.

The Radio Handbook discusses the theoretical and ethical aspects of radi journalism as well as its practical side, enabling students to develop a informed understanding of how and why radio works. It will be essen reading for anyone studying or hoping to work in today's radio indus

Pete Wilby is Senior Lecturer in Communications Studies at Cove University and an experienced broadcaster. **Andy Conroy** is a produ specialising in news and current affairs at BBC CWR, the BBC radi Coventry and Warwickshire. He has worked for the BBC since the of fifteen.

Media Practice

edited by James Curran, Goldsmiths' College, University of London

•••

The *Media Practice* handbooks are comprehensive resource books for students of media and journalism, and for anyone planning a career as a media professional. Each handbook combines a clear introduction to understanding how the media work with practical information about the structure, processes and skills involved in working in today's media industries, providing not only a guide on 'how to do it' but also a critical reflection on contemporary media practice.

•••

Also in this series:

The Newspapers
H A N D B O O K

Richard Keeble

The **Radio**
H A N D B O O K

Pete **Wilby** and *Andy* **Conroy**

London *and* New York

First published 1994
by Routledge
11 New Fetter Lane, London EC4P 4EE

Simultaneously published in the USA and Canada
by Routledge
29 West 35th Street, New York, NY 10001

Typeset in Times by Florencetype, Kewstoke, Avon
Printed and bound in Great Britain by Biddles Ltd, Guildford and King's Lynn

British Library Cataloguing in Publication Data
A catalogue record for this book is available from the British Library

Library of Congress Cataloging in Publication Data

Wilby, Pete (Peter)
    The radio handbook/Pete Wilby and Andy Conroy.
        p. cm. – (Media practice)
    Includes bibliographical references and index.
        1. Radio broadcasting–Handbooks, manuals, etc. I. Conroy, Andy
    (Andrew) II. Title. III. Series.
    PN1991.55.W56 1994
    384.54–dc20   93–44370

ISBN 0–415–09466–6 (hbk) 0–415–09467–4 (pbk)

Contents

Illustrations

Note on the text

Personal pronouns can lead us into a maze of complex forms of written expression which may be politically correct but can prove tiresome and confusing to the reader while distracting her/him (QED) from the main point of the argument. We have therefore decided to maintain 'gender consistency' in chapters; in some chapters we refer to presenters, listeners, engineers, station managers and all other protagonists exclusively as 'he', 'him', etc. and in other chapters we refer to them all as 'she', 'her', etc.

Acknowledgements

We would like to thank all the staff at BBC CWR for their help and co-operation, in particular Paul Carlisle, Steve Woodhall, Kevin Atkinson, Gordon Fudge, Caroline Wilson, Richard Ventre and Charles Hodkinson. CWR staff, past and present, also feature in the photographs. Our thanks to them: Maurice Dee, Daniel Markham, Jim Lee, Fran Daly, Bernice Williams, Rachel Hele, Sally Pringle.

Special mention needs to be made of the station's Managing Editor, Andy Wright, whose support and wisdom ensured the successful completion of this project. We are especially grateful for his agreement for CWR to provide a case study for Chapter 3.

There were two other key players for BBC in the Midlands without whom this book would not have been possible. Owen Bentley, for so many years a champion of BBC local radio, was one of the first to offer his support to the idea of a practitioner and academic working together on this project. His successor, Head of Local Programmes (Midlands), Rick Thompson built on this with detailed advice as well as vital support.

Also within the BBC, we thank: Keith Salmon – Managing Editor, BBC Radio Norfolk; Andy Shiells – BBC Journalist Training Department; Gerald Hyne-Haycock – Regional News Training Scheme, BBC Bristol; and the Copyright and Artists Rights Department in Wood Lane.

We thank the following organisations for their assistance: the Radio Authority; the Broadcasting Complaints Commission; the Broadcasting Standards Council; the Radio Academy; RAJAR; the Henley Centre; the Radio Training Unit based at Leicester Sound FM; AA Roadwatch; Coventry City Council and Burton Group plc for permission to use photographs. We also thank Kate O'Connor of Skillset; Chris Radley of Mercia FM/Xtra AM; John Spearman of Classic FM; Ivor Yorke of the National Council for the Training of Broadcast Journalists; Rod Pilling at the University of Central England; Liz Green at Stratford-upon-Avon College, Warwickshire; and David French at Coventry University. Special thanks to Lynn Baughan at Stratford-upon-Avon College for her comments on the text and overall support.

For background material we thank Simon Lett; for the photographs, Martin Neeves and Stephen Wright; and for the diagrams, Chris Baxter who was also one of the final group of people we would like to target for our appreciation. These are the PDQ pioneers – students, some from Coventry Polytechnic (as it was then called) and some from schools in the city, who came together in January 1991 at CWR to produce the youth programme *PDQ*. They proved – and their successors are still proving – that the marriage of theory and practice can generate a better, more challenging radio experience. Their success in securing full-time employment in both television and radio in Britain and the rest of Europe also shows that programme makers do reward talent and innovation when they see it.

PW/AC
October 1993

Introduction

....

Radio is an intimate medium. These days, people rarely sit round the kitchen table in groups to listen to the radio. It addresses each listener as an individual. When a radio is playing to a group of people, it is often to function as 'background' sound in a place of work activity – the hairdressers or the garage – where listeners are able to entertain their private thoughts, their silent dialogue with the presenter or their personal associations with each record played, while performing their routine tasks.

The obvious distinctive feature of radio – the fact that it does not demand the virtually exclusive level of audience attention that the press and television require for effective communication – emphasises this quality of intimacy. Listeners can carry a radio with them. It can provide company in the kitchen, on the factory floor, in a traffic jam on the motorway, or in a hostage cell on the other side of the world. Of all the 'mass' media, radio offers the greatest potential for building up a one-to-one relationship with each member of its audience.

Radio's product is a combination of sound and silence. The chances are that its sound will consist mainly of music if you are listening to an independent local radio station, or of the human voice if you are listening to a local BBC station. Whether music- or speech-based, a radio station usually develops its own 'voice', not only through its jingles or even the accent of its presenters, but also through its timing, its mood, its intonation, its rate of variation (or lack of it) in presentation style, its method of packaging its pre-recorded items, its sense of urgency, its sense of humour. Listeners may be hard-pressed to define the 'voice' of their favourite radio station, but once the codes and conventions of the radio text – its content and its mode of delivery – have been 'learned', most experienced listeners are able to search the tuning dial at random and quickly guess what *type* of station they've found, if not identify the actual station.

The purpose of this book is to look behind the station's 'voice' to uncover the organisational structure and operational principles that underpin the listening experience that radio constructs. We shall highlight the influence of three factors in determining the organisational structure of a radio station and the way this 'constructs' the station's style of output: the application of available technology, the performance skills of the broadcasters themselves and the conditions of the 'market' in which radio operates.

Technology

When people visit a radio station, technology is the most visible feature, which arguably has considerable impact on their understanding of what radio is 'about'. Many courses and textbooks may give the impression that an understanding of how the equipment works is the key to successful broadcasting. A presenter sits at a microphone. Her voice is heard through a speaker. Between these points of input and output exists a complex and, for the uninitiated, mystifying jungle of faders, meters, trim controls, telephone balance units, talkback systems, all the paraphernalia of a studio desk which seemingly requires the co-ordination of a space shuttle controller to operate effectively.

Technology is clearly significant in the construction of radio's relationship with its listeners and part of what we will say in this book is about the technical equipment that radio broadcasters work with: in particular, how it may be used in different ways to produce different types of output. It is not our purpose to provide a handbook on how to 'drive' a desk or operate a portable tape recorder and readers will hopefully not require a degree in electronic engineering to understand the 'technological references'. However, we do provide a glossary of specialist terminology used in this book (pp. 249–67) plus some chapter notes where applicable on the basic technical principles of how radio works.

Performance

The performance of the presenter, even with the simplest of technology, has a major impact on listeners' perceptions of the image of a radio station. The presenter may take on one of a range of roles: disc jockey, continuity announcer, newsreader, interviewer, devil's advocate in a phone-in discussion – all of these, and many others, constitute components of the radio station's 'corporate' personality. The ways in which the presenter uses her voice, her choice of vocabulary, her accent and her expression are powerful elements of radio's discourse and determiners of the distance between the presenter and the listener. Thus part of what we will discuss concerns the radio station's mode of address: the ways in which the individual performance of the presenter establishes and reflects the different communicative roles of the station and the different styles of interaction between that station and its listeners.

The 'market'

From within the perspective of the radio industry itself, the 'voice' heard by the listener is further seen as the manifestation of a market-orientated process. This view of radio is not always enthusiastically shared within some parts of the industry. The first few months of John Birt's tenure as Director General of the BBC were characterised by an often heated debate on the language, practices and ethics of business operation and whether these rest easily with the 'public service' role of the Corporation and its traditional working practices. Despite such reservations, the nature and character of British radio in the 1990s – both independent and BBC – have constituted a response to such concepts as the market, competitiveness and cost-effectiveness.

Within the market economy model, radio is a mature product serving a diverse market of consumers (as opposed to 'listeners'). The success of a radio station in building a relationship with its audience may be explained in these terms through its ability to establish a strong brand image and to recognise, or indeed create a niche market. With a greater tendency for stations to specialise in musical styles, or to relate to specific audience profiles and interests, commercial radio can and does attract advertisers through offering access to an audience whose lifestyle and consumer preference can be defined in some detail. Add to this the relative cheapness of radio advertising alongside television and it is not surprising that radio in Britain is something of a growth industry.

In 1993, the United Kingdom was served by eight nationwide radio stations,[1] four BBC 'national–regional' services,[2] thirty-nine BBC local radio stations, 144 individual ILR services[3] and numerous community stations, hospital radio services, special events stations, campus radio stations and other forms of in-house radio broadcasting. As listener profiles and tastes are becoming more clearly defined, the prospects are that radio will continue to grow, diversify and weave a complicated and significant pattern of cultural production.

Foundations for innovative broadcasting

Our aim is to build on a simple model of presenter, microphone, radio receiver and listener to examine current practices in professional radio production. But rather than set out a rigid set of principles, we will discuss the notions of 'good' or 'professional' practices in radio broadcasting by highlighting some of the values and rationales that determine the nature of such practices. At the heart of all radio stations and their systems of organisation lies a common skill – the ability to communicate with a fellow human being. This is compounded by layers of further skills vital to all radio stations whatever their market. Such skills may be identified as generic or, to use today's educational jargon, 'transferable', reflecting the greater level of autonomy and self-management required of modern broadcasters. They include timekeeping, self-evaluation, the ability to take calculated risks, make instant decisions, take on a leadership role or listen to others. Or, increasingly, individual broadcasters are required to demonstrate a wider range of job-specific skills in order to function as adaptable members of a flexible organisation: interviewing, editing, newsreading, producing recorded 'packages' or operating equipment based on wide-ranging forms of technology.

These skills are developed through practice and experience rather than reading books such as this, but do not in themselves add up to an effective broadcaster. This book is based on the premise that a *critical* under-standing of broadcasting practices and a recognition of the values that make up radio's professional framework will not only provide insights into radio as a means of cultural production, reproduction and action, but also produce better broadcasters.

Rather than dwell on a possible 'conflict of interests' between media training and education, we would argue that broadcasters who possess the ability to think critically about their own values and practices are necessary if radio is to function as a dynamic medium that relates effectively to its listeners' values and experiences. A 'do as we do' approach to radio training can only expect to (and only deserves to) produce a generation of broadcasters who work to a formula and provide the foundation for broadcasting which, while 'slick' and 'professional', tends to become bland, anodyne and cliché-ridden.

Students well versed in the techniques of criticism and able to apply these to current practices in media production are in a good position, as future members of media organisations, to innovate and articulate arguments for reviewing and sweeping aside the ingrained ideas and practices that lead to stale and unimaginative broadcasting. To be valid and worthwhile, however, criticism should be based on an informed view of working practices and principles in media organisations.

Media and communications courses, based on a strong tradition of critical theory, could run the risk of 'falling from grace' through incor-porating such instrumental knowledge. The pressures on courses to gain recognition from professional bodies in the media industry, and to meet students' own vocational aspirations in this area, have opened up ques-tions about whether the more distanced, academic 'position' adopted by media and cultural theorists up until now is likely to be undermined. This concern has been highlighted in our professional experience with Communication Studies undergraduates at Coventry University on work placement with the BBC local radio station for Coventry and Warwickshire, BBC CWR.

The placement scheme encourages students' capacity to evaluate and analyse critically the production of 'popular' radio and reflects both an 'academic' and an instrumental priority. The academic aim of the scheme is to inform the students of the working environment of radio such that their analysis of media texts and practices carries greater authority and draws on the evidence of their own experience. The instrumental priority is to 'put the skids' under existing practices and to scrutinise unspoken assumptions, such that radio genuinely relates to the cultural experience of listeners and perhaps (dare we hope?) enlightens and elevates that experience.

This is not simply a mission to improve radio for the sake of it. Sue Farr, Head of Marketing for BBC Network Radio, states in an interview with Paul Donovan,[4] 'There's a growing realisation that markets are fragmenting and consumers are getting much more sophisticated about what they will and won't listen to.' Donovan remarks that 'radio's new role as a personal medium offering more choice and intense listener loyalty will give the wireless a new lease of life.' As radio enjoys its restored status as a valued and, in Donovan's terms, 'sexy' commodity, it offers a challenge for today's new broadcasters to cross barriers and explore new terrains of creativity.

It is not our purpose here to provide an account of the development of student contribution to mainstream broadcasting but it is worth stating that our experience in co-ordinating students' academic and professional activities through their work in BBC local radio has demonstrated a need for a textbook that supports their learning. In simple terms, what we aim to examine is not only 'how to do it' but also 'why is it done in this way?' and possibly 'is that the best reason you can come up with – why not do it *that* way?' An appreciation of the constraints and opportunities of technology, audience profiles, legislation and commercial considerations should encourage students of media and communication to explore and evaluate alternative ways of constructing meaningful radio texts, to undertake voyages of discovery away from the tried and tested routes often implicit in training manuals, and to allow greater scope for initiative, innovation and dynamism in 'quality' radio.

A summary of our argument

It is with these considerations in mind that we begin this book with a chapter on current education and training provision for British radio within the curriculum and provided by the industry itself. Here we set out a case for promoting students' recognition of the processes of media education and of the values and priorities that these processes reveal. Broadcasters themselves set high standards in assessing the educational background, skills and experience of new recruits and are often rigorous in their own training programmes; this is to be expected in a situation where the maintenance of their autonomy rests on their own accountability. What needs to be recognised, however, is the danger that media training and education that lacks a reflexive and critical approach can foster 'safe' broadcasting practices – a new generation of broadcasters doing what they do well within the terms of a rigid professional perspective but seeing no room for alternative perspectives.

The subsequent chapters aim to describe, discuss and rationalise professional practices and organisational methods that operate within the modern radio station. We begin with style, on the basis that a carefully considered and clearly articulated style policy determines these practices. Thus in Chapter 2 we consider the place of the radio station within a community of listeners (or the market), the nature of the relationship that a station may offer to its audience and the mechanisms for 'branding' and constructing a public image of that station.

From this basis, we are able to focus in Chapter 3 on the working environment and internal organisation of a radio station. The 'tools of broadcasting' discussed in Chapter 4 – portable recorders, desks and various devices and media that play back recorded sound – form a vital part of this environment. A rationale for professional broadcasting practice is developed from the simple model in Chapter 5 of a presenter talking into a microphone to a more complex range of production techniques addressed in Chapter 6 – packages, trails, debates and phone-ins, and so on.

Beyond the identification and examination of production techniques, we consider in Chapter 7 the rationale behind a programme itself: the way it is planned and structured and how this in turn reinforces the station's image and role in the life and community experience of the listener. A number of 'ground rules' may be apparent in the routine broadcasting of regularly scheduled programmes, although the responsiveness and flexibility of a radio station is put to the test in one-off 'special events' broadcasts which are also discussed in this chapter.

Chapter 8 considers the broad topic of accountability and the various perspectives of the audience that underpin much of the preceding discussion: the intimate interlocutor, the member of a listening community whose identity and position are constructed by the discourse of radio, the consumer in a market-led economy. Accountability as perceived by the broadcaster, who some might say is driven by the needs and wants of the audience, is referred to here along with the station's overall accountability to the public in terms of ethical broadcasting practices and operating within a legal framework.

Our book focuses throughout on the practices and organisation of the UK radio industry, local and national. Local radio will often provide the initial working experience for those embarking on a career in radio broadcasting, although much of the discussion in this book relates also to practices and principles in national radio broadcasting. Indeed where examples are drawn from national networks to illustrate points made, this is because these stations are more widely accessible to readers as listeners; the points themselves apply equally to the local radio experience. Our final chapter offers a brief speculation on future changes and developments in local and national radio – from technological, commercial and political perspectives – that could affect the working lives of students who do take up radio as a career.

At the end of each chapter, we provide a selection of activities and points for discussion. This was initially at the suggestion of lecturers in media studies whom we consulted during the preparation of this book, and the process of devising these activities proved revealing. It highlighted some important resource issues in radio education – for example, how does a tutor establish aspects of radio's character, potential and impact with a large class and not enough tape recorders to go round? But more than that, it enabled us to think through and demonstrate the key point of this book – that radio is about creativity first and technique second. A group of enthusiastic students can develop a strong creative sense which will enable them to produce innovative radio, quite often through team exercises and plenary discussion.

However, the success of these activities depends on students' willingness to listen to radio – not just their favourite stations but the whole spectrum available on the tuning dial. Students can probably learn more about radio by listening to it than reading textbooks. Perhaps this book will enable them to listen more effectively.

In designing the plan of this book we have been conscious of the strengths and limitations of existing approaches to the study of radio and have attempted to address issues that have perhaps fallen through the net up until now. Texts that document radio's history or spell out the radio profession's view of 'good practice' in broadcasting play essential roles in students' understanding of this universal medium of mass communication. Equally important in our view is a recognition of the values and experiences, indeed the historical precedents that have created these notions of 'good practice' to allow students to gain a fuller understanding of radio. While this book does not attempt to itemise these factors in full, it is written in a spirit of healthy critical reflection to promote not only students' knowledge of the medium but also their motivation to become involved and seek to produce more dynamic and more relevant radio programmes. Most importantly, it is written in recognition that any 'techniques' in broadcasting that we may suggest could work towards a homogenisation of radio output, but what radio really thrives on is individuality. Therefore, in the interests of securing a future for excellent radio, it is not the purpose of this book to reinforce the tried and tested.

It is designed to unlock the innovation that lies within all of us and it is dedicated to those who dare to be better.

1 Learning about radio

. . . .

Training needs for a developing industry

INDUSTRY-LED training schemes teach the principles of radio broadcasting in terms of what is 'good practice'. Courses in media and communications apply theoretical frameworks to the study of radio, treating it as a communication process, its texts as structures of meaning and its output as evidence of a consuming culture. Radio training and education form the starting point for this study. A consideration of how radio is taught both within and outside the industry offers a basis for understanding how it is organised, how its output is 'constructed' and how it functions as a product of our culture.

One vital factor for radio's healthy development is a workforce which possesses not only the relevant technical skills, but a broad base of academic skills and knowledge, an excellent command of English and other languages and a strong motivation to innovate and create imaginative listening experiences. An insight into the nature of the radio industry, its self-perception and priorities in broadcasting practice can be gained from how it perceives its own training and educational needs. In 1989, the Head of the Radio Training Unit for Midlands Radio plc, Heather Purdey wrote:

> the whole radio industry is crying out for competent, skilled people to work within it in the future . . . Training in basic broadcasting skills is the first step to high quality radio and must be practical, so that trainees can learn the fundamentals of how a studio and its equipment work, editing, interviewing and presentation techniques and the basics of broadcast law.[1]

Equipment, techniques and the law are the three key themes in many in-house radio training schemes. They are areas that can be taught relatively quickly and precisely and, with these 'basics' under their belts, trainee broadcasters may presumably develop skills as communicators with something worthwhile to say to their listeners.

The need for more provision in basic training is regarded within the radio industry as essential, reflecting a recognition of radio's growth potential, particularly in the wake of the 1990 Broadcasting Act and the heady atmosphere of deregulation. The outcome of the Act for radio has been the formation of the Radio Authority which is responsible for regulating and licensing all non-BBC sound services in the United Kingdom – previously one of the roles of the Independent Broadcasting Authority (IBA). The Radio Authority's three main tasks are to plan frequencies, appoint licensees and regulate programming and advertising.[2] While implementing codes of practice on engineering, programming, advertising and sponsorship, the Radio Authority seeks to encourage fair but unfettered competition between these services on both a local and national level as well as aiming to increase listener choice. There are fewer explicit restrictions on advertising and sponsorship, and independent stations are no longer obliged to carry 'public service' items or regular news bulletins.

In effect, this provides fertile ground for more radio stations to be established. On a national level we have already seen the launch of Classic FM and Virgin 1215. The former meets one of the requirements of the Act that there should be a service which broadcasts music that is not pop while the latter specialises in so-called AOR (adult-orientated rock). This ostensibly competes with the BBC's pop and rock music flagship Radio 1, despite its restriction to medium wave transmission using AM as opposed to the superior sound quality of the FM transmissions possible on the VHF wavelengths available across the country to Radio 1.[3] In November 1993, the Radio Authority advertised the licence for a third independent national service, which is required by the 1990 Act to be predominantly speech-based.[4] The climate overall points to a healthy growth in local, regional and national UK radio in years to come.

Two more factors point to a growth in radio and a consequently urgent need for more trained broadcasters. One is technological. Quite simply, it will be possible to broadcast a good quality signal on a larger number of frequencies than at present, thanks to the development of digital audio broadcasting (DAB). This makes it possible to broadcast on many frequencies from one transmitter. Digital signals are already bounced off satellites to enable the simple and relatively inexpensive distribution of stereo sound, such that any local station with decoding facilities can carry live coverage of sports events or rock concerts meeting high specifications in sound quality. Digital technology even offers a potential for telephone lines to carry 'broadcast-quality' signals such that radio stations could simply 'dial up' and transmit music with no discernable loss of sound quality.

The other factor in radio's growth is the audience. Partly because new radio stations are marketing themselves effectively, and partly because of changes in lifestyle anyway, radio has lost its 'television without pictures' status and regained the recognition it had been given in its own right before television's mass popularity. More people are tuning in and incorporating radio's output into their day-to-day lives.

There is at least one radio in most UK households. Radios with sophisticated tuning technology are becoming standard features on new cars rolling off the production line.[5] Every week during October–December 1992, an average of 89 per cent of the United Kingdom population – i.e. 41.6 million people – were tuned into a radio station. Listeners during that time period averaged over twenty-one hours per week of listening time (Policy Studies Institute 1993: 42–3). There is evidence also of an increase in the popularity of radio in the future against a decrease in that of television. This is concluded in a recent programme of research undertaken by the Henley Centre for Forecasting which cites the increasing number of leisure attractions outside the home plus more holidays as reasons for television's relative decline in significance. The research suggests that conditions are right for growth in radio's popularity because of its versatility as a medium: 'more car ownership, the growth of single person households, and increasing time pressure on people, taken together suggest that radio listening will rise over the next few years'.[6] This is compounded by a marked decrease in the attraction of television relative to radio. An opinion survey commissioned by the Henley Centre found that 60 per cent of respondents would 'rather be out doing something than watching TV' while 42 per cent considered that 'most television programmes nowadays are dull and predictable'. Only 16 per cent said the same about radio.[7]

Radio's popularity should not be surprising. It is a medium that touches the lives of nearly everyone. It is accessible, direct, versatile and capable of providing up-to-the-minute information on any topic, to more people and in the shortest time, than any other medium. It can fill and colour our lives without demanding our total attention. It can stimulate imagination; people may watch television with their eyes but they listen to radio with their minds. Furthermore, radio can be therapeutic. It can provide solace, boost morale and enable listeners to make sense of many aspects of their lives. It is especially effective in these ways because radio is an appropriate medium for individual or isolated reception in any location, unlike television which tends to address the viewer in a domestic social setting.

These features of radio illustrate its wide-ranging and pervasive role in our cultural experience. Radio has always been important through the part it plays in our day-to-day lives. As the Henley Centre research suggests, changes in our lifestyles have given radio greater significance. It provides vital, up-to-the-minute information on weather and traffic conditions to a nation in which private road transport is increasingly more widespread (there are currently twenty million cars on British roads), while public transport systems are on the decline, especially for rural communities. Radio offers a forum for public phone-in discussion on any topical issue and greater numbers of listeners are now becoming participators in live interactive programmes. A not uncommon image of the 1990s is that of the private motorist using a car phone to take part in a public discussion on air, a modern echo perhaps of the 1970s and 1980s CB (Citizens' Band) radio culture.

As the medium of radio increases in significance in people's daily routines, and as the political and economic environment encourages a growth in the number of stations competing for the attention of different segments of a listening market, the radio industry is faced with the need to train more people more quickly to make full use of the opportunities available to it. To be effective in developing people with the necessary motivation and skills – and to be cost-effective – training in radio increasingly involves co-operation between the radio stations and other institutions, particularly in further and higher education.

National Vocational Qualifications

I N his discussion on the role of media education in postmodern society, Desmond Bell noted the increasing pressure on educators to design courses to meet the training needs of media industries and commented:

> We must, I believe, reject this narrow vocationalism. For, if media studies students are favoured in recruitment to the media industries – which they are – it is primarily because they represent a pool of very bright and creative young people and not because they possess some specific set of technical skills in media production.[8]

The benefits of co-operation between the media industries and the education sector, in the teaching of media-related skills and knowledge, have demonstrated that the relationship is founded on something stronger than a marriage of convenience. Bell states for example that students' involvement in production work as part of a media studies course might develop those production skills which the industry is seeking, but also serves to teach students about the material and economic constraints on media output and the management of scarce resources. Media organisations themselves are increasingly looking for graduate recruits with broader backgrounds of knowledge to undertake postgraduate training for areas such as broadcast journalism. A leaflet issued by the National Council for the Training of Broadcast Journalists advises would-be journalists to gain qualifications in subjects such as politics, history and economics, but states that these will not guarantee a job in broadcast journalism: 'What you need now is a place on a company training scheme or an NCTBJ recognised course'.[9]

The pattern emerging in media training, therefore, is one in which the education sector is seen to provide basic production skills, transferable skills and expertise in particular subject areas, while the industry itself

11

offers more intensive, hands-on training to develop competence and expertise in media production through in-house and industry-led schemes and through approval and monitoring of specialist courses provided by colleges or universities. In the near future, the development of trainees' competence in radio production techniques will be assessed through the system of qualifications established through the National Council for Vocational Qualifications (NCVQ).

The establishment of national standards in media-related skills leading to National Vocational Qualifications (NVQs) or Scottish Vocational Qualifications (SVQs) is being co-ordinated by Skillset. This is the 'industry lead body' which represents the training interests of the broadcast, film and video industries in Britain and which is responsible for industry standards – detailed statements of areas of competence that need to be demonstrated by trainees to achieve specific N/SVQs at particular levels. Along with the Open University in England and Wales and SCOTVEC (the Scottish Vocational Education Council) in Scotland, Skillset is also able to award NVQs for competences in film, video and broadcasting.

The fact that Skillset does not address itself exclusively to the radio industry means that trainees can build up a portfolio of N/SVQs awarded for work undertaken in, say, video production which also show competences in areas relative to radio. These can act as building blocks; trainees can identify and demonstrate further competences that combine with those already set out in their portfolios to indicate an overall skills level in radio production.

Skillset is managed by representatives of the film and broadcasting industries and trade unions and works with a steering group, key representatives and consultants from a wide range of film and broadcasting interests. The outcome of this consultation is an agreed set of national standards in a number of areas of competence, ranging from camera operation, graphics and animation to set design, costume, make-up and hairdressing. Competence areas of interest covered by Skillset and relevant to radio are: sound, research, journalism and factual writing, production co-ordination and production management.

To gain an NVQ in sound, trainees need to demonstrate competence in a number of operations or 'units'. For example, they provide evidence of ability to use different types of microphone, adjust sound levels, record, edit, playback, as well as ability to work effectively with colleagues and evaluate their own performance. Similar breakdowns of units exist for all competence areas identified; as trainees build up these blocks through demonstrating specific competences – usually through supervised production work – so they will build up a portfolio of NVQs to indicate to employers their proven skills level overall.[10]

One feature of the NCVQ system is that an N/SVQ in a specific area, whether it was gained through work experience, production work on a recognised course or taking part in an industry-led short course, will itself be recognised in all areas of the industry, rather like a form of currency.

Prior to the introduction of this system, trainees could attend all manner of courses or forms of work experience in radio and come away with any of a range of possible qualifications, or indeed no qualification at all, simply a certificate of attendance or name of a referee.

Industry-led training

VARIOUS short courses and programmes of work experience in radio are available to people other than full-time students, all of which focus on competence, technique and developing specific abilities to 'do the job' of radio broadcasting.

The BBC runs courses for would-be broadcast journalists including an eighteen-month training scheme for local radio reporters available to anyone without a formal qualification in journalism who can get through a rigorous process of recruitment. Trainees begin in London but could find themselves sent to any BBC local radio station in the country at different stages of the scheme. If they are successful, their names may be entered into a 'reporters reserve' which makes them available to any BBC radio station that may need them, although there is no guarantee of a full-time job. This scheme is usually advertised in the national press in late September and training itself starts the following summer. Applicants receive a recruitment pack including a cassette on which specified items should be recorded.

There is also a regional scheme for training journalists, run by the BBC for both television and radio. Thirteen trainees are recruited each year such that each trainee is linked with one of the BBC's thirteen regional centres. Most of the formal training takes place in Bristol. To be recruited, trainees need a good academic record (degree or equivalent) and evidence of personal qualities and knowledge of current events to suggest an interest and ability in journalism. Again this scheme is advertised and selection of successful applicants takes place in the summer although trainees are split into two groups starting in early September and early March.[11]

As radio stations become more prolific, opportunities for access to them are also on the increase. Hence the demand for training in radio techniques is growing, not only in schools and colleges but also within the wider community. For unemployed people seeking new vocational skills, a greater diversity of training programmes has developed, ranging from government-funded Community Service Volunteer schemes, often based at or supported by local radio stations, to the training syllabus in Media Techniques (Journalism and Radio) offered by the City and Guilds of London Institute (C&G 779) and taught in suitably resourced colleges across the country. Such training schemes are attractive not only to those contemplating broadcasting as a career but also to people who are increasingly dealing with radio broadcasters in their day-to-day lives, either as interviewees, spokespeople, public relations staff of local authorities or local industry, or indeed members of communities seeking to ensure fair representation in local radio coverage.

Several BBC and independent local radio stations offer CSV places to young unemployed people for whom the level of training is usually fairly basic, assuming no previous experience of radio work by the trainees. Nevertheless, within a short time, participants are recording material on portable recorders, performing basic editing functions and often gaining some experience in audio mixing and operating a studio desk. One advantage of the scheme is that it provides an opportunity to shine for people without academic qualifications but with a flair for radio that may not otherwise be realised. Working in a radio station means that CSV trainees can easily make themselves known to station staff and, if they are reasonably proficient, may be able to produce recorded packages or contribute in other ways to the station's output. In the near future, trainees on such programmes will be able to gain accreditation and recognition of their achievements through NVQs.

Some independent stations offer training opportunities for people already in the industry and for outsiders with schemes either based at individual radio stations or run through consortia of local stations in one area. The Radio Training Unit based at Leicester Sound FM, for example, offers a selection of ready-made and 'customised' short courses for beginners, print journalists and ILR employees in areas ranging from basic radio skills to music presentation techniques. The Unit also makes use of the technical and human resources of the radio station to train those at the 'receiving end' of broadcasting techniques, for example teaching local councillors to perform effectively when being interviewed on air.

Schemes such as these have important instrumental functions in providing vocational training and breaking down community barriers. While many successful broadcasters themselves gained a foothold in the industry through experience in campus and hospital radio, it is worth noting that mainstream routes into radio broadcasting as a career now also tend to cross academic territory. Much is expected of broadcasters in terms of technical, communicative and intellectual skills as well as confidence in a wide selection of subject areas. The terms 'education' and 'training', once widely regarded in media education to be pursuing different objectives, appear now to be moving closer together and complementing each other. Possessing an academic qualification is no longer seen simply as an indicator of a person's expertise in one subject but as evidence that the person has gone through a particular form of educational experience which has helped to develop such personal and transferable skills as self-management, interpersonal communication, literacy, numeracy, and so on. It is through developing these wider ranging areas of ability that a broad educational background, preferably to degree level, complements programmes of training in specific radio production techniques and produces a more flexible and adaptable (as well as a more creative) broadcaster.

The Training Enterprise and Education Directorate (TEED) of the Employment Department recognises this point from its own research into graduate opportunities and destinations in a wide range of careers.

Over half of new graduates are recruited for their general abilities rather than their subject expertise. In either case, evidence from labour market trends and employers indicates that there is a need for better prepared graduates who are able to adapt and learn new approaches. Most graduates are likely to change jobs at least three times during their working lives. Even if they do not change jobs, their jobs will change. Hence the importance of laying the foundations of adaptable flexible learning.

Brown 1991

If the need for today's graduates is to be flexible and adaptable in a changing work environment, this is especially true for radio. The industry looks to its staff to apply a broad range of skills and expertise on a regular basis and to be prepared to take on board new practices and new technologies as part of their day-to-day routine.

Radio as an academic subject

AT this point, it is worth considering the growing importance of radio in the non-vocational curriculum. The glamorous and visual media of film, television and – albeit to a less analytical extent – the press have received considerable academic attention as cultural forms in syllabuses ranging from liberal and general studies, through English literature to the specific disciplines of communication, media and cultural studies. Radio, on the other hand, has tended to be the 'Cinderella' of academic research and study. Its cultural significance is only beginning to receive wider recognition in academic circles. Learning material on radio has largely concentrated on two areas – the descriptive and historical analyses and studies, or the prescriptive, techniques-orientated ('how to do it') writings of radio professionals.[12] Media students have tended to study film and television in terms of their textual qualities, their means of relating to audience experience and their cultural significance, while students' encounters with radio have been largely along the lines of 'this is how programmes are made'.

When radio forms a component of media courses up to undergraduate level, it is often approached through assignments which combine technical competence in production work with the application of communication principles to programme making. BTEC National Diploma courses in Media Studies, while varying from college to college in specific content, place emphasis on integrated assignments where students can work in groups and – if they have opted to study radio – combine a focus on this medium with other 'units' or subject areas in the syllabus. Thus students

15

less interested in radio's technical operations can develop and demonstrate skills in other related areas: for example, the structure of the radio industry, scriptwriting, or relating text to the needs and interests of a clearly defined audience. Similarly, GCSE and A level courses in Media Studies and Communication Studies promote the skills and knowledge related to production work and media practice with a strong emphasis on reflection and evaluation. Project work is assessed not only for its final form but also for the evidence it provides of research, understanding of communication principles and development of generic communication skills.

In line with the academic tradition of British education, it is the university sector, rather than industry, that determines the scope of the A level syllabuses in Media and Communication Studies. However, as British universities take pains to shake off any suggestion of an 'ivory tower' image, they are now keen to emphasise their vocational role in preparing graduates for industry. Thus many undergraduate courses in media, communications and related areas provide opportunities for students to undertake production work in radio either using on-campus equipment or through work placements.

This concentration on broadcasting production techniques alongside an 'official' history of the development of radio reflects not only the industry's immediate priorities in radio education and training but also the demand of many students whose choices in education are largely governed by career aspirations. As a rule, students are not usually clear in their minds on what they will do with critical theory when they enter the world of paid employment. Perhaps not surprisingly, they often have a more focused idea of how they would apply the subject-specific skills of microphone technique, presentation and editing. These are precisely the skills that radio professionals seek in new recruits, along with the more fundamental skills of clear written and spoken communication. Hence, in comparison with the academic study of other media, radio education has taken on a somewhat functional role.

Alongside the descriptive and techniques-orientated approaches, however, students have encountered forms of radio text analysis. This is often designed to stimulate awareness of strategies employed in a 'sender to listener' process of communication. A critical study of scripts and output draws attention to conventions in production methods and representational codes that are specific to identified programme genres or styles. At a basic level, such study serves to demonstrate how radio producers 'deal with' the lack of a visual channel, perceived as a 'barrier' to communication. Arguably, analysis at these levels and for these purposes reinforces a vocational slant to education that became predominant throughout the 1980s with its focus on processes rather than structures. In the case of radio, it seemed to be asking 'what can we do with it?' rather than 'how does it position us?' as members of a listening community or culture.

As the subject areas of media and communication have become more widely available to pupils and students in the 1980s and 1990s, it is

1   On the air: this is a Communication Studies student broadcasting live from a radio car with a commentary on a traffic problem in Coventry, less than a year after she first turned up at the radio station to make coffee for Breakfast Show guests. For students there are three ways of gaining practical experience on radio: taking part in a work placement scheme; contributing to a specific youth programming project (if the station has one); or through individual contact and being there when needed. Reliable students quickly become capable – and are seen to be capable – such that they find themselves helping out in a wide range of responsible ways as and when the occasion arises.

usually the visual media that have occupied positions of the highest significance within the curriculum. One might argue that the pre-packaged, readily encoded visual image brings us a step nearer to a true representation of the world (via virtual reality perhaps?) than anything

that the imagination can produce. Courses address students as participators in a media culture of the tangibly visible. In many classrooms, the
VCR is a more frequently used piece of equipment than the audio cassette
recorder; it commands the attention of the eye more effectively, even if
it leaves the mind to its own devices.

Nevertheless, somewhere in this unco-ordinated pattern of the study of
radio lies the 'creative' use of the medium. This may be explored for
example through exercises in the planning and pre-production stages of
making a radio drama or documentary item. The inherent learning value
of such activities is widely recognised and they are not exclusive to media
or communications courses. Drawing on their familiar experience of
listening to radio – and on the acquisition of the unstated rules and codes
that underpin radio language and narrative – pupils and students have
become increasingly engaged in simulated production or pre-production
work, such as radio scriptwriting. This type of classroom activity is
designed to enhance skills in written communication generally; one has
to think carefully about communication processes when putting together
a message that seeks maximum impact in a verbal and non-visual form.
And it helps to stimulate an interest in radio itself plus an appreciation of
the particular skills involved in writing for this medium. From this, an
understanding may develop of the ways in which radio represents issues
and personalities – clearly a useful objective within the study of English,
drama, foreign languages, politics, and complementary studies to
vocational courses, as well as in media and communication studies
syllabuses.

The pattern of radio education in Britain may be inconsistent and not
clearly defined but this is not for want of academic research in and study
of radio texts, practices and audiences. There is, however, considerable
scope still for bringing these objects of study together to develop a
coherent, theoretically based model of critical analysis marking out radio
as a specific form of mass communication with its own discourse, its own
codes and conventions, and its own cultural impact. Radio provides
meaning to listeners' lives and a sense of identity in very specific ways.
As radio becomes more popular in 1990s Britain, there is scope to
complement research, focusing on demographics and numbers listening
at a given time, by learning more about what people *do* with radio and
what the experience of listening to radio means to them.

If a wider-ranging and coherent model of analysis is to inform the
teaching of radio from the secondary curriculum onwards, the position
and perception of radio audiences should undoubtedly occupy a major
part of this. An enduring image of British radio audiences is that they are
traditional and conservative in listening tastes and, furthermore, it is their
tastes that largely determine the nature of BBC and independent radio
output. It may be the case that the most vociferous sector of British radio
audiences are conservative by nature: hence the barrage of objections that
the BBC seems to encounter whenever it proposes radical change in
wavelength allocation and programme schedules. However there is also

evidence that radio itself is not always successful at keeping in step with social and cultural developments or with public feeling about radio's function. The restructuring of the BBC's national output with the launch of Radios 1 to 4 in 1967 was one example of the 'establishment' or 'Auntie' finally recognising the explosion of popular music that could only find outlets previously through pirate stations and Radio Luxembourg. In 1993, the BBC found itself embroiled in a heated public debate on its proposals to introduce an all-news network and to scrap either Radio 4's long wave service or Radio 5 to provide a suitable frequency for this.[13]

Further breadth and illumination in the study of radio may also be achieved by wresting what radio theory there is from the dry, reflexive terrains of social science and cultural studies and developing its profile in schools of art – perhaps alongside that other academically neglected non-visual medium, recorded music. Creativity on radio has always been an important issue within the industry itself. It has remained a loosely defined quality but one that is recognised on the principle that 'we know it when we hear it'. Usually, creative radio is that which stimulates imagination where visual media would confine it; the post-war adventures of *Dick Barton*, the multi-dimensional diegesis of *The Hitchhiker's Guide to the Galaxy* and the offbeat scenarios of *The Mary Whitehouse Experience* are among the many programmes cited by radio professionals themselves as achieving this quality. Interestingly, television has presented its own versions with varying degrees of success. Resourced with portable recorders, magnetic tape, editing blocks and mixing desks, one wonders what horizons of creativity may be attained by art students applying the same spirit of adventure and exploration as colleagues working with visual media. Underpinning such activity lies a potential for the analysis of style, narrative, systems of representation and the development of skills in criticism applied to audio recordings in ways similar to paintings, sculpture and electronic graphics.

Campus radio and production experience

THE experience of many academic institutions in which radio is studied suggests that students who are able to produce their own broadcast-quality material are highly motivated to learn more about the subject. A growing number of students are able to gain access to the technology of radio production, either through use of recording and editing equipment available at their schools and colleges, or through a supervised work placement at a local radio station. On a longer-term basis, a sense of professional broadcasting practice and a wide range of skills in presenting and producing radio text can be gained from ongoing voluntary work at a local station while studying. This could be a BBC or ILR station resourced with state-of-the-art technology, a community station, hospital radio, or – if one is available – a campus radio station.

Since the 1990 Broadcasting Act, responsibility for licensing campus radio and other restricted range stations rests with the Radio Authority.[14] In 1993, twenty-three campus radio stations based at colleges and universities in the United Kingdom were listed as licensed by the Authority. Whilst these stations offer an educational benefit for students interested in developing skills and knowledge in broadcasting techniques and radio technology, some have been set up for the explicit purpose of enabling students to work with radio as part of their syllabus, while others are primarily offering a service to all students through entertainment, local information and open access broadcasting. The simplest technological form of campus radio is a cable system with a studio at one end and loudspeakers at the other. The latter are usually located in places on the campus where large numbers of students congregate, such as the refectory or the student union bar. The benefit of this system to students is that it is relatively cheap to set up. Also, from the point of view of a student union or group of college or university societies, the service can provide useful, up-to-the-minute information and announcements on events and meetings to a reasonably captive audience. It can provide atmosphere through background sound and is thus best suited to music-based output. The main disadvantage of this arrangement is that studio output, which may be of very high technical quality, is reduced to noise competing with more noise when these places are busy.

If funding is available, campus radio can make use of more sophisticated transmission technology with signals broadcast on airwaves rather than transmitted via cable. The usual method of achieving this without interfering with other radio services, or demands for wavelengths in the locality, is to operate an 'induction loop AM' system. The signal is broadcast on an AM frequency but can only be received within a clearly defined geographical area – such as the campus itself – because it is effectively contained within an induction field, created when the low power signal is fed through an antenna made up of wire loops or lengths of slotted coaxial cable which mark the extent of the transmission area.

An application fee and licence fee are payable to the Radio Authority which sets a number of conditions on matters such as power levels, the eligibility of the licence holder, and the necessity to adopt a call sign and to log output. Call signs – the announcement on air of the station's identification – are required to ensure that programmes can be monitored. The obligation on radio stations to log output, by keeping a tape recording of output for a specified period of time, enables the Radio Authority to investigate any complaints on programme content.

It is also possible for a campus-based station to operate on a short-term basis as a community radio service, using an FM transmitter on a temporary licence. This would function as a special events station and, depending on the signal strength, would be heard by anyone inside or outside the campus tuning into the correct frequency. Some courses set up a radio station regularly on this basis with support from sponsors.

Students – usually but not necessarily on media courses – are then given the responsibility of broadcasting a wide-ranging output of speech and music for a full day or week, sometimes as part of the assessment towards their final qualification.[15]

Apart from its overall value in providing a taste of the broadcasting experience, the specific benefits of campus radio are that it encourages presenters to think in terms of offering a service to listeners and demonstrates the necessity to give a *performance* through every word spoken and every piece of music included in the broadcast. Regular involvement in campus or community radio can prove a particularly valuable enhancement to the study of media and communications by drawing together theory-based studies of radio texts as narrative and value-laden structures and the pragmatic business of operating studio equipment to 'fill the airwaves' for a fixed and regular period. At whatever level in terms of technical resources and the size of a station's editorial area, broadcasting experience demonstrates effectively the extent to which the text of radio and the experience of listening to radio is constructed and shaped by a number of interconnecting factors.

First there is the technological infrastructure of radio itself. The arrangements of microphones and audio sources, mixing and editing facilities, a transmitter and receivers provide the capability to carry over a distance, from one location to potentially millions of locations, the sound of human voices, music, sound effects and silence. Even the most basic campus station enables the presenter to create a style of broadcasting and a text that conveys a mood or atmosphere through the juxtaposition of these elements. In structural terms, these sounds constitute the paradigms of radio and are common to all radio stations.

Second there is the presenter who makes the choices of which sound elements to select and combine – which paradigms to draw on – to create the particular sound of a particular station at a particular moment in time: in other words, the fabric of the radio text, the syntagm of radio.[16]

A third and equally vital factor in the construction of the radio text is the rationale or house style of a station that expresses its specific character and identity and which governs – effectively constrains – the choices that the presenter may make. Students operating a campus station may appear to have greater autonomy than, say, a BBC local radio station that operates within the terms of a charter, or an ILR station that is accountable to shareholders and advertisers, but are at the very least likely to face sanctions if they broadcast comments that are sexist, racist, obscene, prejudicial, offensive to individual members of the institution or contrary to the wider interests of that institution.

Inextricable from this factor is the audience profile – its expectations of the product of radio and the values and experience that determine these. Bring wider, contextual factors into the equation – the legal framework within which radio operates, the political and cultural frameworks and the position and status of radio as a medium of mass communication within the lifestyles and perceptions of listeners, and it becomes clear that the study of radio has the potential to relate practical, production experience to a wide range of curricular and 'live' issues.

Within the terms of a syllabus or a training programme, focus on any of these factors in isolation is only likely to provide a two-dimensional image of the medium of radio. It is through a combination of production experience and text-based study that a more comprehensive picture emerges. The student develops a deeper understanding as well as a greater level of broadcasting proficiency through exploring these factors and making more and more connections between them.

Activities and points for discussion

1 Assume that you have read no further than this chapter and that you have no experience or knowledge of radio other than what you hear on the airwaves. Write down – or, as a group, conduct a brainstorming session and list –

- the different jobs there are to be done in a radio station (start with presenter and cleaner)

- the different skills that are needed by people working in a radio station (start with talking and listening), and

- the different ways you can think of in which these skills can be taught and developed.

When you have completed the last list – hopefully a fairly long one – indicate how many of these ways can be achieved with limited access to technical equipment and how many with no access at all to technical equipment.

2 Again, assume the same knowledge of radio as in Activity 1. In small teams, think of a gadget – something that does not exist as far as you know – which would be an incredibly useful thing for a radio presenter or DJ to have at hand while broadcasting live: something that would add a particular quality to the programme. Let your imagination run free. Work out a description of the gadget, then elect a team spokesperson to explain your ideas to the larger group. That person must not use any form of visual aid to describe the gadget.

3 How many radio stations can you name from memory? For each one, give a brief description of what type of programme it broadcasts. What would a radio station need to broadcast for you to want to listen to it regularly?

4 Organise and conduct a survey on how radio is used in the household or family. This could be done formally with a planned questionnaire or by using a diary which members of that household (and yourself) must complete on a daily basis for a set period – say one week.

Suggested areas to be investigated are: how many people enjoy listening to the radio on their own? How many hours a day do people think they listen to the radio? In what circumstances do people listen to radio in groups? What are people doing when they listen to radio? How many radio sets are there in the house? Is there one in the car? How many of them have pre-set controls? Who tunes them? Who decides which channel should be listened to? Do people in the household take part in radio phone-in programmes? Are there particular times of the day when the radio is always on? Are there particular items that people listen to intently (i.e. tell others to be quiet so that they can hear)?

Once the results of the survey have been collected, analyse and discuss them. What conclusions can you draw about the significance of radio in people's day-to-day lives? For what purposes do people use radio?

5 What would life be like without radio? As a large group or in small teams, consider a scenario in which radio suddenly no longer works because of freak atmospheric conditions that otherwise have no effect on media services (television still works as normal). What would the impact be? Who would be affected most? In what ways would people have to adapt their lifestyles?

6 Assume that you are applying to a local radio station for a short-term work placement. They ask you to provide evidence of your interest in radio and your potential to be a broadcaster. You decide to put together a five-minute demonstration tape although the only technology you have access to is a hand-held cassette tape recorder with a built-in microphone. What would you record and why?

Make the recording and play it back to members of a discussion group. Each member should do the same. Discuss the strengths and weaknesses of each other's recordings and, from this discussion, agree on and draw up a brief checklist for anyone contemplating putting together a low-tech demonstration tape.

7 Is there any demand for an in-house radio station to be set up at your school, college, place of work? What items would it broadcast and when? Organise and conduct a feasibility study, purely in terms of demand and interest rather than technical practicalities.

23

8 Write each of the following words on a separate sheet of paper:

devotion
coincidence
naivety
beauty
aroma
victory
tradition
horror
flavour
pain
frustration
fashion

Form teams of two or three people. Each team selects a piece of paper at random and discusses a strategy for effectively putting across the selected word using sound only. From this, the team should produce a script for a three-minute radio production based on that word. If possible, make an audio recording of the script.

2 Radio style

··

The radio experience

E VERY radio station, local, regional and national, has its own identifiable style. To recognise the style of a radio station is to recognise its character – its image – when locating it on the tuning dial.
Some aspects of style are apparent in obvious ways: the type of music
played, the accent of the presenters, the frequency of jingles, the professional 'gloss'. These are all evidence of a style policy underpinning a
station's specific and characteristic 'sound' or 'voice'. Broadcasters often
talk about their station's style using rather vague, intuitive terms, such as
'brash', 'sophisticated', 'up-tempo', 'lively', 'serious'. Imprecise as these
descriptions may be, they demonstrate a professional awareness that the
manner of presentation is as important, if not more important, than
programme content and that considerable thought and planning lie behind
the overall 'sound' of a station.

In marketing terms – and reflecting the emphasis that a radio station
places on identifying and targeting a particular audience – the development
and creation of a distinctive output style constitutes a fundamental part of
the process of 'branding' a station, i.e. defining and marketing its brand
image. In this chapter we will discuss some of the finer points of branding,
how this relates to style policy and what impact this has on the final output of a radio station. It is logical to argue that the basic pre-requisites for
radio broadcasting are a voice, microphone and transmitter. But to survive
in a competitive environment and to demonstrate cost-effectiveness, a
station proves its viability by attracting and relating to a specific and
defined listener group; style policy should be determined even before presenters are recruited and transmission technology installed.

An appreciation of the importance of style policy requires a consideration of some of radio's basic characteristics as a medium and how these
may be understood and exploited to establish a station's role in the lives
of listeners. That is why issues related to style are considered here before
we move on to station organisation and production techniques. We begin

this chapter with an examination of what it is about radio's product – its output – that makes it different, in terms of how it is consumed by an audience, from that of television or the press. The structure and qualities of the radio message itself are considered – what type of experience does it create for listeners? – and attention is also given to radio's 'hardware' – in what ways must listeners interact with the technology that enables radio to be transmitted and received, before they can interact with the text of radio? Identification of the principal features of the essential radio output will enable us to define in more explicit terms the nature of the radio experience.

A perspective of radio as a commodity – and the radio programme as something that audiences consume – reflects the principle of consumer choice that has been dominant in political thinking on broadcasting since the Peacock Report's application of a market economy model in its consideration of the financing of the BBC (Peacock 1986). Radio, television and the press have their own qualities to offer as 'commodities' and audiences largely base their selections on their enjoyment of the product. Each medium has a function of keeping its audience informed of significant events; each is capable of educating audiences; but policy decisions on the style and brand image of any media form start with the premise that people listen, watch or read through choice and that choice is governed by people's affinity with that service.

Where radio differs from television and the press is in the nature of the relationship between product and consumer. At the very beginning of this book we have argued that radio establishes a relationship of intimacy. The newspaper and magazine are obviously products of professional teams. The mode of person-to-person communication established by, say, a leader column or a byline commentary may reflect a discourse in which the reader is 'positioned' as sharing certain values and beliefs with the writer, but the experience is by no means interactive; the power of the writer to set the terms of reference is countered only by the reader's decision on whether she wishes to read all or part of the article, or ignore it completely.

Television news or news magazine programmes can be closer simulations of the experience of human interaction. The presenter addresses the viewer in spoken language, she establishes eye-contact, she reinforces her message through non-verbal cues and indicates the nature of her relationship with the viewer through her appearance, mode of address and mannerisms which establish her as friend, expert adviser, official announcer or whatever. The viewer is nevertheless still aware of the existence of a production team, evident through the use of nominated reporters and correspondents, the lighting, set construction and camerawork. Like the press, television is manifestly the product of a team and the viewer's pleasure has arisen from the communion of product and consumer, rather than communication between two like-minded people.

Of all the mass media, radio is most successful at concealing its identity as a 'product' and it is this, ironically, that underpins its 'product identity'.

Common to most of the forms that radio programmes can take – music shows, phone-ins, news, – is the simple characteristic of one person talking to another. The voice itself and what that voice is saying is a far more significant part of the radio experience than the programme's status as a 'production item'. The programme does not deny that it was put together by a team; this fact simply seems to be less important than the programme's instantaneous and personal communicative impact.

Popular daytime radio in particular – BBC Radios 1 and 2, for example, and most of the BBC and independent local services – signifies itself as offering friendship and company to listeners engaged in day-to-day activities and establishing an ongoing personal relationship with listeners. Programmes tend to be long – two or three hours as opposed to the half-hour pre-recorded quiz or comedy show on BBC Radio 4 – with little in the way of a developmental narrative structure. The listener can join the programme at any point without the ignorance of what happened before-hand affecting her understanding or enjoyment of what she hears. Neither is she committed to stay with the programme until the end, although devices are used to encourage her to stay – announcements of items to follow, or quizzes and puzzles whose answers are not revealed until later in the show. Links between programmes tend not to be abrupt and often involve presenters engaged in a dialogue with each other, giving the effect of a continuous listening experience in which the listener is gently passed on from one voice to the next. Through such tactics, the station establishes a long-term rapport with its listeners.

'Rapport' is another imprecise term often used by professional broad-casters to explain the relationship they seek to build between themselves and their listeners but it does indicate the station's expectations of the type of listening activity that its audience is involved in. Unlike tele-vision viewing, which requires some degree of attention, concentration and organisation of domestic routines and space, listening to radio is frequently a secondary experience. People rarely sit down and do nothing but listen to the radio – at least, not for very long. Listeners also tend to make less use of published programme guides. Television viewing sched-ules take up more space in newspapers than radio programme listings. Radio listening offers a more spontaneous, less planned experience.

There are in fact many ways in which people listen to radio. It is an activity which reflects developments in culture and technology and may take on a particular significance in specific social and political circum-stances, for example in times of crisis. Radio becomes a primary focus of attention in times of war, or indeed during adverse weather conditions. For armed forces and expatriates otherwise cut off from the world it functions as a link with home, a comforter and morale booster. The BBC twenty-four-hour news service during the 1991 Gulf War – while offering more speculation than hard 'news' in the early days of the war – represented a permanent point of contact for family and friends of service personnel in action, just as the BBC World Service enabled the Gulf hostages to tune in to voices from home.

In less dramatic circumstances, radio listening is not exclusively an isolated activity. Music radio and local radio may stimulate the working environment of the shop floor or hairdressing salon, providing reference points for small-talk or marking the passage of time. Its discourse nevertheless provides a strong contrast with television's spectacularity and menu of ready-made images interpreting events and issues on our behalf. Radio, especially talk radio, calls for greater participation and involvement by the listener, if not literally by phoning or faxing in to a programme, at least through experiencing the simulated social experience of interaction between peers. The human voice becomes the direct and pivotal point of contact.

Radio reproduces most effectively the experience of human interaction through its reference to the code of the spoken word. Crisell points out that 'the primary code of radio is linguistic, since words are required to contextualise all the other codes' such as music, sound effects and silence (Crisell 1994: 54). He states further that 'the linguistic code of radio approximates much more closely to that of speech than writing' (ibid.: 55). In terms of reinforcing a discourse of companionship through chat, banter, jokes, trivia and gossip, the absence of visual codes serves as a strength rather than a weakness in the communicative effectiveness of radio. Visual images must be constructed and are – on film and television – essentially fabrications and illusions of 'real life' visual experiences. Pictures are framed and composed; protagonists wear make-up in artificial lighting conditions; vision mixers and editors intervene and impose a visual narrative through the juxtaposition of shots and the incorporation of graphics and written text. Radio has no need to resort to such blatant production devices. The technical properties of human speech heard on radio are intrinsically the same as those of someone talking in the listener's front room. This faculty to communicate on a personal level therefore enables the radio programme constantly to redefine its own existence as a product and transform itself through each utterance into a spontaneous experience of communication.

Radio 'hardware'

NOT only is the way that people listen to radio a fundamental consideration for style policy, but also the way they use the technology of radio. In this respect, it is again useful to compare radio with television. Television sets are exclusively designed to incorporate pre-set tuning; this is not the case with radio. Thus, it is often easier for television viewers to 'channel hop' at the touch of a button. Whilst pre-set tuning was a feature of many of the early 'wireless' sets which were household items from the war years to the replacement of the valve by the transistor in the early 1960s, the wider choice of stations and the possibility of picking up signals from overseas stations has made it more practicable for radio tuning to the undertaken by a variable tuner and dial.

This was especially the case when the pirate music stations became active in the 1960s. Searching the dial for a signal from these stations may have been tantamount to a subversive act, at least in the eyes of the authorities, but it did offer commercial impetus for the design and manufacture of cheap radios with variable tuning facilities.

Whilst pre-set tuning is more commonplace for today's car radio or domestic hi-fi system, many listeners still go through the comparatively laborious process of adjusting a tuning control to find the station of their choice. This process can be difficult and requires some technical knowledge on the part of listeners. They need to know the frequency of the station they are looking for and whether it is broadcast on long wave, medium wave or FM. They need to be aware that the station could be broadcasting on an alternative frequency in a different part of the country – or indeed of the region. If the station splits its frequency, they need to know how to retune to find the output they want. If a radio does have a pre-set tuner, knowledge is needed of how to reprogramme it, especially if it is a car radio and the listener's work involves frequent travel around the country.

This demonstrates how the limitations of technology create a major challenge for marketing radio stations. In terms of locating stations, radio is not as easy to access as television. Television offers four terrestial plus a range of cable and satellite channels. Each can be located at the touch of a button on a remote control unit. Radio listeners on the other hand must select from approximately 200 radio stations currently operating in the United Kingdom, not counting the illegal stations. Numerous devices have been applied by radio stations to encourage listeners to find their frequency and pick up the best quality signal for their area, ranging from stick-on labels for the radio dial to incorporation of the frequency number within the station name and even within its telephone number.

The introduction of RDS (Radio Data System) is beginning to overcome the difficulties of locating stations. It can automatically retune a radio to whichever station is broadcasting a travel report, provided that station is transmitting an RDS signal, or to the strongest local signal of the preferred station if the car journey takes the motorist out of one transmission area and into another.

Nevertheless, the fact that a listener's initial access to a radio station is problematic highlights the importance for radio stations to develop listener loyalty. If a listener retunes a set which incorporates a variable tuner and dial, she may be less likely to make the effort to tune back. A major consideration in developing a station's style is therefore an identification of consistent elements in the sound and nature of its output that will encourage listeners to leave the tuning control untouched.

Ironically, once the technological barrier has been crossed and the listener has located the station of her choice, the radio experience involves little physical interaction with the medium, compared with television and the press. This reinforces the notion that radio output is experienced less as a 'product' – in the same sense as television output or the press – more as a form of ongoing human interaction. Newspapers and magazines are picked up, their pages are turned, their coupons are cut out, their margins are scribbled on. Television channels are changed at the slightest provocation with a remote control unit. The television set is also used for watching videos – both pre-recorded and home-made – or for computer games, either for family entertainment or for education. However, once a radio set is switched on, it is often left to provide a background for work or domestic routines or a car journey. The listener may use a pre-set tuner to change channels although even this form of interaction is reduced in car radios fitted with RDS.

The relative ease with which radio can reach a large group of listeners is a reflection of its simple organisational structure – simple, that is, compared with that of television and the press. Modern newspapers and television stations function through complex technology. Admittedly, desk-top publishing has facilitated the professional production of a newspaper or magazine to a relatively limited and local audience although samizdat publications are nothing new. It is true also that well-resourced radio stations contain some very complicated equipment. The point here is that the smallest newspaper office and television station need more sophisticated systems of organisation and a wider range of specialist skills than the smallest radio station. At a minimum, the press requires expertise in writing, keyboarding, computing, printing and distribution, and a system of management that enables these functions to relate together efficiently. Television in its most basic form requires technical expertise in image and sound recording, editing and transmission as well as creative skills in scriptwriting, graphics and setting up the right appearance of anything front-of-camera. But with nothing but a voice and a means of transmitting that voice, radio is possible.

Underpinning the type of interaction that people can have with radio is the fact that its output is ephemeral and evanescent. The 'product' of radio is a sound from the ether that exists only for the moment it is heard. If it is missed it is gone forever – unless the programme has been recorded at source and is repeated later. It does not have the capacity of television or the press for audiences and readers to become involved in different parts of the product at the same time, for example by following a television computer graphic display while listening to a voice-over report or by cross-referring to a chart or photograph while reading a feature article. Radio is nothing but instant sound and the listener cannot move about within the structure of its text.

The use of technology to record media output provides further indication of how radio appears to 'play down' its commodity status. Most products are tangible; they can be stored, referred back to or consumed in a more obvious and literal sense. Most media products in particular can form the basis for an archive. Newspaper articles can be reread, cut out and retained; copies of news photographs can be obtained. Television programmes can be stored on video either for 'timeshift' viewing or for storing as part of a personal collection. Indeed, domestic technology reflects (and arguably reinforces) the patterns of consumption of mass media products. Timeshift viewing is now a common part of cultural experience. Timeshift listening is not. Unlike video cassette recorders, most domestic audio cassette players do not have timed recording devices built in. It is possible to fit a timer unit into a domestic hi-fi system for the recording of radio programmes although this facility is not widely used by listeners apart from Open University students or teaching staff recording items from schools' broadcasts.

Audio cassette recorders are more widely used for the illegal copying of music from compact discs or albums than they are for recording radio output. There is no tradition of recording and keeping favourite radio programmes. This does not mean that radio is not as memorable as television or the press; people just use it in different ways. Radio's mode of address is more appropriately that of the immediate. Radio's ubiquity – its large number of stations, many of which are on the air for twenty-four hours – is such that the news item, the presenter's comments, the phone-in discussion are capable of being superseded and updated almost immediately. Quite simply, there is less need to store a radio programme.

There are of course obvious exceptions. Radio drama and documentary – in fact, any pre-recorded radio programme – tend to create greater distance between themselves and listeners as 'set piece' items than a live presenter-led show and hence proclaim themselves more self-evidently as outcomes of a production process. The human voice is more likely to be 'framed' or contextualised by background sounds and atmospheric music, or treated through such technical processes as fading, distorting or producing an echo effect by adding reverb or delay. Many 'classic' programmes from the BBC archives – from *The Goon Show* to *Knowing Me Knowing You* – have been marketed with considerable success over recent years as pre-recorded and packaged audio cassette tapes. But even in this form, the programme lends itself to a personal and continuous listening experience. People tend to playback audio cassettes when they are on their own, driving the car for example or listening through head-phones while doing the housework or travelling on public transport. There is no visual cueing device to enable the listener to refer back or locate a particular part of the recording with ease.

Often radio listeners interact with programmes themselves rather than the technology that transmits them. A television viewer who strongly disagrees with a view expressed in a current affairs programme may change channels, but it is possible for a radio listener to reach for the tele-phone rather than the off-switch, give an instant response to live output and even contribute to that output. Not all who phone in can get on; indeed callers to national radio phone-ins such as BBC Radio 4's *Call Nick Ross* or *Any Answers* may count themselves lucky to cross the first barrier – hearing a ringing tone rather than an engaged signal. However, it is only on radio that listeners might expect to give their opinions on the air, live, in their own words and unedited, possibly affecting the direction the programme is taking. In this sense, the distance between broadcaster and listener is smaller in radio than it is in television.

It is a tribute to the radio experience that television has enhanced inter-action with viewers by adapting radio techniques rather than creating truly televisual ones. Daytime television's phone-in features basically constitute radio with pictures and with less need for viewers to exercise their imagination. The practice of viewers phoning in to enter television competitions or vote for artists on talent shows can hardly count as inter-active; so far only the video-box style productions can be said to offer the greatest potential for televisual technology to involve viewers in an innovative way.

The emancipated listener?

SO far we have established the radio experience as one which is personal but also secondary. The listener can get on with her life while she is taking part in the radio discourse. The increase in people's access to – and choice of – all mass media forms is afforded through developments in interactive technology. In his commentary on a study of how media technology was used in households of four Midlands towns,[1] Hartmann argues that in many respects new communications technology opens up consumer choice and appears to give people greater control over their own lives as a result:

> Video equipment, for instance, is often used to record television programmes which can then be watched at a time of the viewer's own choosing. People need no longer be concerned that they will miss favourite programmes if they go out. This helps to explain why video owners claimed *more* visits to the cinema and other out-of-home activi-ties than non-owners.
>
> *Hartmann 1992*

The research points to a conclusion that enhanced access to the 'impor-tant resource' of information, brought about by new communications technology, has an impact on the location and exercise of power and control in society.

> The new technologies bring with them a tendency towards greater centralisation of social control, but simultaneously they also contain the potential for greater decentralisation. Satellite television might be thought of as representing a definite centralising tendency; community, local and regional radio and television . . . a decentralising one. People not only consume information, they generate it.
>
> *ibid.*

This is an important issue for radio. Given that listening to the radio is more likely to be an isolated activity than that of watching television, much of radio's output is heard by choice, particularly in out-of-work hours. We have already referred to listeners' greater access to the production process of radio's output through the telephone and the fax machine. This is all evidence to suggest that radio's capacity for the 'empowerment' of listeners as active and participating members of society is considerable. After all, what other medium offers daily opportunities for any citizen to pick up a telephone and talk at length to an audience of millions?

Detractors to this argument might point to radio's capacity to propagate an illusion of greater public participation and create a mythologised listening 'community'. Presenters frequently play the role of devil's advocate when conducting interviews or hosting phone-in discussions, reinforcing radio's cultural role of stimulating discussion, providing a forum for debate and maintaining a neutral position within 'consensual' and ideological boundaries of acceptability and non-deviance. Theirs are the terms of reference. They can – and do – reach for the fader if a contributor to a phone-in programme is boring, inarticulate or expressing an unacceptable point of view. Programme makers – not the public – determine the location of outside broadcast units or the range of themes, styles and listener interests to be addressed within a programme schedule. News editors decide on the selection and order of items in a news or current affairs programme. Radio stations themselves are physically difficult to get into; presenters might be visible behind sheets of glass in the main studio or a satellite studio located in, say, a busy shopping centre, but members of the public cannot get past the security door unless invited in as programme guests or open-day visitors.

Some research has suggested that radio's function of representing the genuine interests of all listeners is open to question. One BBC and two commercial radio stations in London were criticised in 1982 for seeming to be 'unable or unwilling to get to grips with London issues in the way that was promised when stations opened' (Local Radio Workshop 1983:10) while a study of how women are addressed as listeners and employed as workers for Independent Local Radio in the 1980s accused ILR of 'failing to meet the changes facing women' and reinforcing 'the classic female stereotype: the woman whose sole interest in life is her home and children' (Baehr and Ryan 1984: 7).

What is at issue here in the formulation of a radio station's style policy is a lesson that is sometimes hard learned. Because listening to the radio is often a personal experience, a station can only survive if sufficient numbers of listeners take it 'into their hearts' and feel that its output genuinely relates to their own experiences, values and self-image. The geography of the transmission area might be technically convenient, but does it reflect the listeners' own perception of their community? The presenter might be providing important information, but will her tone of voice or accent make her sound patronising or insincere to a particular age group, ethnic group or social class? Where is the line drawn between interesting discussion and – to repeat a term used by the Annan Committee – 'prattle'?

The radio experience can be liberating in providing contact, companionship and community involvement for listeners. Or it can subjugate listeners by reinforcing a self-image that operates against interests other than those of the consumer. The power of radio lies in its purity of form as a means of modern communication. Radio is a disembodied voice. It does not need the clutter of high technology; it works when one person relates successfully to another. It is a relationship between producer and consumer that is based on trust and challenge; the consumer is encouraged to trust the broadcaster that there is more to consume and she is challenged not to switch off in case she misses something she would like, or need to hear. One aspect of radio's creativity is taking that challenge as far as it will go. The relationship is compounded by the fact that the consumer does not appear to pay for the product (though in fact she does through the BBC licence fee and the price of consumer goods and services that are advertised). To the listener, radio's output is free and only pulled from the air when she wants to hear it.

Neither does radio force the listener to construct single or dominant meanings. The production process of radio takes place effectively in the mind of the listener – not the studio. Television and newspapers offer a single and fixed range of images. Radio listeners provide their own details, their own colour, their own picture of the speaker's appearance, the studio layout, or the farm kitchen in the radio soap opera.

However, the relationship between radio and listener is one that can be easily broken. If listeners are offended, isolated, bored, confused or simply of the belief that a better sound can be found elsewhere on the tuning dial they will change their allegiance with little hesitation. For the programme maker, it is considerably easier to lose a listener than it is to persuade her to return.

Output quality

BECAUSE the connection between radio output and the listener is so tenuous, stations look for strategies to nurture and protect the relationship that they have established. One such strategy is to monitor and review regularly the quality of the product itself and its capacity continually to engage the listener. Bodies such as listening panels and the BBC's advisory councils provide regular feedback on whether radio stations are providing the best and most appropriate service to their audiences. Furthermore, everybody in a radio station listens to each other's output, discusses new ideas, provides support and constructive criticism – at least they should do, if only to achieve homogeneity in output.

Station management in particular takes a lead in listening and providing comment on output to production team members and, most important of all, broadcasters themselves are encouraged to listen objectively to their own programmes and constantly to seek means of improving them such that they relate more effectively with the listener.

In some stations, presenters are asked to enter 'incidents' in a station log, recording occurrences of technical or human failure during a broadcast. The advantage of this system of self-monitoring is that it highlights areas of frequent technical breakdown that need attention and points to specific needs for staff training. Used in the spirit of seeking constantly to improve output quality, the log book is useful, entertaining to read and reassuring to presenters that they are not the only ones to have disasters on air. The disadvantage is that the log becomes regarded within the station as a confessional and that presenters feel a sense of failure every time they have to write something in – even if the incident was not their fault.

The overall difficulty with monitoring and controlling quality is that the term itself is ambiguous and relative. High quality programming is a goal shared by broadcasting watchdog organisations and the broadcasting industry itself, but it is hardly an absolute term in the context of broadcasting. The industry does not apply common quality standards to its own practice; to do so would be to aspire to standardisation rather than innovation. Systems – informal as they might be – for overseeing the quality of output may ensure the continued professionalism and technical expertise of radio broadcasters, but they do not guarantee an audience and therefore cannot in themselves act as safeguards for maintaining viable listener figures. Indeed a long-standing issue related to all radio and television production, in the environment of commodification and concern with value for money, is whether a reverse-correlation exists between programme quality and audience figures, although this again depends on how the term 'quality' is defined.

Anthony Smith suggests that quality is a 'slightly apologetic term' now that quantity is guaranteed by the 1990 Act:

> there are some who think that quality and commercial success are the same thing and others . . . who argue that quality is synonymous with the specialist, minority, avant-gardist, or otherwise mentally demanding varieties of programme which require subsidy.
>
> *Smith 1990: 2*

Rather than identify and work to a universal standard of output quality, a radio station aims to represent the values and ideas that are regarded as positive, appropriate and relevant for its potential audience. The business of maintaining and increasing its appeal to listeners is based on a process of continuous appraisal, not of quality in a vacuum, but of how well the station has identified with *this* particular audience on *that* particular issue.

This is not the same as working to an audience-led definition of 'good' broadcasting, or of being satisfied with the level of output achieved as long as the listeners are 'happy'. One might argue instead that the 'best' quality radio is that which surprises its audiences and makes them aware of new forms of output that they enjoy but had not previously experienced. The pioneers in radio are those who recognise that innovation sometimes puts quality at risk. The 'safe' format of a presenter in the studio with guests and records might provide seamless and innocuous broadcasting, and may achieve high standards of professional quality, but is this really exciting, dynamic radio compared with a lively and complex network of voices coming in from radio cars, telephones, remote studios and backpacks (see Chapter 4)? The same argument can apply in a station's consideration of whether to let inexperienced broadcasters (dare we suggest students?) loose on the air. Quality consciousness results in the use of 'damage limitation' strategies whereby a station does take risks and allows for planned innovation but mostly at non-peak listening times.

Notions of 'good radio' and 'effective output' thus relate to a measure of what is appropriate for a particular station broadcasting to a particular group of listeners. The link between broadcaster and listener becomes less tenuous when there is a clear station identity that the listener feels she can relate to and that the broadcaster is able to reinforce. The station identity says something about its character and its role both within the community and the day-to-day experience of each listener. It can provide the terms of reference for monitoring the quality of that station's output and identifying its scope for innovation.

Branding

BRANDING is a shorthand term for establishing a radio station's identity and developing a particular form of relationship with its listeners. Beyond broadcasting, branding is a widely used term for establishing and communicating a product's identity and that which makes the product distinctive from its rivals in the marketplace. We have already indicated, however, that the ethereal nature of radio output and its location in the minds of listeners – rather than, say, on a screen in a living room as a part of people's *external* reality – renders its status as 'product' a problematic one. The fact that radio output *is* a product or a commodity is unquestionable if one considers it as (a) the result of a production process and (b) something possessing monetary value. However, we have established that on both these counts people's *experience* of radio output is different; the listener engages with, rather than simply receives, the radio programme and she does not perceive herself as incurring costs when she switches the radio on.

If radio's identity as a 'product' or 'commodity' *per se* is so problematic, one might suppose that there are special difficulties in branding individual radio stations. It is true that the personal level at which radio engages each of its listeners makes branding particularly crucial. If it is the case, however, that radio constantly and routinely works to deny its own commodity status by replacing this with the status of a personal experience for each listener, this in itself may serve to establish and strengthen its brand image. Even within an ideological climate in which everything has its price, the term 'commodity' is value-laden, suggesting a functional purpose for each product in meeting a specific and defined need within a market. Radio serves human needs like any other commodity but aspires to a higher status than that of a product picked off the supermarket shelf. In a culture dominated by visual icons, radio operates on an experiential rather than tangible plane.

One might argue that insurance companies and manufacturers of air fresheners do much the same! The unique and specific quality of radio, however, is that it provides the catalyst for a constant, textured, ever-changing and individualised experience for each listener. Objectively, radio produces 'an experience'. Subjectively, listeners work on the sounds and silences of radio to produce their own mental images and live out their own experiences whenever they engage with a radio programme – from a simple shipping forecast to a pop-gossip-and-trivia show. For a marketing consultant this may constitute radio's unique selling point. For the purposes of branding a radio station, it points to the creation and reinforcement of an image that relates to listeners' self-image, sense of identity and deeply held values rather than what they can do with the product.

To demonstrate further the difficulties of effectively reducing radio to the level of functional commodity: this would be to place radio, as a cultural artefact, in the same category as, say, a bar of chocolate. Both artefacts may be marketed on a purely functional level of needs-fulfilment. Chocolate staves off hunger. Radio tells you which traffic jams to avoid. Or they may be marketed on a level that relates more directly to the consumer's self-image. Eating this particular chocolate bar signifies your sophistication, sensuality or lorry-driving techniques. Listening to this particular radio station signifies your sense of community involvement, your intelligence or your identity as a cool connoisseur of dance music. Such comparisons might be of value if the business of establishing a radio station's identity were purely a marketing exercise, but a vital consideration is that 'consumers' do not internalise the 'product' of radio in the same way they do confectionery. As listeners, they experience and participate in a form of communication, taking on board a set of values that are vital to their comprehension of the terms of that communication. If the broadcasting organisation appeared to regard its output as simply a product to be marketed, to meet consumer needs, to make the shareholders rich, listeners would probably be less inclined to relate to that product at a personal level, to become so involved in its discourse, to allow it to create pictures in their minds or to generate emotions. The station would cease to address their humanity but become analogous with the deployment of mass media in a 'big brother' scenario, having no further function than to keep consumers happily consuming.

Thus, ironically, the process of successful branding is one which does enhance and objectify the image of a radio station in the minds of its listeners and potential listeners, whilst playing down its status as 'commodity'. Frequently, the process involves 'humanising' the station having established its viability through cold, hard calculations of market conditions and likely consumer response. Anyone establishing a radio station will seek to identify a common factor of a sufficiently large number of people living within a 'footprint' or editorial area. This factor will form the basis for branding the station. Market research may reveal that many people living in this area share an interest in market gardening and keeping allotments. Perhaps there is a potential here for a radio station serving market gardening enthusiasts as a niche market – Veg FM. The viability of such a station, however, depends not on how many market gardeners there are, but on how many of them are likely to tune in for long enough to satisfy advertisers or stakeholders that they can be sure of a return on their investment. The chances are that people actually escape to the allotments to avoid the sound of radios blaring in the house!

This example shows the difficulty of identifying an audience which is (a) sufficiently discrete to merit targeting and (b) sufficiently large to make it worthwhile. This level of identification is a fundamental part of branding. The attempt to define an audience more tightly has the effect of reducing the potential size of the audience group; the most viable station is that which locates the critical level of audience where it is small enough to be defined but large enough to interest investors and/or advertisers. It would be impossible to brand a station in the United Kingdom which relates only to the common feature of all its potential listeners that they speak in the English language, as this would not constitute a sufficiently strong bond of identity to provide a basis for the listening group – although it might do if the station were broadcasting to a niche of expatriates living in France or Germany.

The question of demand and supply is not unique to radio. The same formula may be applied to television, the only difference being that the level of investment and running costs are considerably higher than radio. To be viable, television has to attract a much larger audience with a more loosely defined set of common characteristics, for example in terms of age range and socio-economic class rather than specific interest or geographic location. Hence BBC1 presents itself primarily as a family viewing channel, BBC2 as a channel for the selective viewer, Channel 4 for the viewer with cosmopolitan tastes. The demand and supply curves simply cross higher up the graph.

The need to establish a radio station's identity, and hence its viability, through branding, is one that is increasingly important as deregulation enables more stations to go on air. A station which has a monopoly within its editorial area, or a set of stations which exist without branding, could theoretically function quite successfully provided that people are willing to tune in and listen. But if a rival station were to set itself up to target one specific group of listeners, or one of the existing stations were to break ranks and decide to broadcast in a determined, branded way for a particular niche in the listening market, there would be pressure on the other stations to follow suit or risk losing their audiences.

With so many radio stations for listeners to choose from, each with its own brand identity, there is no space for a general purpose, general interest station. Each of the five BBC national services occupies a clearly defined area of broadcasting in terms of musical taste, listener interests and listener activity. The two independent national stations now operating are identified in terms of their listeners' musical preferences whilst the proposed third independent national station with its talk-orientated output may aim to appeal to the news-conscious or the socially and culturally aware. Meanwhile, the growing number of regional and local stations creates ever-tighter definitions of listener profile, opening up niches that were not fully realised before deregulation. The process has been not unlike shaking a jar of sweets so that they settle into more unseen spaces, leaving room at the top of the jar for more sweets to be added. One might assume that a point will eventually be reached where the full potential for radio to meet the needs of British listeners will be achieved. But in an evolving culture in which the market is constantly changing, there will always be new opportunities for radio to connect with the audience.

A total sound package

BRANDING a product on a supermarket shelf is achieved through packaging, marketing, public relations and images conveyed through advertising. The same could be said of a radio station to the extent that significant differences in brand image may be recognised through the promotion of, say, BBC Radio 4 and Kiss 100 FM, each reflecting distinctive consumer profiles. Where radio differs from the packet of washing powder is in its immediacy. Promises of a 'cleaner, fresher wash' on the packaging and in the advertising may encourage the consumer to select a brand of powder, but only time will tell if those promises are fulfilled. Once a listener tunes in to a radio station, the promise must be simultaneously made and kept.

To identify the factors that constitute a station's style, therefore, is to identify the elements that make up its brand image. Branding is achieved through careful and planned consideration of the language style of presenters and announcers, the quality of their voices, jingles, the type of music played, topics discussed and relevance of output to listeners' needs and interests (e.g. travel and weather reports, news bulletins, sports reports). For all their spontaneity, such factors are subject to careful planning and control, reflecting the radio producer's constant nightmare of people switching off the moment they hear something they do not like. Professionalism in radio broadcasting means, perhaps obsessively to the outsider, attention to detail whereby the cliché 'every second counts' reigns supreme. Every link matters. Every record played is subject to a well-formulated process of selection. It does matter to a presenter that the programme – indeed, the last disc played on the programme – finishes precisely in time for the top-of-the-hour news summary, or that the wording of a public service announcement conveys exactly that sense of immediacy and dynamism that reflects the style of the entire station.

Stations often 'format' their broadcasts by applying strict rules on structure and presentation, governing for example how long a presenter may talk between records. While imposition of this form of discipline clearly helps to build up a particular style, stations also pay attention to the 'total sound package' by developing a holistic concept of voice, music, language and topic which fit together in a coherent and inter-related way to create the station's own distinctive sound or 'signature'. The nature of a station's 'total sound' is articulated through guidelines on style issued by station management, circulated to all who have access to a microphone, reinforced through training and in-house refresher courses, and monitored with feedback by station managers to pres-enters and announcers of live and recorded output. Decisions on the 'total sound' do not always rest with stations themselves. The BBC is pushing its own local radio services to a format of more speech and less music (see pp. 47–9) and, whilst the Radio Authority is less prescriptive on content than the IBA was in its regulation of independent radio, the 1990 Broadcasting Act itself has specified the type of output to be broad-cast by the three new independent national radio (INR) stations, Classic FM, Virgin 1215 and the forthcoming speech-based station, currently referred to as INR3.

As the number of stations increases and more niches are identified in the UK, it is becoming increasingly important for stations in the 1990s to be able to characterise their own output in precise terms in order to define the niche that they are targeting. This does not mean that a station must operate in an unduly small and restricted market simply because there are more stations taking a slice of the total audience. Independent franchises offered in London, for example, attract interest because they offer a potential audience of 6–7 million listeners within the M25 boundary. It does mean that radio has recognised a need to refine itself and target its output with greater precision to maximise its potential listening figures. This is why the independent sector of radio experienced considerable upheaval in the mid- to late 1980s prior to the deregulation of radio and the establishment of the new Radio Authority, announced by Home Secretary Douglas Hurd in 1988.

Stations which had been broadcasting on FM and AM – 'simulcasting' – since the introduction of independent local radio in 1973, were now being encouraged to increase listeners' choice of output by 'splitting' frequencies and providing alternative sound packages. Some franchises offered in the final years of the IBA were for FM services only and the

Government's 1987 Green Paper, *Radio Choices and Opportunities*, proposed an end to simulcasting as part of the move to fuel a major expansion in independent radio services in Britain. Independent local radio's response was often to brand the new FM- or AM-only services in terms of the style of their music output. Red Rose, the ILR service for Lancashire, became Red Rose Gold and Red Rose Rock FM: the former broadcasting a fare of 'classic gold' music, the latter concentrating on 'current and 80s pop and rock'. Alternatives to music-based stations were also opening up in the advent to deregulation. The former news and talk service for London, LBC, was split in 1989 to form two speech services for the capital: the AM London Talkback Radio which 'emphasises the light-hearted side of life with almost continual phone-ins' (Gage 1990: 17) and LBC Newstalk (initially called LBC Crown FM), maintaining its more 'serious' news and talk service.[2]

The range of radio services now operating in the Greater London area alone is proof of the industry's realisation that the market is more mature and sophisticated in its listening loyalties and habits. The pattern that has emerged after deregulation is one in which areas are served by a bedrock of big mainstream stations, surrounded by a plethora of smaller and more focused radio services, able to operate on lower running costs and specialise in relatively narrow editorial areas defined geographically and/or intellectually.

Options for identity

I N the last decade, both independent and BBC radio at local and national level have become more conscious of the need to target output. One consequence of this for the independent sector has been the increased potential to generate advertising revenue.

It is now the norm for stations to target more accurately specific groups within any age range which can be clearly characterised in terms of locality, musical tastes, self-image, educational background, linguistic style or interests. With such detailed consumer information, branding becomes a 'precise science'. There is less wastage – a higher percentage of the audience is likely to respond positively to the message. And as a bonus, advertising on independent radio is much cheaper than advertising on television.

Radio's appeal as a medium for advertisers was less obvious before deregulation. From the outset, independent local radio had been obliged to operate in a highly competitive environment and with a range of restrictions relating to output, availability and size of transmission areas and overall methods of operation imposed by the IBA as a condition for being able to broadcast. Barnard summarises the 'traditional difficulties of ILR':

its brief – to be a local medium, catering for the whole community – only enables it to offer the advertisers a generalised profile of an *homogenous* audience: a station's scope for hitting the socio-economic groups most favoured by advertisers is hampered by the very terms of its IBA franchise.

Barnard 1989: 80

Pressure to deregulate throughout the 1980s, especially from the AIRC (Association of Independent Radio Companies), arose from a recognition of radio's potential to make money through untying the hand behind its back and later to compete more aggressively for audiences watching breakfast television and to lure advertisers away from the local press.

The problem for a new radio station entering the marketplace today is identifying which 'niche' to chase or create. The options are likely to be determined by such factors as age, sex, ethnicity, taste in music and interest in current affairs or sport as much as the geographic location of listeners. Local radio stations in particular need to be aware of these factors in their own editorial areas. Quite clearly, a station specialising in heavy metal music would probably not be viable economically in areas with a high population of retired people, but could fare better in urban areas with a large student population.

Many ethnic and non-English speaking local stations and networks are proving successful, partly because nationwide radio stations, which are dominated by white, English speaking broadcasters, do not adequately reflect the diversity of ethnic cultures in Britain, and partly because some parts of the country have larger ethnic populations than others or different breakdowns of particular nationalities.

Classic FM has demonstrated how a market can be opened up through basing a station's identity on a particular style of music. It has created new listeners to classical music on radio; indeed the number of people who tuned in to Radio 3 since Classic FM began broadcasting in September 1992 has also gone up slightly.[3] Virgin 1215 is branded through its appeal to sophisticated rock and regularly broadcasts thirty-minute segues of records – 'music marathons' – interrupted only by pre-recorded 'station ident' jingles and placing the presenter in a relatively low-profile, non-interventionist role. The formula has proved attractive to the extent that 3.3 million listeners were tuning in each week during Virgin's first year of operation.[4]

Nevertheless, a station's geographic location still provides the most common definition of a station's brand identity. The name of almost every BBC local radio station refers to the area in which the station is broadcasting,[5] whilst some independent stations use names that reflect the character of their location; coastal areas are served by Ocean FM (Portsmouth, Southampton and Winchester), Pirate FM (Cornwall) and Radio Wave (Blackpool). Listeners in Blackpool and Preston can also tune in to the Lancashire identity of Red Rose Gold and Red Rose Rock FM.

Where the locality provides an explicit basis for the branding of a radio station, knowledge of the demographics and local culture of the editorial area is necessary to build up the station's identity to ensure that it is appropriate and economically viable. The station should also remain sensitive to structural, economic and cultural changes within that area and be ready to respond to these changes by constantly reviewing its identity as perceived by listeners. It should consider whether its image and output are still appropriate if, for example, a large number of local people lose their jobs because of factory closures, if more young people leave the area when they get married because local property prices are too high, or if rural communities within the transmission area are becoming urbanised with the building of new housing estates. Changes of this nature are slow and their effects on audiences are not always easy to recognise. The art of a business person investing in radio may be to spot an opportunity for a niche but the art of a broadcaster in tune with the life experience of an audience is to be aware of the subtle changes in that niche.

Just as important as the physical characteristics of a locality – its infra-structure – in considering the brand identity of a radio station that serves that area, is the character of that locality as perceived and expressed through the thoughts, values and customs of the people who live there. Listeners may take pride in their area's sense of history, strong local heritage and richness in folklore and traditions. Or they may picture them-selves as part of a forward-thinking, mobile, prosperous, cosmopolitan and confident community. There may be a perceived need to boost an area's positive self-image, if for example it suffers social deprivation and a high crime rate. A radio station should be aware of such social and cultural characteristics, and be able to reflect them through its output.

This may seem an obvious concern for speech-orientated stations, but music stations are particularly prone to criticisms that they do not project any sense of being local if their output comprises mainly popular music that can be heard on any other frequency. This places even more pressure on presenters to achieve local branding while using fewer words.

Radio 1 – keeping pace with youth culture?

Radio 1 DJ Dave Lee Travis stopped the music during his lunchtime show on Sunday to announce live that he was resigning after 26 years. He blamed the 'sweeping changes' within the BBC for his decision to leave when his contract expires in October.

'Recently there has been a lot in the press about the BBC . . . changes are being made here which go against my principles, and I just cannot agree with them.

'I have the greatest admiration for what the BBC has stood for, but nothing stays the same. The only option is for me to leave.'[6]

In the context of changes in the BBC, Radio 1 has undergone a painful transition with 1993 witnessing the departure of key presenters – Simon Bates, Alan Freeman and Dave Lee Travis – within months of the announcement that Controller Johnny Beerling was leaving the station. While the station's branding was relatively unproblematic when it came on air in 1967, its long history as an 'institution' in British radio broadcasting provides an illustration of how a radio station constantly has to rethink brand identity, to respond not only to changes in British culture, listening habits and audiences' self-image, but also to developments in economic thinking and management style within the BBC itself. Most recently, this involved major changes in the station's line-up of presenters.

From the beginning Radio 1 was designed to attract the young listeners who had been deprived of the 'pirate' stations' output, taken off the air six weeks before Radio 1 played its first record, although its brief went beyond that of appealing to the teenage market. Barnard described the new service as 'aimed primarily at "housewives", which looked back rather than forward to seek a musical identity . . . in contrast to the conventional media view that Radio 1 was a carbon copy of pirate radio' (Barnard 1989: 52).

However, the station passed its own silver anniversary with a listener age profile spread broadly across three decades.[7] Until the new schedule was announced in autumn 1993, there was also speculation on whether the service would be sufficiently distinctive to justify continued public funding. The Peacock Committee's proposal that the BBC should take advertising was turned down by the Government in its Green Paper *Radio Choices and Opportunities* (1987) although the notion of taking Radio 1 outside the BBC licence fee and opening it up to sponsors and advertisers is still attractive to some believers in the principles of the free market, especially as the service appeals to age groups that are of most interest to advertisers.[8]

The BBC's discussion document *Extending Choice* (1992) describes all of the Corporation's national network radio as having undergone 'substantial evolutionary changes in . . . format, schedule, presentation style and target audiences' (1992: 45) and that it is impossible to determine their future development precisely 'given the fluid and dynamic nature of the radio marketplace' (ibid). In a lecture to the Royal Television Society, however, John Birt reaffirmed the age of Radio 1 listeners as the key to its future identity:

We need to develop Radio 1, so that it reflects youth culture in all its richness and inventiveness: with a style of presentation that keeps pace with the humour and outlook of its audience, with programming that feeds young people's needs and curiosities as well as a wider range of music which makes it the leading station for young listeners in the United Kingdom.[9]

The BBC's delivery of pop and popular music radio is discussed in *Extending Choice* in terms of its 'added distinction' through 'authoritative news coverage, original programming, social action initiatives and live performance coverage' (1992: 45). The document declares the BBC's commitment to develop these distinctive features further, including 'a higher degree of speech content than commercial radio stations, with news and information, humour, drama and social action' (1992: 46). Radio 1's present Controller, Matthew Bannister, confirmed this when he announced the new schedule:

> Radio 1's role is to innovate in popular radio, develop new formats, encourage new talent, play new music. As a publicly funded radio station it has the ability to do all these things and take risks . . . I am interested in finding new ways of putting speech into music radio, but not in great slabs of speech.[10]

Radio 1 demonstrates the difficulties of focusing on age as the primary characteristic of a target audience. Such an approach suggests the existence of a homogeneity not only in musical taste but also in programme format. With the exception of schools' programmes, output aimed at young listeners tends to be dominated by music, albeit a wide range of popular styles of music. The move by local and national commercial radio to reduce speech to a minimum in popular music programming – and the fact that young audiences listen to and seem to enjoy this format – suggests that in pure marketing terms, at least, increasing speech content for radio aimed at young people is a recipe for disaster. In terms of public service broadcasting, however, it is the incorporation of speech-based output – record reviews, news programmes, 'rockumentaries' and even the so-called 'talky bits' in music and entertainment shows – which provides Radio 1 with the 'distinctiveness' that the BBC seeks to promote in its output.

Part of the difficulty in branding a station that has attracted listeners in their millions for so long is that the target audience that forms the basis of that branding process inevitably changes, especially when the audience is identified in terms of its age. Undoubtedly, many young listeners to the brash new Radio 1 in the 1960s – with its quick-fire presenters, mid-Atlantic accents and catchy jingles ('Radio 1 is wonderful') – finally 'grew out' of listening and changed their allegiance to Radios 2 or 4, while others remained loyal as they, and the station, grew older.

The connotations of a national station that 'reflects youth culture' are important for listeners' self-identity and choices as consumers. People of any age group may tune in to a pop music station because they want to hear a fresh, lively and 'fun' sound, but the station itself must choose whether its branding will reflect the interests and tastes of a specific age group. If a wide range of listeners' ages was catered for to maximise ratings, the station would be committed to playing 'past hits' as well as up-to-date music and reflecting the diversity of age groups in its topics for speech output. Bannister argues that

> Musical tastes are not a coefficient of age. Radio 1 for the future will not be targeted by age or income. It will offer a diverse range of music and entertainment to anyone who chooses to listen.[11]

It remains to be seen how the recent reorganisation, with its emphasis on innovation and risk-taking, impacts on the age profile of Radio 1's audience over the next five years.

A local identity

THE launch of BBC Radio Leicester in 1967, followed by another seven BBC local stations that same year, was part of an experiment which would establish a pattern of local broadcasting across the country. Initial hopes for this new style of output were high, with plans for the BBC to set up 250 local stations even though it was acknowledged by the Pilkington Committee on Broadcasting that there was little evidence at the time of public demand for such a service.[12] The experiment was indeed considered a success and a structure of local radio was projected by the BBC as a replacement for the BBC Regions.[13] In 1969, the Labour Government approved BBC plans to raise its total of local stations to forty, all broadcasting on VHF (FM) frequencies only. The election of a Conservative Government the following year, with its commitment to introduce independent local radio, plus the restrictions that the BBC itself experienced in budget as well as available VHF frequencies, resulted in a less ambitious but nevertheless significant growth in BBC local radio.[14] The BBC were allowed to launch a further twelve stations, bringing the total to twenty, now broadcasting on medium wave as well as FM and hence increasing their potential audience as many listeners were unable to receive VHF signals at that time.

The need to establish and reinforce a clear role for these services within their localities was strengthened by the expectation that sixty independent local stations would be given the go-ahead by the Government. The first independent stations were broadcasting by 1973 but, following the return of a Labour Government in 1974, only nineteen were on the air before expansion in both ILR and BBC services was temporarily halted. This was while the Annan Committee was being reconvened and another four years passed until more BBC and ILR stations were introduced.

Now at least there was an opportunity for local radio to establish its own role within a greater number of listening communities and for listeners to absorb their local radio service as part of their community experience and day-to-day routines. The novelty of hearing local place names, discussion on local issues and – in the case of ILR stations – local businesses advertised, proved attractive and local radio audiences discovered, as Pilkington had indicated they would, that here was a service that they could enjoy and find useful.[15]

Therefore to a greater or lesser extent, local radio gained its foothold precisely through building the concept of 'locality' into its branding. A station's local identity was clearly more prominent if a high proportion of its output consisted of talk, incorporating reference to local place names, voices of local people, information on local traffic and weather conditions and, most importantly, local news. With greater emphasis on talk in BBC local radio than in ILR services, BBC stations had access to a larger resource of people, often with a local knowledge, who could form part of a local news-gathering infrastructure. However, prior to deregulation, ILR was obliged by the IBA to perform a public service role through providing local news and information and today many ILR stations covering large population areas still provide a high quality service of local and community news and current affairs.[16]

Following the commitment given in *Extending Choice* for BBC local radio to provide a comprehensive, in-depth news and information service (1992: 45), BBC's Managing Director for Regional Broadcasting, Ronald Neil, has stated that journalism is the heart of BBC local radio output – 'by far its single most important activity'.[17] *Extending Choice* committed BBC local radio to provide 100 per cent speech output at 'key times' in the morning, lunchtimes and early evening when the largest audiences are available to listen. But Neil adds:

> No radio station in future will pass muster by simply hitting speech quotas. The 100 per cent is much more than that. It is underpinning a philosophy for BBC local radio for the rest of the century.[18]

BBC local radio draws national and international stories from – and feeds stories to – GNS (General News Service) which provides each station's news computer with access to a complex and comprehensive network of news and information available for broadcast on radio. It is a resource that stations are exhorted to use to its fullest extent such that local, national and international news material may be included in local radio output at any time of the day. Neil says further:

> Backing up the straight news service must be output that puts flesh on the hard news. More extended reports and interviews on the big stories that really do affect people's lives at local level – the Council Tax, health reforms, education, benefits, transport and a hundred others. These are not dry dusty subjects that make listeners turn off. These matters are at the heart of everyone's daily lives – they want to understand them, they want to be involved, they want to question the decision makers and comment on the issues.[19]

A news-based approach as advocated here is designed to position BBC local radio within a distinct niche in the market – that of sole provider of local talk radio. Neil argues:

> Analysts predict that ILR will be even more dominated by pop/gold music with less and less speech and less and less of it of local relevance.[20]

Not only does local news in itself provide the key to the brand identity of all BBC local radio stations; they are expected to act as the coalition point for local information on such issues as the arts, social action, religion and the environment, and to talk about this information on air. For Neil, all local and regional broadcasters within the BBC should be orientated towards

- in-depth reporting and specialist expertise
- high production values and innovative reportage
- incisive studio interviewing – live interviews with key decision makers and people in power should be the core of the regional output
- strong journalist-based presentation
- originality and relevance – local radio should be recognised for breaking stories, and for moving stories on
- intelligence and maturity – no items or strands must detract from our clear focus.[21]

One important consequence of this policy for the branding of any BBC local radio station is that it is likely to appeal to the older listener. This is not to say that young listeners necessarily have little interest in news, but that older listeners are more likely to have a vested interest in the topics covered by news-based talk radio. Homeowners, for example, will be more concerned about local developments affecting the quality of the area in which they live, or the value of their property. Parents will be interested in local educational issues or child-care facilities. Thus branding for BBC local radio works at two levels: its geographic location and its appeal to older listeners through the harnessing of its news-gathering resources to provide plenty of information and discussion.

This results in a common pattern for BBC local radio's weekday output. Some stations include 'softer' material – music, light entertainment, human-interest interviews, phone-ins and outside broadcasts – in between the more intensive, news-based time slots: breakfast and evening times, attracting the greatest number of listeners as commuters listen on their car radios, and lunchtime when listening figures also tend to peak and when the first of the day's news input has been received, digested and written up or packaged. Speech is the most prominent form of output at these hours of the day. Other stations keep up a steady barrage of news and information all day.

BBC local radio journalists in particular need to be familiar with the infrastructure, personalities and geography of the area in which they work. Clearly, knowledge of institutions in the region and contacts with key personnel in local industry, government, church and community groups will enable them to identify and develop news stories, but branding through locality also means that they need to remain credible with listeners through attention to detail, for example in using the correct pronunciation for local place names.

Music style

WE have suggested that as a general rule (and as with any rule, there are exceptions) speech radio appeals to older listeners. Music radio on the other hand can appeal to all age groups. What should concern a radio station that attempts to identify itself with a particular audience group is the extent to which listeners are tolerant of different styles of music.

Listener tolerance is one of the complicating factors generally in the process of branding radio and devising an output style. Older listeners tend to be more tolerant of output not specifically targeted at them and often seem quite happy to listen to younger presenters playing more up-to-date music, whereas younger listeners seem to be more demanding of material that reflects their specific interests and less interested in 'older' music.

This level of tolerance is not one which changes dramatically when an average listener reaches a certain age. It is relative and variable. Listeners of any age between 18 and 45 may be orientated to some aspects of speech output in local radio. However, there is usually a critical point in people's 'listening careers' – often at age 30–35 – when their lifestyle is resettling having gone through some fundamental changes. There is greater commitment to family, career, mortgage and ultimately to the area in which they live. People at this stage of their lives are therefore more likely to share an interest with older listeners in speech output that relates to issues in their locality. However, the process of growing older does not take away enjoyment of modern popular music. Listening tastes become broader and this is compounded by the fact that listeners become more experienced consumers of music and arguably more immune to changes in musical fashion as they grow older.

Most radio stations in the United Kingdom are music-based; their identities are determined primarily by the type of music they play. Even those stations more orientated to speech usually broadcast several hours of music each week. To whatever extent music is incorporated in a station's output, it is governed by a strict music policy that has been drawn up and clearly defined to ensure its compatibility with the station's overall brief.

Three key principles are recognised within the broadcasting industry as pointing to a need for a music policy that has been carefully thought through by the radio station. First, music is expensive. Every piece of music played is paid for. Every radio station has a system of logging what music has been played (see p. 118) and details of this are sent to the PRS (Performing Right Society) which then requires stations to pay royalties for distribution to artistes. Even if a presenter sings *Congratulations* down the telephone to a listener while on air, the song must be logged and the PRS must be informed.

Second, music is not regarded as an easy way of way of filling the transmission hours. If a station plays the 'wrong' disc, the listener will retune just as readily as if the station had talked in the 'wrong' way about the 'wrong' topic. Music has important associations for listeners and, despite the general points we have outlined on listener tolerance, a listener of any age may be intolerant of a particular record or style of music and immediately switch off.

The third principle is similar in that it highlights a danger of misinterpreting the function of music in a radio programme. Music is not a means of providing a break or relief from speech, even if it effectively enables a presenter to set up the next guest interview in the studio. From the listener's perspective, music is an integral part of the station's output. A production team is responsible for presenting its programme as part of the station's overall flow of output and to ensure that the music is blended in to prevent an undue impression of the programme lurching from one item to the next.[22]

Music is positively selected, programmed and presented with these principles in mind, but this process is still capable of provoking more argument within a radio station and abuse from listeners than any other aspect of that station's output. Somebody's favourite style of music may be seen as unrepresented or marginalised, while tracks that are selected may not be regarded as covering the full range of that particular style. Listeners often hold deep-seated opinions on musical preferences to the extent that a choice of record could be perceived as more offensive than a studio guest making a controversial political statement on air. A central problem for the programming of music radio is that it involves juggling with generalities and attempting to articulate factors relating to the indefinable concepts of taste and listening pleasure.

The initial stage in the process of selecting music is that of buying the records and setting up a music library. Record companies and promoters also send in samples to increase the chance of airplay, often accompanied by invitations to interview the artistes. However, the station's own choice of stock music constitutes a major value judgement.

From this point on the selection process becomes increasingly formularised and, for many popular radio programmes, is achieved through computer technology. Individual presenters, or indeed station managers, are not 'trusted' with the responsibility of meeting a music style policy through their own choices of tracks. People inevitably tend to pick out records of their personal preference, effectively disenfranchising segments of the potential audience with differing likes and dislikes. People are also not as effective as computers in remembering what tracks are available. There are several computer systems designed to select music and produce a running order of records to be played within a given time slot. The system works through someone – say, the station's head of music – listening to pieces of music and describing them according to fixed criteria: duration, vocal type, pace, arrangement, whether recorded in the 1950s, 1960s, or whenever, and other categories as appropriate. The computer is then furnished with specifications of the sound that the radio station wishes to feature at different times of the day.[23]

This programming also takes into account the need for variety in pace and style of individual records during a given programme. Thus a formula might be applied in which the first record played after a top-of-the-hour news bulletin has plenty of pace and bounce, followed by a track that is gentler and steadier by comparison, and so on until the track leading to the next news bulletin carries authority and has a strong, resolved ending to announce the newsreader's presence. Another formula may determine that records played in the morning tend to be shorter, more dynamic and cheerful and less mellow than those played in the mid-afternoon.

The more sophisticated the computer programme, the more control the station's head of music can exercise in determining the shape of the musical output. For example, a computer can be instructed to avoid unwelcome clashes or repetitions, such as a record by Wings immediately following one by The Beatles, in turn following a George Harrison number. Or it can be programmed to achieve precisely that type of sequence for a special musical feature. It can be told to avoid a run of more than four records featuring female vocalists, or more than three songs from the 1960s. Or it can be instructed to pick out a sequence of songs for a thematic segue in which a particular word is common to all their titles.

Most radio stations have a 'playlist' which might comprise, for example, forty records that they want to highlight in a given period of time. These are usually new or recent singles or album tracks but the playlist could just as well be the 'best of Frank Sinatra' or the 'Top Twenty classical favourites', depending on the style policy of the radio station itself. A playlist may be fed into the music computer, perhaps with the instruction that at least two records from the playlist are played in any hour and that no record should be repeated within a period of twenty-four hours. Stations may even have two playlists, one of contemporary hits, the other of long-standing popular tracks.

If audience research, or the emergence of a competitor station within the transmission area, suggests that a station should make a minor alteration to its target audience – aiming perhaps for slightly older listeners – it is possible to 'fine tune' the computer programme to ensure that the most appropriate music is selected. The combined factors of (a) the ability to programme a music computer to considerable detail and (b) the emergence of common trends in listener preference if the audience is sufficiently large, highlight the potential of computing technology and marketing techniques to transform the personal and individual activity of listening and relating to musical output into a precisely targeted and, some would argue, sinisterly manipulated process of managing a mass audience.

No matter how much information is fed into the computer, however, the business of selecting music is still problematic; the choice of music to be included on a playlist, or the description of a musical style to be programmed into a computer is based on individual human perception. One person's 'jazzy' record can sound 'bluesy' to another. A 'pleasant and catchy melody' can be perceived as an annoyingly jangly tune that you cannot get out of your brain.

One of the broadest ways in which music can be categorised as a basis for identifying what to play is to distinguish that which is popular and innocuous from that which is specialist and caters for a particular taste or interest. Records in the first category may include Whitney Houston's *I Will Always Love You* or Band Aid's *Do They Know It's Christmas*: tracks with a long-established and wide appeal that listeners may at best enjoy, at worst tolerate. The second category may cover obvious specialisms like folk, jazz, blues, country and western, classical orchestra, opera or music with a specific cultural or ethnic appeal. The extent to which any of these musical styles may be termed as 'specialist' is debatable and a definition may finally be determined by record sales.

To maximise its musical appeal to listeners, a radio station may consider the 'popular and innocuous' category as one which relates to a 'lowest common denominator' in taste but discover adverse reaction because listeners find the output to be too bland and unvaried. To select anything from the 'specialist' field is a risky exercise, however, in view of the highly personal nature of the experience of listening to music and radio stations tend to avoid the 'esoteric' or any sound that does not relate to 'acceptable' musical codes. Hence stations which are branded through playing predominantly British and American popular music concentrate on records with an even and recognisable rhythm and time signature, the use of familiar musical instruments, harmony, 'professional' contemporary production techniques including 'reverb' or 'delay' on the voice and an evenly mixed, 'glossy' sound.

Many stations identify a 'watershed' time when they are willing to be more experimental in their choice of music. A typical scenario would be one in which a station schedules its 'mainstream' programmes with computer selected music to run up to 6pm each weekday, followed by special interest programmes featuring different styles of music each day of the week. The presenter of a programme on, say, folk and roots music, would make her own selection of records but on a 'rule of thumb' basis that anything played during the first half-hour – the tail-end of 'drive time' when commuters are still likely to be listening on car radios – should be accessible to non-folk audiences. Hence, the beginning of the programme may be dominated by contemporary, folk-rock or 'easy listening' forms of folk music – Suzanne Vega, Fairport Convention or Joan Baez – before the rest of the programme indulges in more traditional folk styles – unaccompanied singing, morris dance music or wordy pre-Victorian ballads.

The distinction between specialist and popular music is just one approach to the establishment of a music style for a station. Another is to treat music as a marker of time and relate it to a targeted age group of listeners. Certain tracks may appeal because listeners associate them with key events in their lives – their first kiss, first sexual encounter, first holiday without parents, first pay packet, first car, first house – memories that have strong emotional content or are based on significant personal relationships. Thus a radio station in 1995 targeting 40-year-olds may concentrate on music that was popular twenty or twenty-five years earlier and play the hits of 1970 to 1975 when many of these key events occurred in the lives of its listeners.

Music selection may also be based on the intrinsic qualities of a track and relate to a formula sometimes referred to as 'MFH'. No matter when it was recorded, a piece of music selected on this basis must possess two of the following qualities: it is melodic; it is familiar to listeners; or it is (or was) a hit. Listeners already have an orientation to the tune because it is memorable through its strong, 'catchy' melody, it has been heard before and it has an established status as a 'hit' record.

The extent to which a track reflects the tone and atmosphere of a programme is a further consideration for selection. Raucous, modern pop songs or simple to the point of twee ballads may not be considered appropriate for a programme which features long conversation pieces or in-depth pre-recorded reports. Songs with banal and cliché-ridden lyrics would be unlikely to be included in, say, an arts programme. Even the time of year will determine music selection. The overall sound of a station may be subtly altered or controlled to reflect the moods of listeners during different seasons. Summer is 'celebrated' with 'summer-sounding' songs referring to sunshine, holidays, etc.; Christmas songs are gradually phased in during early December until every other record proclaims Christmas by 24 December.

Selection of otherwise 'safe' songs can prove inappropriate in specific circumstances. Presenters are expected to show care in the choice of the first record immediately after a news bulletin and not necessarily rely on the computer's selection. Queen's *Another One Bites the Dust* or Shakespears Sister's *I Don't Care* would sound insensitive coming out of a main news story about a terrorist assassination of a public figure. Similarly, air disasters, bombings, mass starvation or the outbreak of war are news stories that can be difficult to follow. On a longer-term basis, many radio stations kept their own list of records *not* to play throughout the entire Gulf War in case their themes or titles suggested negative associations for listeners with family members involved. Lighter examples of unfortunate musical choices are Chris Rea's *The Road to Hell* following a news item on improvements for the M25 motorway, and Manfred Mann's

Oh No, Not My Baby in the middle of a phone-in discussion on fostering and adoption.

Presenters may also depart from the computer's selection if an appropriate alternative choice becomes self-evident after a news report. A BBC presenter once selected Lionel Richie's *Three Times a Lady* after a report of the death of a much respected local personality. The station received numerous congratulations from listeners on its tasteful and moving treatment of the story.

While computer technology allows control over a station's music policy – in turn facilitating more effective targeting of a specified audience – its consequences for the future direction of popular music are worthy of consideration. Both the application of too rigid a formula and the over-reliance by radio station staff on that formula reduce the scope for innovation in music and remove the opportunities for listeners to encounter alternatives to that which is tried, tested and proven popular. Creativity takes second place to commodification, whereby the piece of music is selected for the structural qualities that constitute its popular appeal rather than the less definable (for computers) but more significant (for humans) interweavings of melodies, lyrics, instrumentation and production features that create its own appeal within its own terms.

Whenever radio has opened up new definitions of popularity in music, it has usually been when a station has related to those listeners who see themselves as outside the identity 'constructed' by mainstream radio and has built up its following precisely because it broadcasts something that is different. Or it has happened when an audience has discovered an affinity with a 'minority interest' or specialist programme featuring 'indie' or ethnic music. Programmes or stations which do function at the 'periphery' to cater for wide-ranging musical tastes outside the shared definitions of 'pop', 'gold' or 'middle of the road' music, may indeed constitute fertile ground for musical innovation, or a waiting room for artistes whose efforts are yet to be recognised by the major record labels. There is nevertheless no obligation for ILR stations to feature any style of music other than that which is well established and 'safe' and the existence of minority interest music programmes may depend on the enthusiasm of a producer or presenter to build up an audience at non-peak times.

Barnard argues that apart from the large metropolitan independent stations with a relatively high proportion of young listeners, the success of programmes that feature independent or specialist music may depend on the availability and credibility of specific presenters.

---

they are very much individualistic affairs, presented and put together by local would-be John Peels, in which station management takes no particular interest: the presenters are employed to provide a music show of appeal to young people and are left to interpret that brief as they think fit.

Barnard 1989: 168

Specialist forms of music may not be condemned to these shadowy corners of the schedules for ever. 'Progressive' line-ups of the late 1960s and punk bands of the 1970s have made their impact on popular culture and notions of musical taste with and without the help of mainstream radio and the process of renewal continues unabated – even if this means that the music computer needs the occasional reprogramming.

Music off the record

WE have discussed music branding so far in relation to singles and CD tracks which may constitute part if not all of a programme's substantive content. There are three other ways in which music is regularly used on radio which also merit consideration through their ability to reinforce a particular station identity. These are: jingles, signature and theme tunes ('sigs') and live performances.

Jingles

Whether they incorporate sung words or are solely instrumental, jingles are designed primarily to fulfil a basic branding function – to state the name of the station in a musical context that conveys a specific mood and atmosphere. Nearly all radio stations use jingles and can pay thousands of pounds for a jingle package to be made up. Jingles are regarded as vital in fixing the station's role and identity within the consciousness of the listening community.

The station's management supplies the 'jingle factory' with a detailed brief of the brand image and the types of message that the station is aiming to convey. The station may wish to present itself as a key centre in the big metropolis, its finger on the pulse of local, national and international news, or as a rural service with a shire identity and a focus on popular melodic music. The jingles are written to reflect the station's characteristics: perhaps a loud, up-tempo, modern sound with a thrusting and staccato rhythm to suggest traffic, industry and the urgent transmission of radio signals, or a more orchestrated, bright and friendly pastoral musical theme. The 'sound' suggested by the jingle composition is one which sets out not to alienate the listener or to give a message that conflicts with the programme content itself. Obvious examples of inappropriate jingles which would confuse the branding would be the use of heavy metal lead guitar breaks for a service aimed at listeners aged 40-plus, or of electronic 'blippy', synthesised musical sounds for an 'old-gold' station.

Beyond constructing and reinforcing the station's overall brand identity, jingles can be used to name programmes, establish the status of presenters and reflect the time and related 'mood' of the day. 'Morning' jingles tend to be bright, brassy and energetic, perhaps with voices singing in joyful tones 'Good morning from CWFM', while evening jingles repeat the melody line but against a gentler and more mellow arrangement.

Radio stations frequently pay for someone to 'voice-over' jingles. It can prove expensive to have every presenter's name and every programme title sung as an integral part of a jingle, especially if there is a high turnover of staff or regular changes to the programme schedule. The use of voice-overs on top of a set of standard jingles, stating the name and/or the show title is not only cost-effective but provides further opportunity for the station to promote a particular identity that is appropriate for the target audience: an excited voice that oozes with enthusiasm for a young listenership, a mature, friendly and 'educated' voice for a 40-plus, professional audience, and so on.

Jingles reinforce the station identity through repetition of a common aural theme: the sound of the voice, the 'catch' melody line, the name of the station itself. While the familiarity of their sound contributes to the station's brand image, a selection of different versions is available for presenters to use, ranging from the rapidly sung two-second announcement 'CWFM!' to the more comprehensive message lasting for much longer and including details such as the frequency or name of the station's transmission area. Stations have gone as far as producing epic jingles lasting for over two minutes and 'name-checking' all the main presenters, locations covered by the station and main regular on-air features. Again, these are only usable for as long as all the presenters stay working for the station and the programme schedule remains largely unchanged.

Detailed programme content also hinges on the use of a variety of jingles to create a total sound or atmosphere. Jingles work both as signposts and as aural punctuation for output; they mark particular points in a programme by acting as bridges between items and enabling the presenter to 'round off' one item before changing the direction or mood of the programme to set up the next one. A choice of jingles of different durations allows presenters to indicate the significance of the 'break' between two items and also serves the practical function of providing a sound that will 'fill' an exact number of seconds: a useful facility for 'backtiming' (see pp. 211–13) and when a presenter is aiming to finish output at a precise moment before linking with another station in the network (see p. 211).

A jingle package contains key jingles – the most dramatic or distinctive – which are used to take listeners into or out of the most significant parts of output: news, weather bulletins and traffic reports. They ensure that listeners do not have to wait too long for confirmation of which station they are tuned in to and they effectively provide a pedestal upon which the personality of the presenter is placed. A professional-sounding jingle that proclaims 'Chris Shendo on CWFM' contributes to the presenter's authority and 'personality' status.

Jingles express a range of moods and emotions. 'Cheerful' jingles are there to remind listeners of what a good time they are having tuned in to the station. 'Urgent' jingles signify output that is live and news-orientated. 'Mellow' jingles may emphasise a station's relaxed, 'easy listening' style. Mood messages of this nature would seem wholly out of place on a station that presents itself as serious, intellectual and orientated to political and international news, such as Radio 4, or where they would clash with the atmosphere generated by a lengthy passage of classical music or opera, as presented on Radio 3. Neither of these stations use jingles and this absence makes its own contribution towards branding. However, the purposes served by jingles to reinforce station identity and provide punctuation points in output are just as important to such stations; therefore they use continuity announcers or the presenters themselves to brand the output at appropriate breaks or in the middle of news bulletins, perhaps by stating 'You're listening to . . .' alongside a timecheck. At certain points of output – leading up to the Greenwich Time Signal, for example, or after the final echo of the final note of an orchestral symphony – an effective bridge to the next item is a few seconds of pure silence.

Signature tunes

As a means of signifying the identity of a station, the theme of a programme or the personality of a presenter, 'sigs' have similar functions to jingles with the obvious exception that they usually signpost the programme only at its beginning. A shorter 'reprise' of the signature tune may be used to re-establish the programme after, say, a five-minute break for news. Programmes on stations which present output as a series of discrete units – as opposed to a continuous flow – sometimes finish with a repeat of the signature tune; however, unlike the opening, when the tune is often faded to provide a 'bed' of music while the presenter is introducing the programme, the tune that 'plays out' the programme often ends on a decisive note or chord.

Types of programme that use 'sigs' vary considerably. Radio drama productions open with any musical style appropriate to the theme of the play, reflecting among other things the time period and geographical location in which the action is set. Signature tunes for comedy shows give an indication of the type of comedy the listener might expect: a happily banal tune may be ideal for a radio sitcom but wholly inappropriate for a sequence of satirical sketches. Specialist music programmes obviously use 'sigs' to reflect the style of music featured but which also serve to suggest the atmosphere of the programme or its style of presentation. A programme about musicals for example may discourage fans of modern West End or Broadway shows by using a dated theme from, say, *Oklahoma* or *South Pacific*

Signature tunes are sometimes made up of existing and well-known pieces of music that already carry popular associations. A long-standing 'trade mark' of Radio 1 presenter Alan Freeman has been the 'big band' sound of his own signature tune *At the Sign of the Swinging Cymbals*[24] which used to herald *Pick of the Pops*, while his *Saturday Rock Show* launched itself with a lengthy edited montage of loud electric guitar solo clips juxtaposed with lively extracts of popular and orchestrated classical tunes. Radio 4's light-hearted comedy panel game *Just a Minute* opens brightly but 'intelligently' with a delicate performance on piano of *The Minute Waltz* while the comic banality and lack of subtlety associated with Radio 4's fictional talk-show host 'Alan Partridge' is indicated through the use of Abba's *Knowing Me Knowing You* – also the title of his programme.

Presenters often design introductory sequences to their programmes in which set phrases are incorporated within the structure and timing of 'sigs'. A common technique is to select a tune with a regular up-tempo backing to a melody line made up of a short runs of notes interspersed with pauses. The programme is then introduced with phrases spoken by the presenter during the pauses. An example of this is the opening of Radio 4's *PM* programme.

Programmes may incorporate more than one signature or theme tune to introduce and set the mood for different sections or regular features. A tune may also be used as a 'bed' for, say, a regular 'what's on' feature of a specialist music or magazine programme on local radio; the familiar opening bars of the tune signal to the listener that this feature is about to begin, then the music is faded to form a background for the presenter's announcements of local events. The closing bars of the tune are recorded on a separate tape so that the 'bed' can be faded out at the same time that the ending is faded in just before the presenter completes the voice-over. This gives the impression that the music exactly fits the number of items to be read out.

Many radio stations keep a stock of commercially available CDs which carry a selection of tunes that express different moods and might be suitable for 'sigs' and music beds, plus a choice of 'stings' – chords or melodies that run for four or five seconds – and 'stabs' – blasts of music of no more than one or two seconds to punctuate the aural narrative.

Live performances

The development of a music policy necessarily involves consideration of live music. Whether a local radio station provides access to local musicians depends on the brief to which it is operating. There may be little likelihood of the neighbourhood rock band or amateur operatic society being featured on a station that sees its role primarily as playing records and commercials, but a station which bases its appeal on serving a community may regard the regular featuring of home-grown live music as an essential role.

A frequent outlet for local guest musicians is the specialist programme. They may be featured during an interlude for a 'magazine' format programme on local issues, or appear as guests on a big band, classical music or reggae show. Should the composition of the song or tune, or the circumstances in which local artistes are to perform, constitute a 'newsy' story, a sample of the performance may be featured as an item for broadcast during daylight hours, although this would probably be set up and presented as a recorded package, complete with reporter's voice and interview, such that the 'live' performance is clearly distinguished from the CD tracks that surround it. Sadly, it is not uncommon for stations to package raw musical talent in this way to make it 'fit' with an overall sound reflecting a brand image.

Radio stations often set up live on-air music events as a promotional activity. These may vary from the big concert – hiring a venue, booking the artiste, distributing the tickets – to the musical feature on an OB (outside broadcast) programme – a jazz quartet on the station's own stage at the annual county show, or a folk group singing in the pub at the end of a broadcast tour of the local canals. Some stations also provide facilities to record local musicians in a studio for later broadcast – a boon for up-and-coming acts who cannot afford to hire a sophisticated studio to produce a broadcast-quality demonstration tape. However, the radio station's provision is usually quite basic in comparison with a purpose-built recording studio, requiring a rock band for example to give a 'live' one-off performance and making a true recording of that without sophisticated special effects or overdubs.

Live broadcasts of musical material usually have to be paid for. Artistes appear on air according to the terms of a contract which specifies payment but also ownership of the recording and whether the station is entitled to make repeat broadcasts. Even if artistes are not paid, the title, composer and publisher of a piece of music, and the duration of the version or extract that was played, must be logged and its broadcast reported to the PRS along with due payment for distribution to the owner or composer of the item. This applies even if the performed piece of music is audible in the background of a recorded interview or is included in a montage edit of recorded extracts to convey the atmosphere of a local music festival. In this latter case, it is the responsibility of the reporter to make a record of all details to be reported to the PRS, or to ensure that clips in which details of background music are not available are not included in the final edited package.

Whose voice?

PERHAPS the most difficult aspect to define of a station's output – and its overall contribution to the establishment and reinforcement of that station's brand image – is its speech content. We have demonstrated that recorded music may be classified, albeit controversially in some cases, to the extent that it can be selected via a computer programme to reflect with some precision the station's style policy. By the nature of its spontaneity, speech is not subject to this form of scientific control. While formal and informal guidelines do exist on things that may or may not be said on air, speech cannot be subjected to a rigorous formula, not least because much of what is said on air comes not from a presenter, but from interviewees, phone-in participants or studio guests.

Nevertheless, the impact of speech on listeners' perception of a radio station is considerable. Music radio may be more popular than speech radio as a general rule, but stations which do give prominence to speech are usually selected by listeners precisely for that reason. Thus stations monitor speech output with care and base their consideration on three aspects of the spoken word: content, language style and manner of delivery.

Content

An obvious but vital way in which speech contributes towards branding is through the type of topic discussed. A presenter of a mid-morning talk and music programme on local radio may include items ranging from brief announcements to in-depth discussions but risks alienating listeners if the topic of these items has no connection with their own experiences or interests. A recorded package in which an arts reporter reviews an exhibition of pre-Raphaelite landscapes may be a beautifully crafted piece of recording and editing but have little relevance to the lives of listeners whose interest in painting extends no further than whether to use matt or vinyl silk. This is not to argue of course that a skilled reporter cannot present a review of an arts exhibition in a way that makes it interesting to the most philistine of listeners.

The manner in which a topic is approached also reflects the perspective of the target audience. A local radio station that seeks to appeal to listeners in the 35–55 age range may well discuss a forthcoming rock music festival but probably in terms of its effect on the local area and how well controlled the event will be to prevent fights, drug dealing, convoys of new age travellers or other popular fears. It is less likely to broadcast any of the music itself.

The relationship of speech content to a station's brand image is also subject to careful consideration in relation to self-promotional output and competitions. Promotional messages are often recorded with appropriate music or sound effects, exhorting listeners to display car stickers advertising the station (owners of cars 'spotted' with stickers on display can call in to the station and claim a small prize), to collect free tickets to attend a local concert to be broadcast live, or simply to buy merchandise – pens, mugs, T-shirts which feature the station name and logo. Research or experience will tell station staff whether their target audience is likely to participate in promotions of this nature or even whether they would be seen in public exhibiting the station's name and logo on their clothes or vehicles. It is an indication of listeners' self-image and preferred forms of self-presentation, for example, that Radio 1 and not Radio 4 sunstrips are often seen decorating car windscreens.

PSAs (public service announcements) contribute further towards branding. These may be recorded or read out from a list, permanently located in the studio and regularly updated, and can provide a wide range of information: forthcoming events in the area, training opportunities for local unemployed people, recreational courses and evening classes, appeals for volunteers in charity events or announcements of items lost or found. The type of information given out is selected on the basis of whether it is likely to be relevant to the interests of the target audience. It also builds up the station's branding as serving a local community of listeners, especially if each announcement of a 'what's on' event is preceded by the name of the place or district where it is happening.

Language

Broadcasters place great emphasis on the style of language used in speech radio and the need for clear and simple expression when talking to listeners. There is a concern common to all radio stations that presenters use direct and uncomplicated language for two reasons – first because words spoken on the air are not permanent and cannot easily be referred to like words on a newspaper page; and second because there is no visual reference to fix or confirm the meaning that the words are conveying, as there is on television.

Textbooks on radio broadcasting technique are very explicit on the use of language. Boyd argues for 'conversational writing' when preparing speech for broadcast. This should mean 'tossing away literary conventions, including the rules of grammar, if the words are to make sense to the ear, rather than the eye' (Boyd 1993: 38–9). Chantler and Harris describe several writing devices for radio journalists to sound spontaneous on air including the use of contractions – 'He is becomes He's, Do not becomes Don't' – and the avoidance of jargon – 'Assistance (help), Request (ask), Terminate (end) . . .' (Chantler and Harris 1992: 28–9).

Horstmann offers advice on how to make speech on radio interesting by creating pictures and sensations in the mind through the use of words.

> Brian Hanrahan gave a classic demonstration of this in a famous despatch during the Falklands War. He was describing an air strike from a British carrier, and was not allowed to give details of the forces involved. Instead of saying 'Our aircraft suffered no losses', he said 'I counted them all out and I counted them all back' – and in imagination his listeners stood on the deck with him.
>
> *Horstmann 1991: 14–15*

Crisell argues that radio news is only recognisable as such if it is 'couched in quasi-objective language' (Crisell 1986: 82) and that this is vital to the authority of the news broadcast which is presented in the voice of an individual newsreader or reporter, otherwise:

> such statements would sound idiosyncratic – be attributed to the news-
> reader, dismissed as propaganda, or even more likely, misunderstood as
> drama or comedy.
>
> *Crisell 1986: 82*

The use of a language style may contribute towards a station's branding
by signifying the relevance of its output to listeners who are local, of a
specific age group or socio-economic group and, obviously, of an ethnic
group for whom English is not a first language. To enhance the authoritative and informative branding of its local radio stations in the Midlands
region, the BBC has produced a book called *A Style Guide – Writing News
Scripts for Regional Television and Local Radio* which covers clichés,
Americanisms, journalese and the need to use language that does not
imply sexism, racism or unfair representation of people with disabilities.

Radio station staff form judgements on a daily basis on what is and is
not appropriate language to use for that station's image and target
audience. There are numerous examples that highlight different
approaches by stations to the use of language – the use of modern idioms,
shorthand phrases, acronyms, slang or dialect. There are stations that still
prefer to use the word 'homosexual' rather than 'gay' in news reports,
others that happily condone the word 'crap' as a more forceful term than
'lousy' and others still that revel in the melodramatic and sensational –
'his face was slashed by the attacker' – as opposed to the more objective
'his face was cut'.

Delivery

As with language style, there are aspects of speech delivery that should
be common to all radio stations. Chantler and Harris advise on some of
these – sounding interested in the story, understanding the material that
is being read out, breathing correctly, identifying which words to stress,
etc. (Chantler and Harris 1992: 41–8).

Hutchby identifies certain features of talk in phone-in programmes that
'liken it to everyday or "mundane" conversation' as well as the 'more
"institutional" forms of verbal interaction' such as formal news interviews or courtroom exchanges. He states:

> In general we can say that mundane talk is designed, interactively, *ex-
> plicitly for co-participants* and is differentiated from institutional talk by
> the fact that the latter is designed, and displays itself as being designed,
> *explicitly for overhearers.*
>
> *Hutchby 1991: 119*

From this distinction he argues that radio phone-in programmes provide
an 'intermediate' form of talk that resembles the structure of a private

conversation but which is 'projected . . . into a public domain' (Hutchby 1991: 120). This observation offers a useful conceptual model for characterising how the delivery of speech serves to underline a station's style policy. A formal, authoritative and ostensibly objective position adopted by a station is indicated by devices of speech delivery that signify it as 'institutional' – in Hutchby's terms 'explicitly for overhearers'. The listener is being talked *to*. By contrast, an informal, friendly style of delivery may be more appropriate for the branding of a local, entertainment-orientated station whose output is predominantly geared to 'co-participants' – the listener is being chatted *with*. The point occupied by a station between these two positions provides an indication of what style of audience address is regarded as the most suitable for the station's brand image.

One indicator of how speech is delivered which effectively highlights the distinction between the 'institutional' and conversational approaches is the extent to which the personal pronoun 'you' is used. The formal, authoritative delivery style may include phrases such as 'those willing to assist are asked to contact . . .' or 'listeners can obtain tickets from . . .'; the informal, conversational approach addresses the listener directly: 'if you want to help, get in touch with . . .'; 'you can get tickets from . . .'.

Three important variables in the way in which speech is 'delivered' by a station's presenters are tone, pace and accent. These reflect the choices of station management on the type of voice that should personify the station and the brand image that it seeks to project. Different combinations of these variables can produce modes of address that range from the authoritative 'voice of the establishment' to the local voice that oozes street-credibility. The station is by no means confined to a singular and universal 'radio voice' technique.

A visible image

THE style of a radio station – its 'total sound' – is itself 'packaged' by the station's visual identity. Like any company or public organisation, a radio station projects its image through a logo which is designed to communicate the essence of the station's style and preferred public image. The logo is presented on station literature, in advertisements, on car stickers and merchandise. Importantly for local stations, the logo is visible on vehicles seen in the area – cars driven by advertising sales team members, radio cars and vans. While it is technically feasible for a radio station to broadcast from any location, local stations are based on sites that are central to their editorial area to enhance their visibility and accessibility – as we will discuss in the next chapter. Some stations also set up satellite studios in populated areas such as shopping centres to make themselves more visible within their listening communities and to enable the public to watch the presenters at work occasionally.

Station presenters have a role to play in establishing the station's concrete and visible presence. Fundamentally, presenters *are* the radio station – it is their voices and personalities that construct the station's 'human' identity. Hence, foyers of station headquarters are often decorated with large colour photographs of the presenting team. Some radio stations market themselves through the publication of a newspaper or magazine delivered free of charge to houses in the editorial area and carrying 'personality' stories or 'behind the scenes' features to humanise the station's identity and reinforce its visual image.

Presenters themselves take on the task of making public appearances as part of their job. On or off the air, they compère rock concerts, super-vise the switching on of Christmas lights, or take part in public stunts in the spirit of *Challenge Anneka* or *Jeux Sans Frontières*. Their photographs are printed in the local press as often as editors can be convinced that there is a story worth running which promotes the station.

Occasionally radio stations hold open days for the public and seek to break down the barrier of the microphone and loudspeaker by allowing visitors to watch presenters in action, demonstrating how the news studio works, showing the faces behind the voices of the travel and weather announcers and providing opportunities to chat with staff about the work they do. Alternatively, the station team moves out into the area that it covers with OBs, roadshows, canal tours or 'drop in' surprise stunts – for example, a presenter with a backpack (see pp. 108–9) calling at a listener's house while on air to deliver a bouquet of flowers for her birthday.

Whether it is local or national, radio establishes its viability with audiences (and wins franchises) through appearing to meet public needs or to supply a service that is responsible and conducive to the interests of its listeners. The construction of the station's visual identity – through design, marketing, public relations and opportunities for public access – is controlled and driven by a style policy but indicates the station's own accountability as a service operating in the public domain.

Scope for innovation?

AS the increase in the numbers of radio stations in the United Kingdon offers potential for more specialist and focused output, the process of branding might appear to create a straitjacket for each station – establishing a formula of music and speech such that virtually every note of music played or word uttered appears to reflect a pre-determined and desired brand image. In practice, the existence of a style policy need not be experienced as a constraint, but as a set of guide-lines for presenters' choices of music, topic of discussion or priority news story.

2 *Satellite studio – exterior:* this is BBC CWR's studio located at the West Orchards shopping centre in Coventry and overturning the notion of a presenter broadcasting from a secluded corner of the station building. The presenter in this picture is on air in what amounts to a 'goldfish bowl'. Passers-by can see the process of making radio and may even take part in the programme.

Here is an obvious opportunity to reinforce branding with the station name, logo and frequencies clearly displayed along with publicity photographs of presenters. There is even a sign which lights up to declare that this studio is on air while a discreet loudspeaker to the far left of the top name panel broadcasts output – as does the internal public address system of the entire shopping centre.

The challenge for radio in the 1990s is to open up new markets and increase the total audience size, rather than fragment further the existing audience. The Henley Centre's research (see p. 10) indicates that this is beginning to happen and that radio's popularity is increasing, relative to that of television. The key to radio's success thus lies in building on this expansion and convincing more people that listening to the radio is a useful, informative and entertaining activity that enhances the quality of their lives. This highlights the relevance of branding as a means of encouraging a specific and targeted group of people to engage personally and directly with a station's output and to accept that station as part of their routines and day-to-day experience, as they would a close companion.

The growth of stations that do specialise, rather than design output for a wide appeal, can also open up opportunities for more creative and inno-vative radio. Populist radio tends to tread safe ground in its choice of music and its treatment of news stories and information. Its mode of address and the structure of its output function as a form of compro-mise; individual listeners may have their own tastes and perspectives but

3   ***Satellite studio – interior****: the presenter might be visible to the world outside, but the reverse is also true and the presenter can emphasise the immediacy of radio by commenting on what is happening in the shopping centre. The desk is simpler than the one at base although a sufficiently wide range of audio sources is at hand to maintain a full programme from this site – carts and cart machines to the left, CD players (not visible here), grams and guest microphones to the presenter's right.*

populist radio caters for those tastes and perspectives that are common to them all. Similarly, the act of listening to populist radio is also a compromise; listeners do not expect their individual interests to be addressed and instead take on roles as members of a taste and interest consensus when they tune in. A listener might be a particular fan of modern jazz but accept the musical offerings of Abba or Phil Collins on the car radio in the afternoon as part of the companionship and information that the nearest local station can offer at that time.

Specialist stations on the other hand can afford to take risks. A station that *does* specialise in modern jazz twenty-four hours a day would attract listeners primarily because they love the music. The station would be branded through its music output and listeners would be less likely to retune if it varied its presenting or newsreading styles. Indeed its listenership would probably be enhanced if the station included lengthy interviews with exponents of modern jazz or fifteen-minute-long album tracks – features that would be totally contradictory to the style policy of a more populist station.

No matter how a station's branding is determined, the essence of radio is its purity and simplicity as a form of human communication. The voice of the presenter suggests a style of communication that is interactive, that pre-supposes a response from the listener in terms of a reaction, an emotion or a recognition of shared experience. Style policies may be simple or complex, intuitive or scientifically calculated to maximise listening figures, but they are invisible at the point of interaction when presenter and listener are both firmly embedded within the discourse of radio and participating within its own terms of reference. Branding is the construction of a theory on how a radio station is most likely to connect with its listeners and as such is only the first stage of the process of making that connection. It does not guarantee the success of this communication. This is down to the individual presenter and the extent to which she encourages the listener to relate to her as a human being.

Activities and points for discussion

1 What does the logo for BBC Radio Norfolk (Figure 1) suggest to you about the station and its role within its transmission area? In terms of promoting a brand image, how does it compare with the logo for Classic FM (Figure 2)? What indication do both logos give of the type of output you might expect to hear from these stations and the type of listener that they are targeting?

Figure 1   *Logo for BBC Radio Norfolk*

Figure 2   *Logo for Classic FM*

Now consider the logos for four of the national BBC radio networks (Figure 3). To what extent does each logo signify (a) the style and special character of the individual network and (b) the overall public image of the BBC itself?

Figure 3   *Logos for four of the national BBC radio networks*

Brand an imaginary radio station on the basis of these three factors:

- what its listeners are interested in
- what its ratio is of talk to music
- where it can be heard.

For example, your station could be aimed at people who like soul music, and could broadcast 70 per cent music against 30 per cent speech in a built-up, metropolitan area. Think of a name for that station and design a logo which incorporates that name. Display the logo. (You might also think of a slogan and combine this with the logo to design a car sticker.) How many colleagues are able to identify correctly the three factors behind the branding of your station?

2 As a group, select two contrasting radio stations. Organise a campaign for members of your group to listen to as much output as possible within a week. Record samples of the output. Listen out for characteristics such as: the accent and language style of the presenters; the structure of output (seamless flow or individual programmes); the use of jingles and sound effects; the amount of airtime given over to members of the public phoning in; any indicator, in fact, of style policy. Use this evidence to make a report in the form of an oral presentation, comparing the styles of each station and suggesting how their output sets out to target a particular niche in the listening market.

3 As a group, draw up a playlist of fifty records for a music radio station aimed at 16–25-year-olds. Which records would be more likely to be played

- 6–7am?
- 3–4pm?
- immediately after a news bulletin?
- as the first item of a late afternoon 'drive time' programme?

4 You are in charge of marketing a local radio station that needs to increase its profile in the community, especially as a listener survey is to take place during the next four weeks. You want the station to be very visible in the area during this time. How would you go about it? Individually, or as a group, draw up a list of strategies to give your station a strong visual presence.

5 Listen to the BBC World Service and to foreign stations, even if they are broadcasting in a language different from your own. Discuss how they differ from stations you would normally listen to in terms of style, presentation techniques, music–speech ratio, access to interviewees and listeners phoning in. How many indicators can you identify of the station's style policy (for example, jingles, music selection, presenters' style of delivery) and to what extent are they common to stations you are more familiar with?

6 Listen to a phone-in programme and pick out the characteristics of people who call in and get put on the air. What range is there of their views, apparent expertise or knowledge in the topic under discussion, communication skills, language style and overall performance? What strategies does the presenter apply in discussing their views with them and to what extent do these strategies reflect the brand image of the radio station?

3   Getting organised

....

The essential components

THE style and character of a radio station determine the nature of investment into its operation and the emphasis placed on its resources of people, equipment and an appropriate base from which to broadcast. A station whose output is entirely music-based and where no physical public access is needed could feasibly operate from a bedroom, a ship out at sea, or even a computer (see p. 84). A community talk station needs to be in the middle of the community it serves to enhance public access and also in a building that can comfortably accommodate the larger number of staff needed to provide the material and voices for its output.

Having identified the main considerations behind the establishment and reinforcement of a station's style, we will now turn our attention to the means of translating a style policy into a product – output itself. Before identifying the specific 'tools of broadcasting', we will focus in this chapter on the working environment of a radio station and investigate the extent to which this is controlled and organised to reflect its policy on style and branding. To illustrate the physical environment in which broadcasters work and the channels of communication that are available to them, we will describe and discuss the rationale behind the organisation of a BBC local radio station. As to the social environment of the radio station as a workplace, we will consider the different areas of responsibility that exist within a station team, again with a view to how this influences – and is reflected by – the nature of the station's output.

Clearly, where variations do exist in the organisation of radio stations, these arise from differences in emphasis. There are a number of common structural features to all radio stations, some of which are quite basic but all of which are instrumental to the nature of mass communication that radio offers. The essential components of any station are a source of sound and a means of transmitting that sound. The most vital source is the human voice.

A source of sound

The strict definition of radio as a generic term is the capability to transmit a signal through space without the use of wires to connect the signal source with its receiver.[1] In terms of the product itself, however, radio may be defined by the way it is heard rather than the way it is delivered. Hence, a basic public address (PA) system, in which source and receiver are indeed linked by a cable, could constitute the means of providing a 'radio' service, for example in a hospital, factory or student union building on a campus. Following this definition, a club DJ who can be heard in more than one disco might be perceived as providing a listening experience which is, to all intents and purposes, radio.

To qualify as 'radio' in these terms, even the simplest means of broadcasting involves orientating the source of sound to the radio listener. It underpins a particular style of audio text and a discursive framework that presupposes a group of listeners adopting a specific mode of reception. The radio experience is about being entertained and informed, but more than this – as we have already suggested – it is about companionship and being part of a mental and cultural environment in which consciousness and intellect can 'breathe', an external alternative to the 'inner voice' that drives our moment-to-moment thoughts in a linguistically based, interactive manner. Hence the essential means of broadcasting radio take it beyond the status of a telephone tap or baby alarm. Even in its most basic form, it is designed for the transmission of a structured performance and organisation of sounds and silences. 'Eavesdropping' technology conveys signals which are unwittingly produced of sounds generated almost by accident and not designed for consumption by a mass audience. Such signals are not necessarily intelligible without any visual reference. In contrast, signals generated from the radio performance compensate for the listener's lack of visual access; the verbal descriptions are more explicit, the organisation of sounds within the radio text are such that the listener is openly invited to take them into his consciousness and construct his own pictures. In his discussion of the characteristics of radio, Crisell argues

> The risks of ambiguity or complete communication failure are high, and so in all kinds of radio much effort is expended on overcoming the limitations of the medium, on establishing the different kinds of contexts which we would generally be able to see for ourselves ... Physical objects or processes which are normally self-evident have to be described: 'Tell the listeners what you are doing.' 'Can you describe this object to us?'
>
> *Crisell 1994: 5*

Such a characterisation places focus on a perceived 'weakness' of the medium of radio, set out at the very beginning of Crisell's study:

> What strikes everyone, broadcasters and listeners alike, as significant about radio is that it is a *blind* medium.
>
> *Crisell 1994: 3*

A seemingly more positive perspective of radio, offered by McLeish, suggests what the minimum capability of a basic radio station should be.

> Unlike television, where the pictures are limited by the size of the screen, radio's pictures are any size you care to make them. For the writer of radio drama it is easy to involve us in a battle between goblins and giants, or to have our spaceship land on a strange and distant planet. Created by appropriate sound effects and supported by the right music virtually any situation can be brought to us. As the schoolboy said when asked about television drama, 'I prefer radio, the scenery is so much better.'
>
> *McLeish 1978: 16*

What must be remembered in the creation of the experience of radio – as illustrated here by McLeish – is that the broadcasting equipment, even at its most basic, should be designed for a distinctive form of communication that is not a 'poor cousin' to television. It is a form that allows mobility to the listener and, more importantly, requires conceptual and intellectual 'work' by the listener, effectively transforming his status from that of 'receiver' to that of 'participator'. The simplest public announcement – 'The AGM is about to start in the Main Hall' – could well constitute part of the 'experience' of, say, campus radio, but unless the station's facilities can be used to evoke images and experiences in the minds of listeners, and to provide some form of structured aural narrative, it will be unable to function effectively as radio, only as a PA system.

This is not to argue that to produce a genuine radio experience, a station must consistently transmit sounds from more sources than that of the single human voice. Imaginative, captivating and mentally stimulating radio broadcasts can be – and frequently are – achieved through one speaker talking into one microphone: telling a story, expounding a theory or performing a comedy monologue. It is essentially the *performance* of the speaker, whether a news correspondent, continuity announcer or DJ, that signifies a sequence of broadcast sounds as 'radio'. Nevertheless, the auditory codes of radio and its conventional forms of address are such that the listening experience would be incomplete without a variety of sound sources to package, contextualise, co-exist with and punctuate the spoken word. In Chapter 4, we will examine the range of devices available to professional radio presenters to achieve this. Here we wish to emphasise a fundamental point to the organisation of any form of radio: that sounds from a range of sources, both live and recorded, are gathered in and marshalled to construct the essential radio performance.

A means of transmitting sound

The basic operational principle behind radio is the construction of an audio text – produced by mixing and editing sounds from a range of live and recorded sources – and channelling that text in such a way that its final form can be heard simultaneously by anyone within range of a suitable receiving device. The cable that links the studio to the PA loudspeaker, or the wire that is run round a building to transmit an AM signal through an induction loop system (see p. 20) are technically capable of achieving this outcome, albeit with a more limited scope than the transmitter that radiates a signal across a large geographical area, or bounces a signal off a satellite.

The size and shape of the area that can be covered by one radio transmitter is determined mainly by the strength of the signal transmitted and the physical height of the transmitter. A finite number of frequencies is available on both AM (long and medium wave) and FM wavebands and international agreements govern the allocation of these frequencies and signal strengths to the broadcasting organisations of different countries. It is possible for more than one radio station to operate on the same frequency provided the transmitters are far enough apart and the signals are not so strong that they overlap. It is also possible to broadcast a stronger signal on a frequency already allocated such that the legitimate user of that frequency is blotted out; this was the practice of William Joyce who, as 'Lord Haw-Haw', made pro-Nazi broadcasts on BBC wavelengths during the Second World War in an attempt to demoralise British listeners.

A signal generated by one station can be fed through to other stations for them to broadcast via their own transmitters. This is networking; it effectively transforms a local station into a regional or national station at the flick of a switch. Many local stations link in to a network for part of their output, simply because they cannot justify the expense of producing local programmes for small audiences at non-peak listening times. Some ILR stations, for example, broadcast their own output between 6am and midnight and then network with other stations in their group during the 'dark hours' or switch over to a jukebox (see pp. 83–4). They may provide local news between 6am and 6pm and link to the national IRN service during the evening. Many BBC local radio stations finish their own programmes at 7pm or 9pm and thereafter join a regional network until midnight. Then they may opt for the national Radio 2, World Service or jukebox until their own early morning programmes start up again.

Transmission technology has consistently exerted an important influence on the way that radio has developed in Britain, both in style and usage. It was the combination of the BBC's determination that post-Second World War radio in Britain should not become 'Americanised' and the availability of wavelengths to listeners across the country that formed the basis of the tri-partite Light Programme, Third Programme and Home Service provision, the forerunners of Radios 2, 3 and 4, along with a structure of regional broadcasting (Briggs 1979: 52 and 84–7).[2] The greatest impact on the scope of post-war BBC radio, however, was created by what Briggs refers to as 'the changing technology of Sound' (Briggs 1979: 561) allowing the introduction of very high frequency signals (VHF). Test transmissions of VHF signals with FM began in 1950 and the possibilities opened for more frequencies, providing signals free of interference, just as the BBC was considering the regional structure to be insufficiently focused for non-national audiences and the need for a more localised pattern (Briggs 1979: 562). Indeed, as Crisell points out, 'it is VHF which has made possible the extensive development of local radio' (Crisell 1986: 31).

The current availability of FM frequencies on the VHF waveband has enabled a dramatic increase in the number of radio stations operating across Britain. FM frequencies available in this country range from 87.5 to 105 MHz[3] and are grouped roughly into sub-bands dedicated to BBC or independent national or local services.[4] The 'technology of sound' alone, however, does not guarantee that radio stations will hit their target audience. As the 1992 Green Paper *The Future of the BBC* points out, 'About one million people have difficulty in receiving the BBC's national radio services on FM' (para. 5.9) whilst the Radio Authority reminds listeners that 'More and more services are becoming available on one waveband only' (Radio Authority 1993a: 7). The current problem of transmission technology therefore is one of convincing the public that they should possess radio sets capable of receiving clear signals on FM and AM (medium and long wave) to maximise the listening choices open to them.

Transmission by cable and satellite has also provided opportunities for new applications of radio. Satellite services currently licensed range from a national in-store service (Asda FM) to a twenty-four-hour country music service (QCMR – Quality Country Music Radio). Cable services include a Westminster-based twenty-four-hour community service for Arab and Muslim listeners (Radio Orient) and a community service for listeners in Milton Keynes (CRMK). Again, scope provided by the transmission technology is effectively limited by listeners' ability to receive the signals: hence the tendency for satellite and cable services to be aimed at very specific listening groups pre-disposed to having access to satellite and cable receivers. However, viewers of satellite television are able to tune in to satellite radio by linking their radio sets to the receiving equipment and selecting the appropriate audio channel.

The next major development in transmission technology is the introduction of digital audio broadcasting (DAB) which should be operational by the end of 1996 when the BBC's current charter is due to expire. This will have two important effects on radio: it will further improve reception quality and it will open up even more services. The Government has set up the UK DAB Forum to consider how DAB may be most effectively utilised and a national policy is being formulated on the organisation of – and frequency allocation for – local and national radio DAB.

By tracing the technological developments in radio transmission it is possible therefore to gain some insight into the changing nature of the radio experience. With more channels available, radio could become more relevant to the interests, tastes and life experiences of listeners as members of a niche market. Improved reception makes radio easier to listen to; arguably the reduced necessity to concentrate in order to hear the signal renders the message conveyed by that signal as more powerful, pervasive and, for the benefit of advertisers, persuasive. Radio as a technical phenomenon requires the means of transmitting a signal, but the nature of radio as a listening experience is to some significant extent influenced by the state of play of transmission technology.

It is worth qualifying this point however with two reminders that the means of transmitting a radio signal is by no means a sole determinant in the nature of the radio experience. Firstly, reception technology and its availability to all listeners are important factors in the viability of radio. Wider listener choice is only possible if listeners have sets capable of receiving all wavebands. This point was illustrated in 1992 by the remarkably strong and co-ordinated opposition of Radio 4 listeners, not usually noted for their militancy, to the BBC's proposals to transfer the long wave frequency to the all-news channel and forcing fans of *Woman's Hour* and *The Archers* to retune to FM – not an option for those without FM receivers or living overseas. Changes in reception technology itself have also considerably influenced the role of radio in listeners' lives, no less dramatically than the introduction of the portable and inexpensive transistor radio. The 'trannie' re-established listening as a solitary and individual experience (see Crisell 1994: 11–12) and fuelled the growth of the pop music industry by providing a medium for young listeners to tune in to all-music stations. Two decades later, technology created further isolated listening experience when the Walkman became a vital fashion accessory.

Second, whether necessity or ideology has been the mother of invention, it should be noted that the 'discovery' of new and better means of transmitting radio signals has not occurred in a political vacuum. The notion of radio operating in a free market with maximised choices open to 'consumers' would have less resonance if the opportunities for growth and the availability of new frequencies were not so visible. Usually, technological developments flourish provided the political and economic environment is conducive and they are considered to offer a good return for investment. This suggests that, at least within the perspective of a free market economy, a third essential element is necessary for radio: the likelihood of sufficient 'consumer' demand.

The location

FOR the listener of a national network radio station, the distance between him and the studio from which the signal is being broadcast is immaterial. If he and the presenter share the same language, hold the same sense of national or cultural identity, perceive the world in similar ways or enjoy listening to the same type of music, the studio location is of little relevance. The presenter's voice comes clearly through and the essential elements are in place for the unique form of communication that radio offers. For local radio, however, the whereabouts of the studio is crucial to the station's credibility with its target listeners.

Local credibility can be won or lost in a number of symbolic or intangible ways: the local knowledge of presenters, perhaps their accents and language style, the station's focus on urban and rural issues, the accuracy of information given out and the station's sensitivity to local feelings and attitudes in relation to particular news stories. Similarly the bricks and mortar of local radio – the station's physical presence in the area – can make an important impression on listeners, effectively reinforcing the bond that has developed between them and the station's own persona. Listeners' knowledge that the voice they hear is from the building in the centre of town – and that when that voice says 'It's raining' they can look out the window and see the same thing, or at least the clouds heading their way – is an essential part of that station's local branding. Not just the building but all aspects of the station's physical presence within its editorial area can influence that credibility. A station's local image could suffer, for example, if its editorial area included a leading car manufacturer as a major local employer and it bought in a different brand for its own vehicles; this may not endear a hapless reporter trying to record *vox pop* interviews with the workers on the day of a strike call.

A radio station's position within the main population cluster of its locality can provide positive publicity, although this is a factor that must be weighed against the costs incurred. The ideal location for local radio is likely to be on a premium site with high rent and land costs and a talk station with a large number of staff may take up a considerable amount of space for the building itself and parking for radio cars and vans. Some stations reduce these costs by establishing their main base in a less expensive area whilst setting up a small satellite studio in a visible and more populated central location.

By establishing itself physically in a city or town centre location, the station allows two relationships to develop. First it provides an opportunity for members of the public to walk in through the front door. They may be collecting competition prizes, leaving information for social action broadcasting slots, buying merchandise or attending open days or public meetings. All these activities work towards building up a more tangible relationship with listeners based on a familiarity with the station as part of their living environment. Second, a central location enables programme guests and contributors to have better access to the station itself. Face-to-face interviews are more spontaneous, natural and easier to conduct than interviews down a telephone line. The interaction between contributor and presenter can create better integration of that item into the rest of the programme and thus improve the overall flow of output.

The editorial area of local radio usually takes in more than one major population cluster and could well cover several major towns. If output is largely speech-based and involving the regular use of local guests, it may be cost-effective and desirable in broadcasting terms to install a series of remote studios or unmanned satellite studios in convenient locations and capable of linking with the main studio without loss of signal quality. These studios are simple to operate in contrast with the station's main studio and sometimes comprise little more than a microphone in a sound-proof booth (see p. 90).

An alternative to inviting the listening public into the studio, or setting up remote studios, is literally to transport the studio to the people. Local stations have been known to convert a suitable vehicle – a double-decker bus or canal narrowboat – into a mobile studio and use it for outside broadcasts in different locations. The studio need not be fully equipped; CDs and tapes may still be run from the central studio provided the presenter on location and his colleague at base have agreed on a running order or worked out any necessary cues.

The internal structure – BBC CWR

THE organisation of a radio station reflects the type of service that it offers. The presenter's performance on air and the type of material that he includes in his programme are determined partly by the physical and technical resources available to him; these in turn are governed by the station's overall style and function. Very few radio stations operate on a 'stand alone' basis with sole responsibility for their entire output. Usually, stations carry additional material brought in from external sources, either by linking with other stations in a network to share a programme, or connecting with specific sources for news, weather and travel information.

The channels of communication built into the organisation of a station are frequently complex, placing the broadcaster in the centre of a large web of editorial or advertorial commitments. For example, member stations of a large independent group may take shared programming but broadcast different advertisements at set times on local frequencies. Many ILR stations also have contracts with IRN (Independent Radio News) or Network News for a supply of national and international news to be incorporated into their output at fixed times. BBC local radio stations are themselves enmeshed in the Corporation's intricate news-gathering operation with items fed from one station to another either off or on air.

As a radio station's product becomes more complicated and its sound more varied – a jigsaw of items from different sources within and outside the studio – so the need increases for a bigger building to operate from, accommodating more people and equipment. Similarly, the bigger the proportion of output that is taken up by speech, the more people are

77

needed to prepare and present the material. In resourcing terms, it is easier for a station to play a three-minute record than to conduct a three-minute interview. The interview needs research, a guest, a question plan, another studio if the guest is unable to be there in person, or time to record and edit prior to the broadcast if the interview is not live.

The local radio service for Coventry and Warwickshire, BBC CWR provides an illustration of the elaborate internal organisation and communications structure of a local radio station. It is no more sophisticated than many other radio stations in these respects and it does demonstrate the extent to which one station is linked to other broadcast services. It also indicates the ways in which advanced communications and computing technology are applied to create the spontaneous sound of radio, establish its instantaneous links with sources across the world and maintain an output that consistently reflects the station's style policy.

BBC CWR is a talk station and more than 70 per cent of its output is speech-based. Therefore it needs more than a studio and a handful of presenters in order to fulfil the remit of a BBC local radio service. A cross-section plan of the CWR building in Coventry (Figure 4) reveals the range of day-to-day activities that take place for the station to operate effectively. The ground floor houses the main studios and a reasonably spacious reception area. The first floor contains a large working area – the production office – where, in broad terms, material is gathered in and prepared for broadcast. The two ongoing activities on the second floor are the collection and preparation of material for 'Action Desk', the station's social action broadcasting function, and training potential broadcasters through the Community Services Volunteer scheme.

The production office and newsroom

A more detailed examination of the production office (Figure 5) highlights not only the complex organisation behind a talk radio station but also the news-orientated nature of its output. The main working area is an open plan office where nearly all the people involved in generating programmes, news output and recorded items work together. Journalism lies at the heart of operations of all BBC local radio stations (see p. 47); it is not confined to hourly bulletins but underpins a large part of total output, whereby individual stories are covered in greater depth through live interviews or recorded packages. At BBC CWR, integration of news-based material into overall output is achieved through organising staff into small programme teams working in the same office as the journalists. Here, different working areas for individual programme teams are marked out by the positioning of desks. In other stations, there is greater integration with programme makers and journalists working together without any 'team territories'.

The 'newsroom' half of the production office is equipped with devices to collect in material from various sources. Hard copy for national and

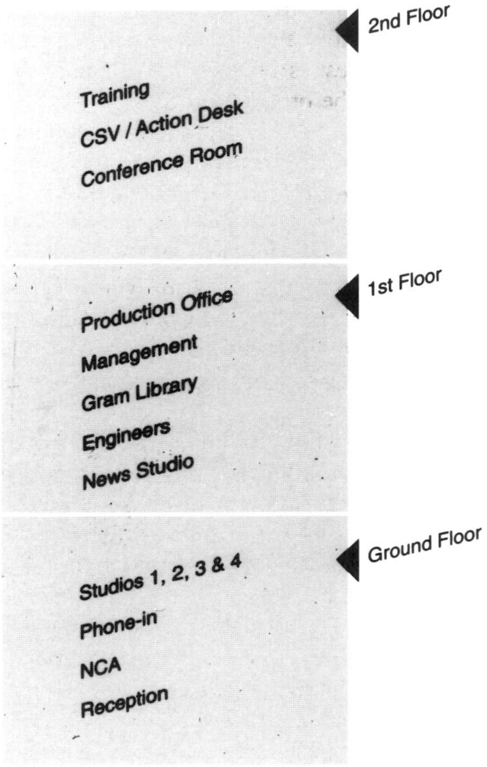

2nd Floor

Training
CSV / Action Desk
Conference Room

1st Floor

Production Office
Management
Gram Library
Engineers
News Studio

Ground Floor

Studios 1, 2, 3 & 4
Phone-in
NCA
Reception

Figure 4   *Cross-section plan of the BBC CWR building in Coventry*

international news is sent by the BBC's central newsroom, GNS (General News Service) to the station every hour via landline to be received by two teleprinters. GNS also sends audio material – interviews or correspondents' reports already recorded and ready for broadcast – through a system of lines that links all BBC local radio, referred to as 'the circuit'.[5] This material used to arrive at set times, but the tendency now is for a continuous flow of stories to be fed down the line along with an increasing amount of material from regional newsrooms. Audio material (or 'feed') is recorded automatically at each radio station onto cartridge (cart) tape machines so that it is ready to be used if required on the next news bulletin. The system sends a tone down the line that automatically activates the recording. All the station has to do is to ensure that carts are fed into the recording equipment to take the signal. A reel-to-reel tape recorder also records this material as a back-up and is left on for twenty-four hours a day so that stories can be received even when the station is unattended.

BBC CWR's production office is also equipped with telex and fax machines. Telex is now only used for collecting copy on travel conditions

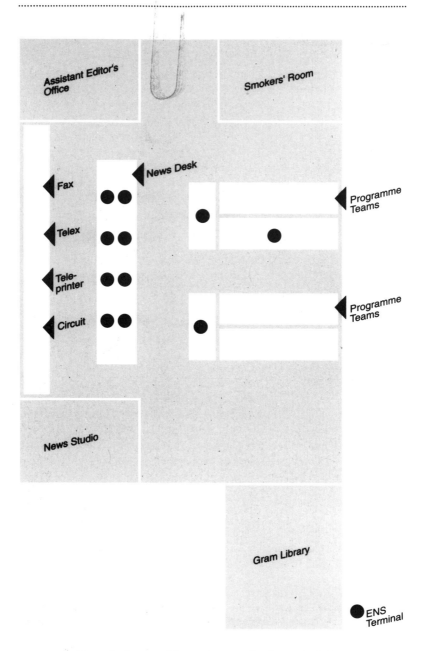

Figure 5   *Layout of the production office floor at BBC CWR*

from the AA Roadwatch service and updated weather forecasts from the regional weather centre, while the fax machine is in almost constant use with more and more press releases arriving through this rather than by post.

4   *News-gathering*: *the reporter here is scanning incoming material on a printer in a BBC local radio newsroom. Material on this printer comes from local sources and can be fed in at any computer workstation in the building. The teleprinter at the front of the picture provides a continuous supply from GNS – the BBC's main London newsroom – of cues, background information and editorial advice, for example on the treatment of national stories.*

Note the stock of blank carts in the background. In front of them (just discernable) is the 'circuit', which is the newsroom's means of receiving audio material from GNS. This is recorded on reel-to-reel tape and carts, both of which have been bulk-erased. Carts are ready to load into a recording machine, automatically activated as material is fed to the station.

Facilities for receiving and processing news and information at BBC CWR are similar to those found in any local BBC or ILR station. The major source of national and international news for independent stations since 1973 has been IRN which supplies two- or three-minute live bulletins every hour for local radio stations to put on air alongside their own local stories. It also feeds audio material to stations for use in local news reports plus supporting information and cues on teleprinter. Since 1991, independent stations have also been able to subscribe to Network News which provides live bulletins only for broadcast at the top of each hour. Both IRN and Network News send their audio material by satellite.

Local radio stations can have access to wire services. These include major international agencies such as Reuters, Associated Press and UPI (United Press International). British national news is supplied in this way by the Press Association. BBC local radio can call these up through their news computer and the information required is fed through by GNS. ILR news staff can access wire services via IRN.

The news computer

A further aid towards integration – within the station and between all stations in the region – is the use of the news computer or electronic news system (ENS). Most radio newsrooms are computerised. The BBC uses a system called BASYS, while many ILR stations today use Newstar. These are essentially data storage and distribution systems combined with word processing.

BBC CWR's production office is equipped with over a dozen ENS terminals. From these, any staff can enter their own password and access any file, or create their own, on items not only relevant to that radio station but also to be broadcast anywhere else in the whole region on both radio and television. A file may comprise an individual story to be included in a news bulletin, set out word for word in the way it will be read on air. Or it may carry details of an entire programme complete with running order and cues.

The ENS enables the station to receive regular information – national and international news – from GNS. A keyword facility in the news computer highlights if a story coming through is likely to be of interest to a particular local radio station. Examples of keywords are local place names, the names of major manufacturers in the editorial area, or names of local Members of Parliament or well-known personalities. If a story containing a keyword has been sent through the system it is automatically placed in a holding file while a message is flashed on the computer screen to alert users that the file exists.

Other uses of the ENS are: as an electronic mail system – a user can send a message on the screen to any other user in the region – and as a master file of all contact names, addresses and telephone numbers, saving the laborious task for individual station staff of keeping their own contacts books and no doubt duplicating information held by colleagues. Stations often use their ENS also to book radio cars and studio time.

Through their use of this system, BBC local stations are never isolated in their locality but remain intrinsic parts of a sophisticated communications network. Any station can access ENS files of any other station in the BBC region; the data is pooled and whilst it has been argued that the system is more sophisticated than needed for local newsrooms,[6] it serves as a practical reinforcement of each station's identity as part of the BBC.

The gram library and jukebox

Adjacent to BBC CWR's production office is the gramophone library – a misnomer as nearly all music played on air comes from the station's eight CD jukeboxes which are situated in this room and linked directly to the main studios downstairs.[7] Different jukebox systems are in use in several independent stations although BBC CWR is the first (and, at the time of writing, only) BBC local radio station to have this facility. The jukeboxes provide music for all mainstream programming. Each jukebox contains CDs. Thus presenters at BBC CWR have almost immediate access to a choice of 7000 CD tracks.

The music running order is selected by computer (see pp. 50–2) and is shown in the studio on a visual display unit linked to the jukebox. Presenters can change the order of tracks if they wish, or even access the jukebox in a matter of seconds to find a particular track, say, by an artiste who is the subject of a breaking news story. Otherwise, all they need to do is open the fader on the studio desk (see p. 116) and the next track on the displayed running order is on the air. The fact that the CDs are not physically handled ensures that they do not become damaged or dirty.

Before the jukeboxes were installed, presenters used to call into the gram library before going on air to collect a box of records already prepared for them. Station staff were faced with the time-consuming task of setting up records for each programme, locating them on their shelves in the library, maintaining a written record of where they were located and keeping a booking system to ensure that no albums were misplaced. Outside normal working hours, records and CDs were kept under lock and key and were difficult to obtain at short notice.

With the jukebox system in place, presenters now have only to pick up a paper printout of the music running order. Here the records are listed in the 'ideal' sequence worked out by the music computer (see p. 51) plus bar codes to be scanned whilst each track is playing to log the piece of music for royalties payment (see p. 118). The printout also supplies useful information about each record: the full title and name of the artiste (the fields of the VDU are often too small to give all this information), the duration of the whole track and of the introduction, whether it fades out or finishes abruptly, plus any background information that has been fed into the system about the piece of music itself – whether it reached the charts, reached number one, if so for how long, etc.

A further practical benefit of the jukebox for the busy presenter is that it makes the vital task of 'logging' music – to ensure that all relevant royalties are paid – less laborious and more accurate.

Perhaps the most remarkable – and possibly controversial – feature of the jukebox system is that it enables a station to run an entire programme on air without a presenter and even when there is not a single person in the building. Automated jukeboxes are not only fitted with music CDs, but also CD recordings made in the station of identity jingles and the voice of a presenter linking each piece of music to be broadcast. The system is then programmed to play the CD tracks in a particular order and treats the recordings of jingles and announcements in the same way as it treats any CD track.

The rationale of stations running automated programmes is that it is not cost-effective for a presenter to be live on air at times of the day (or night) when hardly anyone is listening. As the number of stations increases and their range of output style diversifies, this is an argument that will be put forward more frequently for automated programming. The current alternatives for stations at present to address their overnight schedule are to go off air completely, or link into a network. For example, BBC CWR could carry Radio 2's programming in the early hours of each morning. During this time, however, Radio 2 continues to promote its own identity and also broadcasts music from its own playlist, reflecting its own musical branding. It is obvious to listeners that they are receiving a 'fill-in' service instead of their own local service; they may even be sufficiently convinced by Radio 2's self-promotion to retune to that service anyway. By setting up the automated jukebox, a station ensures that its own music profile remains consistent to its style policy.

Nevertheless the irony of automated programming cannot be lost in consideration of the essential personal nature of communication between radio station and listener. While offering more diversity perhaps than the listener's own domestic CD system programmed for random play, the pre-recorded voice of the presenter offers an illusion of human intervention to disguise the fact that the listener is tuned into a machine. The machine compounds its own status as the non-human agent of extra-personal communication by functioning as a replicant of a human radio presenter. The listener tunes in to take part in the radio experience. The station responds by engaging the listener in a pre-programmed simulation of human companionship.

The use of hard disk technology for recording and playing back audio data enhances this illusion by providing a reusable medium for recording the presenter's voice. The ability to store and retrieve audio on computer disk is already being exploited by some independent stations. Presenter links recorded on CD cannot be erased; thus the links tend to consist of comments that can be reused. On a hard disk of a computer, however, comments can be recorded earlier in the day, be geared to specific tracks being played, even relate to recent news events and issues, and then be over-recorded at no material cost to the station. The resulting output is more immediate, topical and 'human'.

The smoking room

At the opposite end of the production office from the gram library is the smoking room. Like most employers, the BBC has a smoking ban in most parts of its buildings. Apart from the obvious health hazards, one important reason why smoking is not allowed in the production areas of any radio station is that they contain a highly inflammable material – audio tape, large quantities of which may be stuffed loose into waste bins around the production office or any other location where tape editing takes place.

Technologically it is now possible for radio stations to function without the use of any audio tape. The transition from the studio to the workstation (see pp. 104–5) will result in dramatic transformations in the day-to-day operations of radio broadcasting plus an even greater reliance on computer technology. Clean air will be as vital as ever for an effective working environment in radio.

The news studio

The only studio on the same floor as the production office is the news studio, a more compact version of the main studios on the ground floor. This is equipped with:

- three microphones to enable the broadcasting or recording of interviews

- two reel-to-reel tape machines

- a cartridge stack – a stack of three machines to play back material on cartridge tape. One of these machines can also record material, say, from a reel-to-reel tape machine onto carts

- a mixing panel – a desk with sliding controls (faders), each control connected to a sound source: a playback machine or a microphone.

The news studio is used for the presentation of the hourly news bulletins and, between these times, as the main production area where news staff can prepare material, record interviews by telephone or via links with other studios, edit recorded material to make up short packages or newsclips and transfer these onto carts ready for the next bulletin.

During the bulletin, newsreaders operate the studio themselves, opening a microphone fader to put their own voice on air, or faders to operate carts containing newsclips.

5 **_The news studio_**: this is used for simple voice broadcasts and recordings; there is no need for a visual talkback system and the only audio sources needed – apart from the newsreader and possibly an additional reporter talking into the microphones – are the studio tape recorder (seen here behind the newsreader) and the stack of three cart machines, one of which is capable of recording (seen here behind the newsreader's microphone).

The desk itself is reasonably simple with only seven faders and (next to the news-reader's hand) a row of buttons for talkback. The desk also has a radio car talkback system. The three lights above the clock indicate, left to right: (a) a mike fader is open, (b) the radio car is calling to base, and (c) the telephone in this studio is 'ringing'. The large light to the right of the clock is the fire alarm.

Note the posture of the newsreader. The script is raised slightly so that his chin is lifted to enable him to form words properly.

The main studios

The public face and public voice of BBC CWR are based on the ground floor of the building (Figure 6), the location for its reception area and main studios. Nearly all the station's output comes from either Studio 1 or Studio 3. Both studios have direct access to the transmitter and are equipped with:

- a studio desk – from which the presenter can select and mix in any source material: his own voice, music, telephone callers, reporters in radio cars, etc. Each desk is equipped with three microphones

- three cart machines – used for playing jingles, trails or trailers (see p. 135), or packages (see p. 144)

- three reel-to-reel tape machines – used for recording packages by mixing together material played back from two tape machines, or

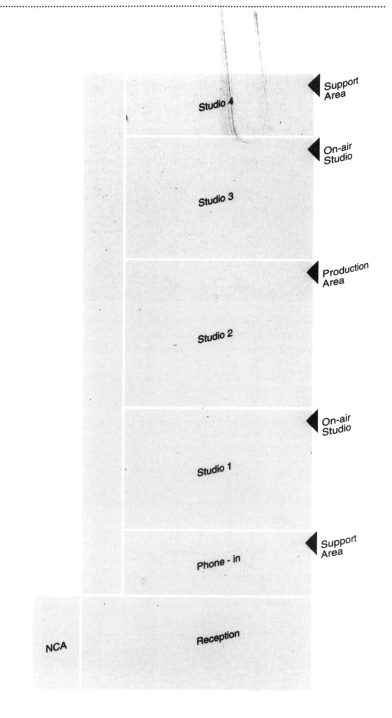

Figure 6   *Ground floor layout of BBC CWR: reception area and main studios*

other sound sources, and recording it on the third machine. Tape machines are also used for playing back packages on air

- two CD players

- two grams (gramophone turntables)

- a DAT player

- talkback systems – enabling the presenter to talk off-air with the producer or other staff located in the building

- a television set equipped with CEEFAX

- visual display units for the jukebox and for information keyed in by the programme producer in the support area, next door to the main studio (visual talkback)

- the small computer to log the music for royalties payment – presenters 'log on' by entering their 'programme number' at the beginning of the broadcast, then scan bar codes to enter details of each record played

- loudspeakers and headphones (cans)

- a hands-off telephone

- an on-air red light

- a clock

- a storage area for carts containing jingles and public service announcements.

(See Chapter 4 for more detailed discussion on items of studio technology.)

Both studios are self-operated – a presenter sitting in either of them can press buttons and open faders to put himself on air and connect with any of a wide range of sources. He could, for example, set up a conversation on air between a member of the public in a radio car in Nuneaton and a film star at the end of a telephone in Hollywood, or reunite family members on telephones in Coventry and Australia.

Throughout the day, BBC CWR alternates the use of Studios 1 and 3 for each programme; thus the mid-morning presenter can prepare his programme in Studio 1 whilst the Breakfast Show is still being broadcast from Studio 3.

Support areas

Both studios have support areas. Programme producers work in Studio 4 adjacent to Studio 3, or the phone-in area adjacent to Studio 1.[8] Here they sift and prioritise news and information to be fed through to the presenter, set up interviewees on telephone lines, in radio cars or in satellite studios,

6   *The on-air studio*: *the presenter pictured here has all potential audio sources at his fingertips and is still able to maintain eye contact with a guest or, in this case, a reporter contributing to the programme from the guest's seat. To the presenter's left are two CD players and below these (not visible here) are two grams. The music running order is on a document stand easily accessible to the presenter's left and near the jukebox VDU. Behind that, a poster prompts the station's address and telephone numbers.*

On the desk next to the presenter's hand is the lightpen for logging music (the bar codes are on the running order sheet). The 'well' in the middle the desk contains the buttons to operate the talkback and a space for the presenter's scripts and notes. Above this are the meters and, above those, two of the three cart machines are loaded and ready to 'fire' (i.e. be activated by the opening of a fader). A selection of jingle carts are on standby on top of the console while all current trail carts are accessible to the presenter's right in a rack above the studio tape recorder.

The visual talkback monitor is to the right of the desk console where the guest cannot see it. Data and messages on this are sent through by the producer located in the support area behind the glass panel. Also in the presenter's line of sight are the studio clock and the on-air light.

and receive listeners' calls on the telephone answering system (known as Telecaster), allocating them to lines which the presenter can open to place the caller on air. Each support area contains an ENS terminal providing the producer, and thus the presenter, with access to files on all current news stories including those that are just breaking. GNS could provide a report through the ENS on, say, the resignation of the Chancellor of the Exchequer such that a local radio presenter could be announcing the news within minutes of it happening.

The producer remains in contact with the presenter throughout the programme through a choice of talkback systems; he can either be heard in the presenter's headphones or through an intercom device if the presenter's microphone is closed, or he can key in data to be displayed on a VDU in the studio (referred to as a visual talkback). This data could take the form of cues to be read out before a recorded item, up-to-date news items or public service information to be given on air, or brief details about phone-in contributors – their name, where they live and a brief summary of what they want to say.

Studio 2

Output from Studio 2 can only go on air via either Studios 1 or 3. It provides more space for people taking part in a live broadcast and can be used for round-table discussions or even live performances by a choir or band provided they do not take up too much space. Studio 2 often doubles as a recording studio. Musical performances may be recorded by setting up microphones in Studio 2 and linking them through to the desk in either Studios 1 and 3, or by running a cable to the radio van parked alongside the building and containing more sophisticated recording equipment.

The NCA

The ground floor of BBC CWR also contains the News Contribution Area which can be linked to any other BBC studio centre. If, say, the *Today* programme on Radio 4 wanted to interview the head of a local manufacturing business, the NCA allows this to happen on a good quality line rather than through a telephone or the necessity of a time-consuming visit by the interviewee to London for three minutes of airtime.

Like all remote studios, the NCA contains equipment which can be operated by the interviewee following a set of simple directions provided. Remote studios contain a microphone, a telephone, a set of headphones and a small control unit. The interviewee enters the studio, telephones London, presses one button on the control unit to switch on the microphone, presses another to receive 'cue' through the headphones and then starts speaking at the appropriate moment. A guest in the NCA can hear the programme in telephone-quality sound through the headphones, but his voice – transmitted through the microphone and along a landline – will be heard by listeners in good studio sound quality.

The editorial area

The nature of BBC CWR's technical infrastructure is governed by the station's brief – to talk about Coventry and Warwickshire. To fulfil this, the station's presence must be evenly spread across the entire editorial area; it should be heard clearly by everyone living in that area and there should be reasonable access for people in any part of the county to make contributions of a high technical quality to BBC CWR's output. To achieve optimum reception, the area is served by three FM transmitters strategically positioned in the north, south and centre of the area, broadcasting on different frequencies to enable listeners to select the clearest signal. Contributors' access to output is enhanced through use of the city centre satellite studio plus an extensive network of remote studios (Figure 7).

These studios have to be booked in advance, especially as some are linked through to others rather than directly to the central studios. For BBC CWR, use of the studios in Atherstone and Warwick plus the Royal Shakespeare Company's studio in Stratford-upon-Avon also ties up, respectively, the studios at Nuneaton, Leamington Spa and Stratford

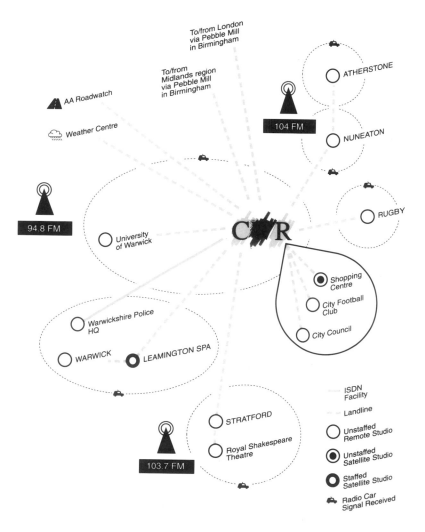

Figure 7   *Map of BBC CWR's range of technical resources beyond the main studio in Coventry*

itself. Remote studios are usually located in a room of the Town Hall or other civic building in a population centre and in any location which is likely to be used regularly for broadcasting, such as a major football club, police headquarters or university.

Most studios, including those used by the AA Roadwatch service and the Weather Centre, are linked to the central studios by landline, although a high quality telephone line – ISDN (Integrated Services Digital Network) – is in increasing use, achieving a sound close to studio quality. This is cheaper to use than setting up landlines and simple to operate.

In addition to the permanent studios scattered across the editorial area, BBC CWR makes regular use of its fleet of three radio cars and one radio van. Like all BBC stations, these vehicles constitute evidence of BBC CWR's commitment to provide opportunities for contributions from all parts of the transmission area through OBs. A person living near Nuneaton or Stratford-upon-Avon can sit in a radio car and discuss on air issues of concern with a Government minister, hooked to BBC CWR from the NCA in Westminster. Radio car signals are transmitted either directly to base or to a local receiver set up in the editorial area before being routed to base along a landline. For the listener, the sound of their voices is of equal strength and quality and the discussion could be that of two people sitting in the same room.

To summarise, the organisation and layout of BBC CWR reflects its role as a talk station and one that is fully integrated into the nationwide network and infrastructure of the BBC. Whilst no two stations are identical, even within the same organisation, CWR is by no means exceptional in the complexities of a station that offers predominantly speech-based output. It serves here to illustrate the relationship between the organisation and resourcing of a radio station and the style and nature of its output.

Resources and staffing

THE physical organisation and network of communication channels within BBC CWR highlights an important principle of working in radio: *whatever resources are available should be exploited to the full*. Broadcasters harness technology to reinforce the station's overall broadcasting style and image. A station cannot hope to convince listeners of its journalistic base, for example, if it is not capable of carrying reports from courtrooms, conference chambers or conflict zones across the world. Communications technology is also applied to enhance the variety and vitality of a station's sound. More fundamentally, it provides a means of promoting innovation and creativity in radio broadcasting.

The network of landlines, telephone lines, computer links and radio waves creates unlimited opportunities for instantaneous communication through audio signals, transmitted print or access to databases. A station resourced with the most basic equipment can fulfil its function of providing a radio experience by transmitting music and talk along a single channel – a cable or radio wave. If it links up with a second station and establishes some means of audio transmission between the two, the station more than doubles its potential. It has access to a larger audience, it can share output with its colleague station, and it can inform and be informed of news and developments with audio material – even a single voice – from another source to put on air as well as its own reports. Add a third station to the arrangement and the opportunities for multi-source broadcasting and exchange of audio material are multiplied further. The basic station now becomes part of a network with access to a considerable variety of voices and material to go on air. Even one station on its own but marshalling input from satellite studios, radio cars or listeners' telephones is in a position to augment a product of recorded music and studio chat with up-to-date news, wider interactive discussion and the more spontaneous style of output that arises when greater public access to the airwaves is made available.

A working environment, in which broadcasters feel motivated to make optimum use of the resources available, works in the interests of a station at various levels. There is the straightforward economic argument that the communications infrastructure is wasted and not cost-effective if broadcasters confine themselves to safe 'music and studio chat' shows. There is the market-led view that audiences' learned expectations should also motivate broadcasters to push technology to its limits. Today's listeners are accustomed to the instant and live sounds and images that bounce off satellites and into their living rooms and would probably think it odd if a radio station did not carry a breaking news story from London or interrupt the normal schedule to go live to, say, a major disaster within the editorial area.

The most important motivation, however, is similar to that of the mountaineer who climbs a peak 'because it's there'. The availability of sophisticated communications technology has its own creative appeal which most dedicated broadcasters cannot (and should not) resist. Technical innovations have often arisen through serendipity rather than necessity. Teletext and viewdata technology, for example, came about through an unsuccessful attempt to design a videophone system. For professional broadcasters, the realisation that something is possible makes it worth trying out. If a radio station were to discover by chance the means of transmitting aromas by radio wave, it would not wait for the result of market feasibility studies – it would simply put those smells on the air.[9]

The 'pioneering spirit' shared by staff of a successful radio station is further encouraged by the personnel structure that most stations adopt. BBC, independent and community stations are usually highly efficient operations with only just enough staff to carry out their tasks. The gap between senior management within a station and the lowliest programme maker is not great as all staff are usually involved in activities that bring them close to actual broadcasting; there are few, if any, penpushers. From the listener's perspective, the roles and levels of responsibility held by individual members of the station staff are immaterial as long as there is a seamless and constant flow of output carrying new ideas and interesting comments.

This offers an argument for the flexibility and adaptability of all station staff. There may be economic reasons for this. In 1992 Chantler and Harris pointed out that many American radio stations operate newsrooms staffed only by one or two journalists covering all the functions of editor, producer and reporter, and predicted with some accuracy that this 'may be the way forward for some British commercial stations' (Chantler and Harris 1992: 14). Whilst staff in any radio station are not wholly interchangeable and do not possess equal levels of broadcasting skill and knowledge, there is arguably a stronger and more necessary degree of understanding of each other's role than in other areas of work. This is reflected, for example, by the open plan production office characteristic of many stations. It is also one of the reasons why trainees and work placement students are usually taught very quickly how to record and edit and are quite likely to hear their efforts on air within a short time of joining the station.

The person in charge of a BBC local radio station is the Managing Editor; the equivalent ILR role is Managing Director. The former title reflects an emphasis on journalism-based speech (comparable with the editor of a large provincial newspaper) while the latter highlights the business orientation of commercial radio. Both report to regional or group management, but make final decisions on station output and tone. Off the air, the ME or MD manages all the station's resources and controls finances, public image and the appointment of staff.

The management role is supported by three broad departments or areas: engineering, finance/personnel and the largest area in terms of staff numbers, which is editorial or production, usually headed in ILR stations by a Programme Controller and in BBC local radio by one or two Assistant Editors.

Engineers maintain the station's technical base – everything from the studio desk to a portable tape recorder – and install new lines and equipment. Furthermore, they are very active in programming. Engineers conduct site tests for all potential locations for OBs (i.e. make sure the location is a suitable place geographically for transmitting signals); they record and sometimes transmit concerts from a radio van or lorry parked outside the venue; they 'drive' a programme from the main studio if the presenter is out on an OB; and they are usually on hand to solve a technical difficulty that may arise during a live broadcast.

Finance and personnel issues may be dealt with by a single person or a small department overseeing the day-to-day financial aspects of an operation with a high turnover, as well as maintaining all personnel records. Naturally, independent radio stations also have advertising departments which are responsible for selling airtime, writing and recording commercials and scheduling them on the air.

The role of Assistant Editor in BBC stations has arisen as a result of the Corporation's journalist-based model for local radio. In effect, at any time that the station is on air, the Assistant Editor is responsible for its overall sound – music, news bulletins, the entire output as a unified result of the interconnected functions of programme making and journalism. The Assistant Editor recruits and deploys staff, organises rotas, looks after budgets and checks the legal status of specific broadcast items. The position replaces the former organisational structure of BBC local radio in which responsibility at this level was held by the Programme Organiser and News Editors, emphasising the current BBC philosophy that all areas of output should be fully integrated.

This also affects the distinction at the level of producing material for output between programme makers and journalists. Whilst radio stations have traditionally run their newsrooms as separate, autonomous units within the overall structure, the division between reporting and presenting in BBC stations is becoming less clear-out. The news team is a collection of broadcast journalists from trainee to senior, acting as newsroom assistants, reporters and bulletin editors or readers, collectively functioning as the intake point of much of the information that informs the station's speech output. Depending on that station's style, the news team's end-product ranges from an hourly or half-hourly news bulletin to a regular supply of updated information and recorded material to incorporate in mainstream programming. News-room staff also feed audio reports on big local stories to national stations. Some BBC radio stations even have facilities for a television crew to feed audio and visual material to a regional or national television centre.

The responsibility for shaping and crafting overall programming falls to a series of programme teams. The basic team comprises the presenter and producer although a larger team becomes necessary as output becomes more complex, requiring greater advance preparation. Thus it could also include one or more radio production assistants (RPAs) to set up interviews with guests either in the studio or at the end of a line, or reporters to prepare packages especially for the programme.

Through liaison and consultation with programme producers on a day-to-day level, the Assistant Editor is able to act on the Managing Editor's guidelines on the overall shape and sound of output. The producers' crucial role in a radio station is to put these ideas into practice, guide their programmes through transmission and then participate fully in evaluation and feedback sessions.

In addition to the station's permanent staff of presenters, announcers, newsreaders and reporters, there are two further sources of prepared speech material. The first highlights the BBC as a bi-media operation with component stations linked in a wider news-gathering structure. The Corporation employs a series of experts or specialist correspondents – for example, in rural affairs, industry or local government – who serve regional television and local radio.

The second source is the group of contributors who offer specialist local knowledge on specific subjects – darts, club and pub bands, amateur theatre, or whatever – and give reports or 'what's on' listings on air, usually as guests of a mainstream presenter during a regular programme slot. When the subject area and potential listener interest merits it, such contributors may even be trained and supported to run their own programmes.

The human factor

THE essential components of radio – a voice, a means of transmitting that voice and a means of receiving it – do not in themselves guarantee the radio experience. A basic set of principles is also necessary with regard to the application of available technology and the mode of listener address that is established. These principles relate to the performance of the presenter, the selection and organisation of source material and the manner in which this material is contextualised and integrated to create a discourse of radio founded on elements of companionship, community or cultural involvement and journalism.

If the radio experience is essentially derived from an audio text that pre-supposes listener reaction and response, its construction must appear to be a human rather than mechanical activity, conveying a sense of immediacy and spontaneity while relating to listeners on a personal level. Hence, the staffing structure and the technical infrastructure are harnessed primarily to reproduce this human communicative experience and to establish radio as something more than a sophisticated public address system for the sole conveyance of announcements and background music. Even the automated jukebox system aspires to creating this personal form of listening experience.

The way in which radio's basic components are developed to create a particular listening experience depends on the niche that the station is aiming to reach. BBC local radio provides a talk service with a journalistic base, functions within a complex national network and represents, at a local level, the corporate identity of the BBC as a provider of public service broadcasting, accountable to licence fee payers. Hence the essential radio service is transformed into a highly complicated, people-centred organisation with an intricate and involved communications system. Independent local and national stations can work from a structure that is similar in complexity, although a much simpler arrangement is more appropriate for music-based stations, capable of creating a radio text with two CD players, a cartridge stack and a microphone.

Incremental and community radio stations also tend to operate from a structure that is nearer to the basic minimum radio model, partly through the need to work on a considerably smaller budget and partly because community access is a more vital element to their style and philosophy than a tightly controlled, 'glossy', 'professional' sound. Access for some community stations is not enhanced through the use of radio cars and remote studios. In fact, these would appear to make access to the heart of the station more restricted, especially if the presenters are known personally in the community and the station is a short distance from listeners' homes and workplaces.

An important conclusion to be drawn from this is that the success of radio does not depend on the level of investment that has gone into a station. *Commercial* success may be achieved through a judgement of the *minimum* investment to create an 'acceptable' sound, attractive to a sufficient number of listeners to interest advertisers. In this circumstance, the propensity for producing an innovative and interesting listening experience rests largely on the inclination and talent of individual presenters. Meanwhile, for broadcasters working within the complicated resource structure of the BBC or the simple organisation of a campus radio station, radio's 'success' is not measured solely on a balance sheet or against objective indicators of market response. 'Good' radio is recognised through a particular resonance created in the minds of listeners – an appreciation of its dynamism, originality and interest, a sense of genuinely stimulating communication.

Activities and points for discussion

1 As a team, you have been awarded the franchise to establish a new independent radio station in a large industrial town. Its output will be a mixture of talk and popular music and the aim of the station is to promote a strong local identity. There are two financially viable locations available for setting up the studios – in the middle of a new retail park on the edge of town or in a shopping centre near the middle of the town. A third option is to set up a mobile studio – a large vehicle that contains all the equipment necessary for live broadcasting that is capable of operating from any location within the editorial area.

Discuss the advantages and disadvantages of each of these options and make a decision on which of these would be the most suitable on balance. What additional facilities would you seek to establish to support the station's service? If possible, base your discussion on a town with which you are familiar.

2 A large, manufacturing organisation is about to open a new factory in the locality, creating hundreds of jobs in the area. The company will become an integral part of the community and aims to promote a positive commitment to community involvement. The opening day of the factory is to be a major public relations event with an invitation for everyone living in the community to attend a 'Fun Day'. The local radio station agrees to give extensive coverage to the event.

Fun Day' attractions include: a 'traditional' fair with stall holders dressed in Victorian costume, morris dancing, live music by a local 'Dixieland' jazz band, a Punch and Judy show, a team of jugglers, stilt-walkers and unicyclists offering tuition for people who want to have a go, a bunjee-jump demonstration and the official opening speech by the company's Managing Director. Two local MPs are also expected to be there.

As a production team for the local radio station, work out a plan for covering the event. Assume that you have use of a large OB vehicle, complete with stage, that can be parked at the 'Fun Day' site throughout the day and linked directly to the base studio. Decide first of all how much coverage you intend to give the event and how it will be integrated into the day's normal programming. Then work out a programme plan that most effectively conveys the dynamism and *visual* aspects of the event. Work to the principle of exploiting your resources to their fullest extent to create lively and imaginative radio.

3 A consortium is offering a small amount of cash to support a community radio station in a small inner-city area, scheduled for urban renewal. The area has suffered from the usual symptoms of high unemployment and previous lack of investment – petty crime, damaged property and overall neglect. A substantial proportion of residents are elderly people with few amenities and sharing a distrust of young people who live in the area. There is also a strong ethnic mix with many local businesses run by Asian, Chinese, Eastern European and Afro-Caribbean families. It is local business people and representatives of the city council who make up the consortium.

As a group seeking to set up the radio station, write up a bid outlining the facilities you would need and the type of service you would seek to offer for listeners. Produce a draft programme schedule with a brief description of each programme. Describe what strategies you would employ to maximise community involvement.

4 The tools of radio broadcasting

....

Components of the total sound

I N the previous chapter we considered the wide picture of how a radio station is organised and indicated at least the scope of the broadcasting opportunities available within a station's overall communications structure. This discussion made reference to various items of broadcasting technology that make up radio's working environment and contribute to a station's capacity to operate fully within its own terms of reference. In this chapter, we adopt a more focused perspective on these 'tools of broadcasting'.

It is not our purpose to provide a step-by-step description of how each item of equipment should be used. For trainees in radio broadcasting, skills in equipment operation are usually most effectively acquired through hands-on experience plus guidance from a station's training unit or an experienced broadcaster.[1] Any detailed description offered here would be subject to variations in the design of particular items. For example, a station may favour the use of a Uher or Nagra portable reel-to-reel tape recorder, or be equipped with Revox or Studer studio tape machines. Furthermore, items which may be essential to the station's operation one day could become obsolete the next as new technological rationales are introduced and applied.

In line with a key theme of this book – that radio is considerably more than the sum part of its components – our aim here is to discuss the contribution that items of equipment make to the station's overall sound and to the listener's radio experience. Thus we are concerned with applications and capabilities of station equipment as a basis for subsequent discussion on performance techniques in live broadcasting.

In this chapter, we will discuss the use of three categories of station equipment: that which is designed to store audio information – tapes and CDs; equipment for use outside the station building to collect or transmit audio for broadcast or later processing – from the basic portable tape recorder to the complete radio van; and the technology of the studio itself for the processing and transmission of live audio, enabling the presenter to maintain control over output.

Tapes and other storage media

Reel-to-reel tape

This is the most heavily consumed item in a radio station. Trainees in radio find themselves handling tape from their first day and developing the dexterity needed to load it quickly onto a tape recorder.

Most radio work is done on quarter-inch (6mm) tape. Speech is recorded at 7.5ips (inches per second) or 19cps (centimetres per second), while music is recorded whenever possible at 15ips (38cps). As tape travels through a tape recorder it passes a row of three heads: the first erases, the second records and the third plays back.[2] The faster the tape travels when it is in contact with the record head, the better the quality of the recorded sound – the audio 'information' of, say, one second is literally spread across a longer length of tape.

The most commonly used portable tape recorder for on-location interviews and short commentaries is the Uher. This German manufactured machine can carry quarter-inch tape spooled onto 5in. (12.7cm) reels. At 7.5ips this enables a reporter to record a little over fifteen minutes of material. Audio tape may also be supplied on 7in. (17.8cm) or 10.5in. (26.7cm) reels which can be used on studio tape recorders or on recording machines fitted into a radio van for longer items recorded on location. Hence the recording of a half-hour musical performance at a concert, at 15ips, would use up most of the tape on a 10.5in. reel.

A regular part of the day-to-day routine of radio broadcasting is the task of editing and banding reel-to-reel tape. Editing is literally cutting out pieces of unwanted tape with a razor blade and splicing together the remaining tape. It is also possible to change the order of items – sounds or statements – recorded on tape through careful editing. The task of editing can be performed on any studio tape recorder with the aid of a razor blade, editing block, Chinagraph (or grease) pencil to mark the tape where it is to be cut, and splicing tape to hold the edited tape together. (Editing techniques are discussed on pp. 121–2.)[3]

Banding involves attaching leader tape to audio tape. Leader tape is thin plastic tape which is also a quarter of an inch wide but cannot carry audio signals. It is spliced onto the beginning and the end of audio tape so that a reel of tape can be spooled onto a machine. Approximately 45 inches (114cm) of leader tape is attached at the beginning of a reel of audio tape to provide up to four seconds of running time before the recorded section is reached. This enables the presenter in the studio to cue

7 *Storage media: from left to right: a recordable CD (approximately sixty minutes recording time); a 5in. ciné reel of quarter-inch audio tape (fifteen minutes recording time at 7.5ips); DAT (usually ninety minutes); an audio cassette (varied durations available); and a cart (anything from ten seconds to five minutes). In the centre is a 10.5in. NAB reel of quarter-inch audio tape which will provide sixty minutes of audio at 7.5ips.*

Regular use is made of each of these media in most radio stations for different purposes. If this photograph had been taken in 1980, the CD and DAT would not have been featured. In the year 2000, additional media in everyday use will be the floppy and hard disk.

the tape – line it up so that the beginning of the recorded section is ready to run past the playback head as soon as the tape machine is activated. Attaching leader tape to the beginning and end of a tape ready for transmission is referred to as 'topping and tailing'.

Leader tape is also spliced into the middle of a length of audio tape to separate out different sections of a recording – providing an easy visual reference for the presenter to cue one of a number of items that have been spliced together on the same reel. Leader tapes are colour coded. There are variations but normally yellow or green leader is used to mark the beginning of a tape, red to mark the end, while yellow or white leader is used to divide up sections of the tape. Red and white striped leader is sometimes spliced onto the beginning of tape recorded in stereo.

Talk radio stations in particular have a large tape budget. Even though audio tape is reusable, it does deteriorate with use and new tape is preferable for optimum sound quality. Radio stations extend the life of their tapestock in two ways. It can be bulk erased and reused as if it were new tape, although reporters should be careful that they do not record interviews over tape that has been banded.[4] Or if lengths of 'slash tape'

8 *Editing: the reporter is using a Chinagraph pencil to mark the point where he will cut the tape with a razor blade (just discernable by his left thumb). He hears what is recorded through headphones, bypassing the loudspeaker so that colleagues do not have to tolerate the noise produced as the tape is manually rocked backwards and forwards against the playback head.*

A reel of splicing tape is kept handy (here to the reporter's left) to join together lengths of audio tape. Reels of red and yellow leader are also within reach (here at the top of the machine) to 'top and tail' and band the edited material.

Editing is not an exercise of depriving listeners of parts of a recording. It involves organising the recording such that it 'tells the story' neatly, clearly and in its own right. Material that is discarded as 'slash tape' is material that adds little if anything to this purpose.

have too many splices from previous editing they are placed into salvage bins and returned to tape manufacturers for recycling.

As tape quality in cassettes and carts has improved, radio stations are using these formats more frequently as alternatives to reel-to-reel tape. This may also prove cheaper in terms of raw material, but additional studio time is needed to transfer (dub) cassette tape recordings onto quarter-inch tape before the recording can be edited.

Carts

Carts (cartridges) are plastic boxes containing a continuous loop of tape. Their great advantage over reel-to-reel tape is that they do not have to be spooled onto an empty reel of a tape machine. Carts are slotted into cart machines and are ready to play. When the tape runs its full circuit, a pulse signal instructs it to stop so that it is cued and ready to play again. Carts can also be programmed to fast-forward to the beginning, by recording a pulse at the end of the recorded material, automatically recuing the tape once it has been played.

The commonest use for carts is for short recorded items such as a thirty-second jingle or a five-second 'sting' of music. Carts are used for advertisements, public service announcements and 'trails' which announce forthcoming programmes or features. Presenters record individual sounds onto cart that they may incorporate in their programme – 'you win' or 'you lose' sound effects for phone-in competitions, 'happy birthday' jingles, fanfares, crowds cheering, canned laughter, any noise that may be required the instant a presenter opens a fader. Carts are also widely used in radio news studios to play back newsclips or inserts – recorded extracts of individual statements or interview responses by people in the news.

Longer recorded items are becoming more frequently used on cart. Signature tunes and backing music (beds) for 'what's on' announcements may be recorded on carts containing tape of five minutes or more in length. High quality carts are available for recording music in its own right and some radio stations have transferred their music playlists onto cart so that tracks do not have to be cued up on grams or CD players.

Part of a presenter's organisational skill involves having the right carts ready at the right time. A typical studio is fitted with three playback machines for cart. Each cart needs a few seconds to re-cue itself once it has been played. If a presenter has to run three commercials followed by a jingle, she has to wait for the first commercial to re-cue itself while the second commercial is playing, remove the cart from the machine, load the jingle cart into the machine, check that it is properly cued and be ready to play it by the time the third commercial has finished. Throughout the programme she has to think ahead so that carts of public service announcements, sound effects, travel news beds or jingles that take listeners into the main news bulletin are all at hand and cued up, with cart machines available to play them.

Audio cassettes

Usually the only role for audio cassette players in a radio studio is to record a copy of output to give (or sell) to studio guests as a souvenir of their appearance on the programme. Standard audio cassettes, unlike carts, are not self-cuing and are thus hardly ever used for playing back material for output. Furthermore, the size of the tape makes them very difficult to edit.

They are more widely used outside the studio for collecting audio material to be dubbed onto reel-to-reel tape and edited. The inconvenience of having to dub material from cassette to quarter-inch tape is compensated for by the lightness and greater versatility of the portable cassette recorder. There are high quality audio cassettes on the market which are capable of providing a reasonable quality recording of speech and even music in stereo. Cassettes hold much more than 5in. reels of audio tape and, like the recorders on which they are used, they are considerably cheaper.

Video tape

As a medium for storing audio material, video has a useful role to play in the radio station. Stations are required to keep an audio record of output[5] and usually do this on VHS format video tape set at long play and capable of holding eight hours of material. Some radio stations are also using video as a playback medium for unmanned, overnight broadcasts (Boyd 1993: 207).

DAT

Digital audio tape is used by some radio stations as a compact means of storing and playing back recorded copies of music. Smaller in size than standard audio cassettes, DAT cassettes carry clean, broadcast-quality, digital recordings. They can be indexed with a pulse signal at the beginning of each track, enabling the user to find the track she wants. It is possible to link a DAT player into a studio desk and cue up a DAT so that the presenter can play the track she wants in the same way she would play a CD track.

The introduction of DAT was thought to herald a major revolution in recording technology and practice whereby all radio stations would abandon the old-fashioned audio cassette and reel-to-reel tape recorders in favour of digital technology. Many stations in fact have chosen not to invest in the digital editing equipment that would be needed if DAT were the sole recording medium. This is partly because they have opted to wait until hard disk audio recording is more widely available before refurbishing their recording equipment. Also many broadcasters still prefer what some may regard as the messy and fiddly work of editing quarter-inch tape with a razor blade and splicing tape. By marking the tape with a Chinagraph pencil, they can 'see' the order of the material on tape and physically move it around. It is one of the ever-diminishing number of tasks in working life that does not require use of a qwerty keyboard.

CDs

Equipped with a compact disc making machine, radio stations are able to save storage space by transferring music from fifteen 7in. vinyl singles onto one CD. With the use of a jukebox (see pp. 83–4), a station can incorporate these tracks into its automated music selection and playback systems. Once the CD is installed in the jukebox, any track on it can be accessed instantaneously by the studio presenter. CDs are also used for recording announcements, links and jingles for automated radio programmes (see p. 84).

Computer disks

Some radio stations in Europe, Australia and the United States have already replaced the studio with the workstation. Here, tape of any format is no longer needed. One terminal is used not only to type scripts and cue sheets but also to edit audio material. This material is stored on hard disk and can be decoded in two ways. It appears as waveforms on the monitor, so that it can be marked for editing. And it is heard as audio through headphones. One advantage of editing material stored in this way is that the original recording is not destroyed and can be edited in different ways. Once editing is complete, the package is given a new filename and can be accessed and put on air at the touch of a key.

The computer system handling the audio material could be integrated into an existing computerised newsroom (see p. 82), enabling member stations of a group or region to have instant access to each other's files containing unedited and edited audio material. The near future could see the demise of portable tape recorders and the appearance of more compact devices loaded with a floppy disk. Audio material would be recorded on this and then transferred to the main computer, ready for editing or transmission, by the reporter on her return to the studio.

Out in the field

The portable tape recorder

This is likely to be the first piece of equipment that radio trainees learn to operate. The Uher tape machine has been in regular use at many radio stations for several years; it is simple to operate, reasonably sturdy and records straight onto quarter-inch tape which can be transferred onto a studio tape machine for editing immediately after the material has been recorded. Specialist reel-to-reel recorders are also available. A 'Mining Uher' is designed not to produce any accidental sparks when switches are operated in a hazardous area. The Nagra portable tape recorder is more sophisticated than a Uher and capable of recording audio to a very high quality, although it is more expensive and less widely used.

Portable cassette tape recorders are usually taken out for longer assignments in which actuality footage may be collected to fill an entire programme or even a series – for example, a reporter making an audio diary of a Himalayan trek. BBC stations tend to use the Sony Walkman Professional, while ILR stations often favour the Marantz CP230.

Uhers are fitted with rechargeable battery cells which should provide enough power to record on four 5in. reels of tape, i.e. approximately one hour's recording time at 7.5ips. Battery time is reduced by use of the fast-forward and rewind buttons. Recharging through a unit plugged into the mains takes between sixty and ninety minutes. For most location recordings it is usual practice to identify the likelihood of material being used in the final edit and to keep interviews short and punchy.

When out on an assignment with a portable recorder, radio reporters can emphasise the immediate, on-the-spot nature of the recorded material

9 ***The portable tape recorder****: pictured here is the machine most commonly used by reporters, the Uher. This is an unobtrusive piece of equipment for capturing the atmosphere of interviews on location. Note the microphone position, not too close to the interviewee's mouth, requiring minimum movement for when the reporter speaks. The recording level is adjusted so that ambient sound is discernable. In a more noisy environment, the recording level would be reduced with the microphone held closer to the speaker's mouth. The lead is coiled to reduce microphone noise or 'mike rattle'.*

The reporter also holds a script for reference but concentrates on keeping eye contact with the interviewee. It is unusual, but not impossible, for the reporter to wear headphones when using a Uher; this could intrude on the rapport between reporter and interviewee.

through incorporation of background sound (atmosphere) and microphone technique. Having found a suitable location for recording the interview or commentary, the experienced reporter will run the tape for ten or more seconds to record wildtrack – traffic sounds, seagulls, wind blowing through trees or whatever – as this is useful audio to edit on to the beginning and end of the final package to fade in or out, or to fill awkward, unnatural jumps which may occur at points on the tape where it has been edited. By holding the microphone close to her mouth and setting the recording level relatively low, the reporter can reduce the intrusive effects of loud background noise such as pneumatic drills or the tide crashing on to the beach. By holding the microphone away from her mouth and turning up the level, she is able to emphasise the background noise – enhancing the impact of, for example, a chanting football crowd, a noisy motorway or the police and ambulance sirens at the scene of an accident.

With the minimum of practice, the portable tape recorder is an accessible and simple form of technology that enables radio reporters to obtain broadcast-quality material in virtually any location. It also plays a vital role in reducing the technological barrier between a radio station and its public. Presenters may be hidden away in the 'strange' environment of a studio and inexperienced studio guests are often daunted by the complexity of the desk and the position of control occupied by the person 'driving' the programme. Out in the streets, the portable tape recorder is much simpler and certainly less intrusive and intimidating than a television camera. Therefore one use for which portable recorders are well suited is the *vox pop* interview which itself signifies the radio station's place among 'the people'. With *vox pops* a station positions the voices of shoppers, schoolchildren and concert-goers alongside those of professional spokespeople, politicians and rock stars.

Recordings made on location convey immediacy and appear to be less staged. Admittedly, much of the 'stagecraft' may occur when the tape is edited, but portable recorders can convey the impromptu, the spontaneous and the 'natural' qualities of an occasion. The comments of a news story protagonist may provide a ten-second sound-bite, edited from a recorded interview, but portable recorders are as effective in 'painting a sound picture', combining statements with sound effects to represent the atmosphere of a bell-ringing session, stock car race or morris dance display. A historian, accompanied by a reporter armed with a recorder and microphone, may walk around a museum and recreate its visual impact through an aural medium.

Portable recorders are popular with students and trainee broadcasters. Provided their own performance and voice work is up to standard, the equipment enables them to produce material that will go on air and nothing is more motivating for a trainee than to switch on the radio and hear her own voice.

The cellphone

Developments in telecommunication technology have enhanced radio's pervasive presence within the community it serves and have proved especially beneficial for news staff. The images of the determined reporter feeding coins into a telephone box, or 'croc-clipping' the phone[6] to feed squawky audio material to the newsroom in time for the next bulletin are part of radio's colourful folklore. Armed with a cellular phone and mobile fax machine, the reporter is now able to position herself at any location relevant to a news story to provide an atmospheric, on-the-spot account.

While a rule-of-thumb for radio is to employ the best quality medium available for sending audio material from a location, the telephone-quality voice of a reporter does endow the story with a sense of both the immediate and the authoritative. These are vital components of the news text which constantly reinforce its own veracity with such a code to distinguish its status from that of opinion or fiction. Telephone reports on television news tend to convey the remoteness and inaccessibility of the location of the news event, such as a blockaded region in a war-torn country, or simply highlight that the presence of a camera would not be reasonably expected or cost-effective, as in a report on a local Third Division football match.

Whatever the circumstance, telephone reports on television emphasise the programme's *inability* to send pictures; viewers have to be content with a still photograph of the reporter or a shot of the newscaster's non-verbal reactions to the report. On radio, telephone reports play a more crucial role. They emphasise the station's *capability* of providing 'pictures' in words given by someone at the scene. Often the report is no more than a description to add 'colour' to what has already been said by the newsreader, but this is often sufficient to suggest that the listener is getting the full picture.

Chantler and Harris suggest that an interview between a reporter in the studio and somebody at the end of a telephone also gives listeners a sense of the news story's immediacy – 'It sounds to them as if you have reacted fast to a story rather than done something which has required planning and a lot of time' (Chantler and Harris 1992: 63). This argument may help vindicate a station's decision to reduce the size of its news team, but a much greater sense of immediacy is achieved if a reporter drives or travels by taxi herself to the scene of the event, armed at least with a cell-phone to file her story. For interviews and more detailed reports, she has other mobile technology at her disposal – backpacks and radio vehicles – capable of sending audio which is nearer to studio quality.

The backpack

This device can be used by a reporter on location in two ways. First, it may function as a self-contained portable broadcasting unit. The reporter receives both cue (the sound of the output that she will link into) and talkback (messages from the programme producer) through her headphones. She uses a microphone that is cabled into the unit to put her own voice on air. The backpack transmits the signal of her voice to a local receiver linked to the studio desk. Its use in this way is limited – the signal from the backpack is considerably weaker than that from a radio car and the reporter would need to be within range of a receiver.

A more common use of the backpack is to receive cue and talkback only, while the reporter talks on air via a radio microphone within the vicinity of a radio vehicle which transmits the signal to base. Used in this way, the backpack enables the reporter to broadcast from almost anywhere within the transmission area.

While it can be worn as a high-tech shoulder bag, the backpack may also be fitted securely over the reporter's shoulders to ensure that she has both hands free. Kitted out with backpack and headphones, the reporter is strapped into the machine of radio; she is effectively a human extension of the sound-gathering superstructure. Her immediate vocal reactions to events witnessed or experienced by her – every utterance and breath – are shared with listeners. It is the equipment of the intrepid and committed radio professional working in any terrain and conveying her own thoughts, feelings and observations rather than acting as an agent for comments and responses of interviewees.

Radio cars and OB vehicles

Hatchback or taxi, the radio car is another means of bringing part of the technical anatomy of a radio station out into the world of people and events that make up the themes and issues of its speech content. With a built-in transmitter and aerial, the radio car is regularly, but not exclusively, used to bring news reporters closer to the scene of action. It may enable the station to give live coverage of a breaking news event or be parked outside the home or workplace of an interviewee whose schedule does not allow her time to come to the studio. It may be driven to a housing estate or high street to include live, impromptu, human-interest *vox pop* material for a local station's mid-morning show. Or it may be one of a fleet of radio vehicles, sent out during a general election to cover the results for constituencies within the editorial area.

While broadcasts of this nature serve to reinforce a station's visible image and presence within the community it serves, there are occasions which call for on-the-spot coverage but which may not be the most appropriate for the station to advertise its presence. Events such as a heated demonstration, street disturbance, prison riot or hostage situation may carry a risk of escalated violence by participators 'putting on a show' for the benefit of the media. It has also been known for reporters to be subject to aggressive attention from people with a grievance against the way the station has reported their cause. Many stations use unmarked radio cars for such occasions, enabling reporters to provide actuality reports at the minimum risk to themselves.

109

Sports fixtures, carnival parades or the switching-on of Christmas lights are routine occurrences for coverage from a radio car although stations may make their presence felt more substantially at events, such as a major concert, church service or public meeting, by sending an outside broadcast vehicle in the shape of a radio van, truck or caravan.

With more space and comfort for the operator, these OB vehicles can also carry more equipment. Leads connected to microphones in the venue can be run through to a mixing desk and the event can be recorded on 10.5in. reel-to-reel tape with a back-up copy on DAT. The operator may also make up edited packages of recorded material on the spot to be transmitted back to the base studio and put on air.

At longer-running events, such as a week-long county show, major sports meeting or exhibition, a local station may book a site at the venue and set up an OB vehicle that also functions as a drop-in centre for the public, complete with somewhere to sit and a retail outlet for merchandise. A station team may arrive in a large truck which converts into a stage complete with PA system for roadshow broadcasts. OB vehicles that are even more sophisticated and luxurious are available to some stations as a group or regional resource. These are equipped with mobile studio, editing facilities, a shop and kitchen.

While radio cars are ideal for reporters covering stories at short notice, longer-running events require more self-sufficient OB units undertaking a greater number of the operations that would normally be covered by the base studio. They also require more technical knowledge to operate. For a news reporter or programme assistant on location, sending in a report from a radio car is a relatively straightforward process. Larger OB vehicles with a wider range of technical functions are usually taken out by one of the station's engineering team.

The studio

THE three main functions of a radio presenter, as we shall discuss in more detail in Chapter 5, are to be the personality of the station, to represent the interests and concerns of the listener, and to maintain a constant flow of output. The studio should therefore be resourced with all necessary equipment to enable these functions to be achieved.

In theory, the 'basic' set-up of one microphone linked to a transmitter enables the broadcast of the simple voice item, such as a thirty-second travel report. In fact, travel centres and meteorological offices are linked to local radio stations through *remote studios* fitted with microphone, headphones and telephone link. The speaker hears the cue down the telephone line and through the headphones. The microphone is linked to a landline so that the speaker's voice comes through as studio-quality sound. The presenter in the main studio monitors that voice and often runs a 'travel bed' or 'weather bed' jingle beneath it to fill out the sound (see p. 58).

10 *The backpack*: this is essentially a portable studio; the interview here is being broadcast live. The signal from the microphone is beamed out by one of the aerials protruding from the top of the pack to a nearby receiver from which it is transmitted via the desk at base to the station's transmitter. Through the headphones, the reporter can hear cue, picked up by a second aerial, and talkback, picked up by a third.

While the backpack highlights the flexibility of live radio, its use is restricted to the vicinity of a receiver. Also, it is a heavy piece of equipment and, for health and safety reasons, not appropriate for wearing on the back or shoulder for a long time period.

11 **The radio car**: *this works as an extension to the studio and as a positive visual image of the station – provided it is kept clean inside and out. An interviewee with a tight time schedule is more likely to take part in a programme in a conveniently parked radio car rather than having to travel to the studio base. Each aerial serves a purpose: transmitting the signal back to base and receiving cue and talkback. Some radio cars are fitted with a larger 'pump up' transmission mast which should be used with care – checking, for example, that there are no overhead cables.*

For reasons of health and safety, the microphone cable is only long enough for the reporter to stand next to the car. A backpack would be needed to enable the reporter to roam further away while on air.

As the radio text incorporates audio material additional to the isolated human voice, so an increasingly complex studio arrangement is called for. *News studios*, also referred to as *contributions studios*, are still dependent on the presenter in the main studio to link the newsreader's microphone to the transmitter; however, the newsreader's voice is combined with material from other sources – usually clips from interviews or press conferences transferred onto cartridge tape. Therefore, the news studio is equipped with a control panel (desk) with faders which open up the microphone and activate each cartridge tape lined up in the cart machine.

If newsreaders are unable to gain access to a news studio to read out a bulletin, they may use one of the studio guest microphones in the main on-air studio. For brief headlines on news and sport this makes it easier for both newsreader and presenter of the main programme to provide cues for each other. However, if the bulletin includes recorded clips, it becomes the programme presenter's responsibility to play the carts – hopefully in the right order – at the newsreader's signal. The newsreader's presence in the on-air studio also makes it difficult for the presenter to talk to the producer or set up contributors for the next part of the programme – things

12 *The radio car interior*: the reporter is talking to base using the talkback. In this car, it takes the simple press of one button to switch the microphone to transmit and divert the sound of output from the car radio to the headphones which also receive talkback. Note the book of street maps on the passenger seat. Being unable to find a location could prove a major embarrassment for a reporter of a station that purports to serve its community.

that would normally be done during a news bulletin. She can only resort to brief verbal exchanges whenever a cart is playing.

Off air, news studios are also used to prepare material for broadcast. They are often fitted with reel-to-reel tape machines and can be linked to other studios in the network to receive and record studio-quality audio. This is then transferred onto cart, ready for the next bulletin.

The main *on-air studio* has all these facilities and more. The presenter can walk in and put herself on air, placing herself in control of the station's total sound for the duration of the programme. It is through her operation of the desk that jingles and records are played and channels are opened up for input from newsreaders, travel announcers, phone-in participators and interviewees located in any other studio in the network. Every fader on the studio desk represents at least one source of sound that could be incorporated into the output. In functional terms, the presenter's role of maintaining a constant flow of output involves ensuring that at least one fader is open throughout the duration of her programme.

Stations are often equipped with two on-air studios, either of which can function as the presenter's workbase and control area during a live broadcast. One studio 'hands over' to the other as each new programme begins. When only one studio is available throughout the day for live broadcasts, presenters execute a 'hot seat' change at an appropriate point of the handover, for example during a news bulletin or while a record is playing.

13   *An OB 'rig'*, *photographed here at the annual Royal Show at Stoneleigh, Warwickshire. The radio station's van is parked alongside with transmission aerial fully extended, sending the signal from the unit to base. There is no mistaking the station's identity. Name, wavelength and logo are clearly visible along with publicity photographs of the station's presenters. Also on display are the logos for BBC's regional service and the AA Roadwatch travel information service. The Royal Show can lead to traffic problems and the station responds with additional bulletins for this area.*

The door to the unit leads to a production area, with facilities for editing and word-processing plus a kitchen. Behind the glass window is a small studio with grams, CDs and cart machines. In front is a stage where the programme presenter can perform to an audience.

When not in use for live broadcasts, the on-air studio provides a location for the preparation of material for future programmes. This may involve recording telephone interviews, preparing programme trails and public service announcements on cart, and mixing voice reports or inter-view responses with music or special effects for recorded packages. The studio may be used for recording entire programmes although this is rare for local radio where the emphasis is on immediacy, linking the listener with the 'here and now' and often enabling the listener to phone in and take part.

Whether recording or broadcasting live, most presenters 'drive' the desk themselves to ensure maximum control over the output. Just as a newsreader in the news studio operates a control panel when on air to 'fire' carts of recorded clips at the appropriate moment in the script, so the presenter responds to her own cues when opening and closing faders in the main studio. Because of her central position when on air within a network of communication channels, she has access to a wide variety of audio sources which she must control while maintaining her roles of 'voice of the station' and 'representative of the listener'. This points to an important ergonomic issue in the design and layout of the studio. The continuous flow of the radio text sounds effortless and self-generating; the listener is unaware of the production process. The presenter says her cue and the CD track or the recorded package begins to play while the technical means of making this happen remains invisible to the listener. Hence the design of the studio enables the presenter to maintain her control and react appropriately to any situation that might arise in live radio. It provides her with ease of access to every potential audio source as well as every source of information needed to drive the show effectively, allowing her to concentrate on speaking to the listener, preferably with a smile in her voice, not with an edge of panic.

There are still occasions when the presenter is assisted by a technical operator driving the desk. This occurs, for example, if the presenter is a guest celebrity in fields other than radio and has no training in desk operation. Or the presenter may be chairing a panel discussion on air, requiring her full attention on which panel members are talking and what they are saying. A solo presenter working with a technical operator can sit in the same studio, using a studio guest microphone. It is essential that the technical operator is aware of all cues so that she is able to open faders at the right moment to play a CD track, jingle, recorded package or whatever items are lined up for the programme. The panel discussion, on the other hand, may take place in an adjoining *talks studio*, equipped with a round table and central omni- or bi-directional microphone capable of picking up the voices of all contributors which are fed through a single fader circuit. Here, programme participants can talk without the technical distractions of the studio desk, provided the presenter is able to hear any comments or instructions from the technical operator through a set of headphones.

The decision on who operates the studio equipment during a live broadcast is based on a perceived balance between two crucial factors – the amount of control that a presenter needs over the programme's flow to ensure that one item follows the next as planned and precisely on cue, and the extent to which the presenter is able to give full attention to the content of output and interact most effectively with other programme participants. Ideally, a presenter in full control of programme operation can provide the most spontaneous and dynamic output. There is no need to plan every programme item in advance to ensure that a colleague knows when to play a jingle or open a telephone line. Nevertheless, complex programmes involving material from various sources are at greater risk of going wrong if certain tasks are not offloaded – answering the phones, collecting news scripts, reading them on air, settling in studio guests, etc. A delicate balance exists between presenter control and the need to delegate; the achievement of this balance is an important organisational issue that reflects on programme output.

The desk

The studio desk is a large control panel that brings together different forms of communications technology. It has a range of distinct functions – one section operates the CD players, another operates the grams, another the microphones, and so on. In this respect, it is similar to the domestic hi-fi stack, only arranged horizontally instead of vertically. It enables the presenter to exercise her control in selecting and mixing sources to go on air. McLeish describes three types of 'circuit function' contained in the studio desk: programme circuits, monitoring circuits and control circuits (McLeish 1978: 24).

Programme circuits

These comprise all channels through which audio material is received, selected, mixed and put on air. The channels are normally controlled individually through the operation of faders; there is one fader for each studio microphone, each CD player, each cart machine, etc. Some circuits include selector switches so that the function of those particular faders may be altered. For example, a fader may be alternated between one of the grams and a DAT machine. Faders are also used to mix in externally sourced material – anything from the voice of a phone-in caller to the entire output of another station in the network. Faders are similar to slider controls on the mixing desk of a music public address system, except that the presenter normally opens a fader by sliding it towards her rather than away from her.

Faders can control volume level of audio material on air. Thus a fader for a 'travel bed' jingle is only partially opened while another fader is opened fully for the travel reporter to speak over the music. Normally, however, audio level (volume) is adjusted in advance, using a trim control above the relevant fader so that when the fader is fully open, the volume of that source is not too loud or too quiet. Adjustment of the audio level is achieved through a 'pre-fade' circuit which allows the presenter to hear the source through her headphones without it going on air. A few bars of a record are usually enough for a pre-fade check. If the presenter is conducting an interview, she will encourage her studio guest to speak while the necessary adjustments are made for level.[8]

Monitoring circuits

These provide the presenter with essential information on output itself. This is achieved both visually and by sound. Meters fitted into the desk act as visual monitoring devices. The VU (volume unit) meter indicates the volume of an audio signal and whether that signal is being transmitted on both stereo channels (for FM stations), while the PPM (peak programme meter) registers the higher peaks of sound and maintains those readings for a short while, making it easier to ensure that the signal does not exceed the permitted peak level.[9] Desks are also fitted with a pre-fade meter, enabling the presenter to check the level of a piece of music, jingle or contributor's voice before it goes out on air. Radio stations have a pre-determined level where output should peak and part of the presenter's responsibility to maintain a continuous flow of output involves checking that the actual output level does not deviate from this. This is to prevent the constant need for listeners to readjust the volume control of their radios. If an automatic level control is fitted into the desk, this may be activated to prevent the output level exceeding the pre-determined peak. This often creates an unnatural effect on the sound when it does peak, however, and reduces the impact that might be required of a sudden, sharp, loud sound.

A crude but essential visual monitoring device is the studio light. The red light comes on in the studio and outside the studio door whenever one of the microphone faders is opened. When the light is on during a live broadcast, anything said by anyone in the studio is likely to be heard by listeners.

The content of output is also monitored. Presenters should listen to their own output as much as possible when lining up music, packages or live interviews. They should be aware of the mood of a song being played or of the key points being made and by whom in a recorded package. A studio is equipped with loudspeakers and headphones (cans) which enable presenters to monitor the station's own output and, when required, output from another station in the network, items being checked on pre-fade, and 'talkback'.

Control circuits

Talkback is the term for the radio station's off-air communications system. It enables the presenter, or anyone in the station, to speak to anyone else in the building, or in radio cars, OB units and remote studios. Talkback combines the function of an intercom with a public address system with some additional features (see pp. 89–90, 119) and constitutes part of the third circuit function of a studio desk identified by McLeish – that of control circuits. These also include the telephone lines and radio links that connect the presenter to phone-in callers, reporters out in the field and external audio sources.

The sound of telephone callers is fed through the desk via a telephone balance unit (TBU). The telephone line is selected to come on air when the fader is opened and the TBU balances the audio level with that of the presenter's studio-quality voice.

Playback machines

A list is given in Chapter 3 (see pp. 86, 88) of equipment in a studio capable of playing back recorded audio. Unless a studio is linked to a jukebox system, all recorded music is set up and cued by the presenter. It is her responsibility to ensure that a CD is always loaded in the machine, or an album on the gram, ready to play when needed. Whilst one disc is playing the next is lined up, checked for level on pre-fade (see p. 117) and cued so that the track begins playing as soon as the fader is open.

Digital playback technology – CD players and DAT machines – can be cued relatively easily. The machine will search for and stop at the beginning of whatever track it is asked to locate; CD players do this instantly, DATs have to be run through on a similar basis to the 'music search' function of a domestic audio cassette player. Analogue recordings on vinyl are cued by physically moving the record backwards and forwards with the stylus on the groove to locate the exact point where the track begins and preceding silence ends. Then the record is turned back part of its circumference, depending on its playback speed, to give the turntable motor sufficient time to pick up speed once the fader-start mechanism is activated.

Reel-to-reel tape is cued on a studio tape recorder by positioning the last inch of leader tape prior to the recorded section alongside the playback head. Again, once the fader is open, the tape recorder mechanism quickly picks up speed so that the beginning of the recorded section is heard clearly. If the digital counter display on the studio tape recorder is zeroed at this start point, it is possible to run the first few seconds of the tape through pre-fade to check the level and then press the RTZ (return to zero) button. This automatically rewinds the tape to the start point although a final manual adjustment is usually necessary.

Carts are self-cuing. The touch of a button on a cart machine runs the tape back to its beginning. If the cart has been programmed with the appropriate pulse signals (see pp. 102–3), the cart machine will automatically cue the tape as soon as the jingle, trail, or whatever it contains has finished playing.

Whatever playback device is in use, the scope for errors by the presenter is considerable. With the predominance of CD recordings, presenters can easily forget to check the playback speed of vinyl recordings. The fact that cart machines have self-cuing devices does not guarantee that a particular cart has been cued at the moment it is needed. Even though fader controls are marked and colour coded, it is possible for the wrong fader to be opened at a given cue. Part of the skill in presenting is being organised enough to avoid such errors and, if they do occur, being able to cover the mistake without getting flustered or giving the listener the impression that an unseen disaster has occurred.

As soon as a playback machine is activated during a live broadcast, any music that is heard must be logged for royalties payment. Many studios are fitted with a computer that automatically registers when any fader connected to a CD machine or turntable has been opened (see p. 88). The presenter must then match up details of music played with the registered times when faders were open and feed this information into the computer either during or immediately after the programme. This process can be simplified by scanning or wiping bar codes containing all relevant details for each track played.

Communication systems

Vital 'tools' for the presenter in the studio are the devices that keep her constantly supplied with the information needed to enable her to host and control the programme. This information is passed to her via both aural and visual channels of communication.

For most talk programmes, whether news-based, phone-in or whatever, the presenter is assisted by a programme producer usually located in a support area adjacent to the studio. The producer may pass information to the presenter by voice through the talkback system: by pressing a button she can cut into the audio that the presenter is hearing through her headphones. Many presenters set up their headphones as 'split cans', with output heard through one channel and talkback through the other. Alternatively, the producer's voice can be heard through small loud-speakers built into the desk. Anyone else with access to the talkback system can also directly contact the presenter in this way. Similarly, the presenter can request information from whatever source she needs in the station through the talkback. If her hands are busy operating desk controls, she can use a voice-activated talkback.

The other main voice contact that the presenter makes with an external source during a live broadcast is by telephone. She uses the studio tele-phone to contact regular external contributors such as the regional travel service, before opening up the studio quality line for their reports. If she is willing to receive calls from listeners during transmission about items on the programme, these can also be put through to her by the producer while a record or material from any other source is being broadcast.

Visual information is fed through to the presenter in many forms. Apart from the obvious printed or written data – scripts, question sheets for interviews (neither of these should be too prescriptive), details on album sleeves – the presenter has access to a regular flow of information on paper handed to her prior to and during a programme.

If she is playing music through a jukebox system, she will have collected a printout detailing the full titles of tracks, artistes' names plus technical and historical information (see p. 83). Any recorded package on reel-to-reel tape or cart should be handed to her complete with a cue sheet prepared by the reporter, specifying how the item should be introduced by the presenter (see p. 144). The presenter may also be provided with telex information on weather or travel, hard copy from the newsroom, a 'what's on' listing of local events, details to announce on air of a competition or promotional event, details of events cancelled and schools or workplaces closed during bad weather (see pp. 227–9) or even clippings from the day's press that merit reading out or commenting on.

Visual information is also supplied through communications equip-ment fitted into the studio. The presenter could have access to up to four visual display units:

The jukebox VDU

This specifies the track currently playing and the one which is lined up and ready. Using a mouse or, if available, touch screen control, the presenter can use this information display to locate a specific track on the jukebox if it relates to a breaking news story.

Teletext

CEEFAX or Teletext UK – is usually included in a well-equipped studio to enable the presenter to check on the current status of national and international news stories and sports results. The presenter can select which information she wishes to read and can even use the monitor as a television set to pick up any visual data flashed on screen – for example, during an election or a budget speech.

A computerised news distribution system

This may also be monitored by the presenter through access to a VDU in the studio, enabling her to call up files containing scripts for specific stories or to respond immediately if the system's keyword function were to register a local news story breaking (see p. 82). Often, it is the producer in the adjoining support area, rather than the presenter herself, who has access to the news computer during a broadcast. She is able to filter out the unnecessary data and pass through the essential information, using the fourth VDU, the visual talkback.

The visual talkback

This monitor conveys data to the presenter as it is typed in by the producer. Its uses range from an alternative to the printed cue sheet – a package is rushed in to go on air and the producer types the cue for the presenter to read directly from the screen – to a list of callers' names, locations, points they wish to make and line numbers, enabling a phone-in presenter to choose what line she wants next to maintain balance or develop a theme for the programme. The visual talkback is of particular value for providing up-to-the-second information to a presenter with the least risk of distraction. A telephone link may be set up at short notice with a leading politician to discuss a breaking news story. The producer can use the visual talkback to feed questions to the presenter during the interview itself. With data communicated in this form rather than through one channel of her headphones, the presenter is able to concentrate more easily on the interviewee's responses.

In addition to visual information on VDU, on documents spread across the desk, and on meters registering output level, the presenter should be able to refer to the studio clock, the labels on the jingles carts and, in particular, she should be able to maintain reasonable eye contact with studio guests, employing those codes of facial expression – smiles, nods and reactions to their comments – to encourage a natural and animated dialogue or discussion. The ergonomic concerns of studio layout are therefore important to ensure the optimum effect both on data transmission behind the scenes and on interpersonal communication both on and off air.

The studio tape recorder and editing kit

The studio tape recorder is a vital component in the armoury of the broadcaster. It provides one means of playing back recorded packages during live broadcasts, although more stations are opting for cartridge tape as the most suitable medium for this. More importantly, it is used for editing material to make up packages – anything from the brief newsclip to a lengthy documentary item incorporating a presenter's voice piece, interview responses, actuality material and possibly mixed-in music and sound effects.[10] It also provides more options for creative broadcasting with devices to manipulate sound – playback at variable speeds and a facility to disguise the voices of speakers whose identities are to be protected.

After the portable tape recorder, the studio tape machine is the next item of equipment in a radio station that a trainee broadcaster is likely to learn how to use as she develops skills in basic editing. This involves taking out the unwanted parts of a recording on quarter-inch tape and rearranging what is left. Complex packages, juxtaposing a number of voice pieces, go through a process of 'rough editing' – whole sections of the recorded tape are run onto separate reels, labelled or marked and put back together in the desired sequence. 'Fine editing' involves a detailed 'cleaning up' of voice pieces, removing individual sentences, words, coughs, sneezes, 'fluffs' and other distractions from the overall meaning that the package is attempting to convey.

Editing creates pace, style and impact through the juxtaposition of audio items. An interview may be transmitted word for word as it was recorded but given greater dynamism through faster pace, simply by editing out the gaps and pauses in the original dialogue. All this is achieved simply by cutting the tape with a sharp razor blade and splicing it with specially designed sticky tape.

With practice an editor develops a sense of timing and a routine to turn an unstructured and regularly interrupted recorded interview into a seamless package with the most elementary form of technology. By listening through headphones as the tape is moved forwards and backwards across the playback head, it is possible to locate edit points with some precision. These are marked with a Chinagraph pencil before the tape is placed in an editing or splicing block and cut with a razor blade. The skilled editor can enhance the atmosphere of the location through positioning of 'wildtrack' – background noise recorded on location such as a heavy downpour at the beginning of a report on a village cricket match, or the wail of a police car siren in a report on rising crime figures. It is also possible for an editor to convert a hesitant and stuttering speaker into a fountain of eloquence although the desire to 'sharpen up' a recording should be weighed against the ethical consideration of whether the interviewee is being fairly represented. The removal of natural speech mannerisms may in fact result in a sterile and unnatural recording.

This highlights the capacity of radio as a medium through which reality may be distorted. The listener has no visual image to confirm the veracity of the recorded item. As an auditory medium conveying a transitory text, radio leaves little room for the suspicion which may arise from, say, reading a quotation in a press report that it has been refined or doctored. It presents itself as a medium most worthy of audience trust precisely through the seamlessness and apparent spontaneity of its output. For this reason – and because individual reporters are not constantly supervised when preparing packages of recorded material – a key issue in the professional ethos of broadcasting is that of individual responsibility. Members of a station team are aware that interviewees lose trust in the station if they feel their words have been distorted through editing. Hence devices such as internal edits – changing the order of statements in a recording – are actively discouraged.

The skill that a trainee in radio is encouraged to develop when editing the spoken word is in fact to create the illusion of spontaneity, such that splices are undetectable to the listener. Evidence of editing is more overt when putting together a 'montage package' – brief extracts of voices, music and sound strung together – although this type of presentation is more effectively produced by mixing different audio sources through a studio desk.

Microphones

HILLIARD (1985: 210) describes five basic microphone positions, each of which locates the listener in a particular orientation to the speaker or other source of sound. These are:

On mike

The speaker talks directly to the microphone and the listener has unobstructed access to her voice as if she were in the same room. This is the commonest microphone position. The speaker may be a presenter, newsreader or continuity announcer, directly addressing the listener. Or she may be taking part in a dialogue or discussion, either using her own words – for example, in an interview, panel discussion or quiz – or following a script as in a radio drama, whereby the listener is positioned as a privileged witness to what is being said.

Off mike

The voice of the speaker is heard some distance from the microphone; it is not only fainter but also integral to ambient sound. The microphone represents the location of the listener in relation to the speaker; the listener 'catches' what the speaker is saying through being within earshot, as if by accident. Whilst this is a common microphone technique for radio drama, it is also used in lively music and entertainment-based programmes – for example, where the presenter is giving the impression of a busy and chaotic studio and appears to be speaking to people who are there with her.

Fading on or fading off

The speaker appears to be approaching or moving away from the microphone whilst talking. The microphone represents a fixed standpoint for the listener; she does not have the unrestricted access to the speaker afforded by moving around with her as she speaks. The effect is produced by the speaker altering the physical distance between herself and the microphone as she speaks or, if the microphone is unidirectional (see below), by the speaker moving into the field of optimum reception of sound. Slow fading – up or down – of the microphone at the control desk produces the effect of moving the listener, through both space and time, into the scene of the action where the speaker is already located. Again, this has applications in live broadcasting as well as radio drama. It is a common convention in radio to fade gently into an OB location, for example during the initial audience applause of a quiz show, to create a smooth transition for the listener out of the atmosphere of the previous programme.

Behind an obstruction

The speaker's voice appears to be coming from behind a door, outside a window, inside a locked trunk, anywhere in fact that the imagination allows. The effect is achieved either through placing a physical obstruction or baffle of some description between the speaker and microphone, or through electronic adjustment of the sound waves. The application of special effects to the voice can also create the impression of someone speaking in a large cave on a planet in the outer reaches of the galaxy or from a call box at Euston Station. Many studio desks are fitted with an echo effect that can be brought in at the touch of a button when, for example, the presenter is describing a local ghost legend.

The positioning of a microphone to signify the listener's orientation to the radio text demonstrates that creative radio does not regard its technology as merely a channel for the communicative performance in front of the microphone, but as a medium in the sense that clay is a medium for the artistic ceramicist. Part of the training of broadcasters involves using the microphone 'correctly' to avoid unwanted 'handling noise' (Boyd

1993: 213) or 'mike rattle' (Gage 1990: 41). This conceals evidence from the listener of the production process of radio while enhancing the text's status as a true recording of aural reality. Effective microphone usage also involves consideration of the location for the recording, the setting of the recording level and the distance between the microphone and speaker. *Creative* microphone usage involves the application of microphones and related recording technology to create the most interesting and stimulating sounds for the listener, rather than the positioning of microphones just to 'pick up' the sound. It may even be the intention of the producer to incorporate 'handling noise' to signify 'amateur' broadcasting techniques in a comedy sketch or to indicate that a reporter was indeed present to capture the action and immediacy of a dramatic news event on tape.

The nature of the recorded sound is further influenced by the type of microphone used. A presenter, newsreader or announcer in a studio usually speaks into a unidirectional or cardioid mike. The unidirectional mike responds to sound directly in front of it while the cardioid is so-called because it is most sensitive to sound emanating from within a heart-shaped area where the mike is positioned at the point where the top of the 'heart' dips to the centre.[11] It picks up the presenter's voice with the minimum of background sound from elsewhere in the studio. The studio mike is attached to a stand or flexible arm, similar to that of an angle-poise lamp; this is normally adjusted *before* the fader is opened as this mike is highly susceptible to 'handling noise'.

Interviews and music performances in a studio are often recorded with a ribbon mike[12] which can be unidirectional or bi-directional, i.e. more sensitive to sounds directly in front and behind it, creating a figure-of-eight pick-up pattern. A bi-directional ribbon mike is often placed on a stand between protagonists of a radio interview. It is normally unsuitable for outdoor work as its receiving mechanism is too sensitive to wind noise. Even a loud cough or sneeze could sound like an explosion and risks damaging the mike. It does however provide a rich tone to the voice through its excellent response to bass frequencies.

The lip mike is a ribbon microphone that can be used outdoors, e.g. for sports commentaries. This microphone is less responsive to wind noise as it has a very limited field in which it can pick up sound. The presenter speaks into it with her lips pressed against the specially shaped casing.

Reporters and correspondents in an outdoor location often use an omnidirectional mike. This is equally sensitive to sound picked up from all directions and thus produces a different 'actuality' type of sound in contrast with the clean and crisp audio produced by a unidirectional or cardioid studio mike.[13] The omnidirectional mike is least favoured in the studio as it is more susceptible to 'feedback' or 'howlround' – an unwanted high-pitched noise produced when a microphone is positioned too closely to a loudspeaker, causing it to pick up its own signal and continuously 'feed' it back to produce an increasing spiral of sound. The strength of this microphone when used outdoors is that it is least susceptible to 'handling noise'.

Some intrepid reporters may need both hands free to drive a car, sail a dinghy or climb a mountain whilst recording or broadcasting. A small unidirectional mike attached to a light headset may serve this purpose. Lavalier and tie-clip mikes,[14] more commonly used in television studios, may be useful in radio for recording interviews or 'fly on the wall' documentary material where the physical presence of a microphone may influence the performance of protagonists.

With a wide range of microphone types available, broadcasters weigh creative decisions with technical ones on frequency responses and pick-up patterns when selecting which one to use. They also take such practicalities into consideration as whether the mike is attached to a portable recorder or linked directly to a transmitter by a lead, or whether a radio mike with its own built-in transmitter to a nearby receiving unit would be the most useful.

Selection and use of microphones, as with all forms of technology associated with radio broadcasting, play an intrinsic part in the process of radio production, both through the qualities of sound that are produced and transmitted and through the associations that these qualities have for the listener, experienced in the interpretation of audio codes and the recognition of radio's significatory conventions.

Activities and points for discussion

1 Radio reporters out in the field sometimes need to apply some innovative thinking when covering special events. Microphones are rigged in all sorts of locations using all manner of everyday devices. Bicycles and railway porters' trolleys have been known to carry equipment for reporters who have to record whilst on the move. Consider the following two scenarios and discuss what devices and strategies you would use to cover them for radio.

(a) *Marathons.* Since their growth in popularity in the 1980s they have been frequently covered on local radio, although the events are often too big to be adequately reported from fixed points. Assume a full twenty-six mile marathon is to be run in your area (work out your own route if necessary). What form of live coverage would you give it? How would you cover it? How many people would you need and what equipment would you use?

(b) *Water events.* A local watersports club is offering cut-price canoeing lessons to the public. As a radio reporter you decide to put together a package of yourself learning how to 'shoot the rapids'. Bear in mind that portable tape recorders are susceptible to water damage and you need both hands free to operate the paddle. How would you record your lesson?

2 A Saturday morning programme on local radio is to include a 'treasure hunt' competition. A roving reporter will be in radio contact with the studio presenter throughout the programme. Her mission is to find the 'treasure' by following clues planted at different locations in the editorial area. Listeners have to solve the clues and phone in with answers (the winners get prizes). As a group, discuss how you would organise this. What equipment would you use and what difficulties would you anticipate?

What other dynamic radio 'events' could you devise to make the fullest use of the broadcasting equipment available to you whilst maximising the station's presence and image across the editorial area?

3 Under what circumstances would you *not* send out a reporter on his or her own with a portable recorder, backpack and/or radio car to cover an event or issue? Give your reasons. What alternative methods might you employ to cover these particular events or issues?

4 Plan and record three short interviews: one in a quiet indoor location, one in a crowded indoor location and one in an outdoor location. Base the interviews on topics appropriate to the locations and use the microphone to incorporate ambient and background sound to enhance the 'picture' in listeners' minds of what is happening. If you have access to editing equipment, record some wildtrack at each location and use it in the final package.

Play back the tapes and evaluate with colleagues the success or otherwise of the strategies employed in microphone usage and editing.

5 As a group of three, adopt the roles of presenter, producer and interviewee. The presenter conducts an interview with the interviewee without face-to-face contact – along a telephone line or via an intercom system, or by sitting back-to-back. The producer 'feeds' the presenter with questions via a visual talkback system. This can be set up with a simple word processor – the producer keys in the questions and other relevant data while the presenter reads the screen.

Record the interview. Does the presenter sound spontaneous in asking the questions? Do the questions flow logically? Do they reflect answers given to earlier questions? Evaluate the exercise. What were the difficulties in thinking quickly to produce a dynamic interview? How could these be dealt with?

6 A rock band is giving a concert in a local venue. You decide to record it so that edited highlights can be included in the next edition of a music magazine programme on radio. How would you set up and monitor the recording? What problems would you anticipate and how would you deal with them?

5 The voice of the station

Natural speech

WHILE the components discussed in the previous chapter provide a foundation for constructing the radio experience, the event of radio itself is not simply a matter of operating equipment and understanding the procedures for bringing in audio sources. Radio is capable of connecting with the listener in two important ways. First, it creates a link between the listener and the 'here and now' of the world in which he lives. Second, it connects with the listener's own social and cultural experience – the listener identifies with the values inscribed in radio's text, recognises and shares an understanding of the codes through which that text is meaningful, and thus relates to and participates in the experience that radio has to offer.

It is essential to radio, therefore, to establish and foster a particular relationship with each listener, one that is personal, positive and based on those values and perspectives that are relevant to the listener. The 'tools of broadcasting' help to create this link by opening up the channels of communication, but the success of the process depends finally on the performance of the presenter. It is through the human voice and how that voice is used that the *link* between station and listener becomes a communication *event*. This applies to radio that comprises mainly back-to-back music as much as it does to talk radio. The number one record in the charts sounds the same, no matter what station plays it. The presenter who introduces it aims to talk for one station addressing one distinct audience. In this chapter therefore we discuss the qualities of human speech in the context of radio and the range of techniques applied in talking to listeners.

One enigmatic quality that the radio industry seeks in would-be broadcasters is a 'good voice'. This suggests that the skills of a presenter or announcer are innate, indefinable but recognisable when that person speaks. Specific features of a 'good voice' are often described in intuitive terms, rather like those used in wine-tasting; one has to be in the business to know what they mean. Boyd defines a 'good microphone voice' as 'reasonably rich, crisp and resonant and free from obvious impediments' as opposed to 'piping, reedy, nasal, sibilant, indistinct or very young sounding' (Boyd 1993: 136). Managers listen out for voices that convey authority and personality, use appropriate variety of intonation and are delivered at a pace that enables listener comprehension.

Installed behind the radio desk, the presenter can provide the listener with access to any of a range of audio sources, but it is the presenter's own voice that establishes the point of contact for the listener – a personality to relate to. The voice may inform, announce, comment, ask questions, pass on gossip or attempt to persuade – whatever mode of address it adopts, it constitutes the key to the radio experience. Records and jingles contribute to an overall style of a station's output but the voice actually says something that listeners should latch onto, remember and talk about.

The professional radio voice can be developed through training. This consists mainly of practice, confidence building and, most important of all, listening. Most people who hear recordings of themselves speaking react with surprise ('do I really sound like that?') and criticism ('I wish I didn't sound like that'). For would-be broadcasters, getting used to the sound of their voice on tape and then working on the inflections and intonations are the best ways to develop its quality.

Undoubtedly, the activity of presenting a radio programme involves a considerable degree of role-play in which broadcasters learn to project a part of their personality that is geared to the radio experience once the red on-air light comes on. It is often a side of the broadcaster that best achieves expression in the context of radio; away from a microphone, some presenters may appear shy and reserved but are able to give voice to an outgoing, demonstrative side of their personality within the structure of a live programme. The voice is more than a 'tool of the trade' and much of the confidence and authority that is communicated through the voice is generated from within the presenter and his attitude to the listener.

Cloistered away in the studio, it is easy to forget that it is the listener, rather than the microphone, that is being addressed. Trainee presenters are often advised to picture a listener sitting in the studio. The voice is more likely to become natural and unstilted, if they are able to develop a sense of a genuine relationship with the listener. McLeish suggests that the relationship should be that of acquaintance rather than friend:

[The presenter] is friendly, respectful, informative and helpful. He has something to offer the listener, but does not use this to gain advantage either by exercising a knowledgeable superiority or by assuming any special authority. The relationship is a horizontal one, he refers to his 'putting something across', not down or up.

McLeish 1978: 103

The consequences of forgetting this relationship are unfortunately still too commonly heard on local radio. Unconvincing presenters range from the forced jollity of the 'wacky' personality ('well we're all leaping about here and it's absolute mayhem in the studio . . .') to the formularised intonation of the scriptreader who delivers cues in the same manner as one announcing the football results ('and we sent our reporter Nick' – up-inflection – 'to find out all about it' – down-inflection).

Presenters do read scripted material – cues for packages, back announcements, up-to-the-minute items of news that the producer may have typed into the visual talkback – but any evidence of a script, whether it is the sound of rustling papers or a vocal intonation that suggests that the item is being read out, produces an effective barrier to communication between presenter and listener. The programme sounds contrived and unspontaneous and the listener becomes an outsider to some private, ceremonial sermon rather than a person who is being directly addressed.

Practice in voice work enables the presenter to reduce this barrier and to transform written statements into conversational speech. Spoken sentences are not always as grammatically or structurally precise as written sentences. Written words are often shortened or abbreviated when spoken and formal written words may be colloquialised: 'the Government' may become 'the powers that be', 'a man' may become 'this bloke' or 'this guy', 'children' may become 'kids', depending of course on the item itself and the circumstances or style of the programme.

Structurally, written words may be referred back to if the reader loses the sense of what is being said. Spoken words must produce immediate comprehension. A press report may read:

> The house had rising damp, falling masonry, cracked plaster and no central heating and was judged to be unsuitable for its 66-year-old occupant, Mrs Marcia Smith, who suffers from rheumatoid arthritis.

The impact of this statement would be lost if it were read out as an introduction to a studio interview with a housing officer. Stating the age and health of the occupant towards the end of the sentence makes it necessary for the listener to think back to the list of faults affecting the house. Furthermore, the passive verb 'was judged' carries a sense of formality about the statement and turns it into a pronouncement. A more suitable structure for speech would be:

> Now here we have the case of Marcia Smith – 66, suffering from rheumatoid arthritis – and she's living in a house with rising damp, falling masonry, cracked plaster and no central heating . . .

Even when fully scripted, the spontaneity of the statement and the sense of concern felt by the presenter could be lost through inappropriate use

of stresses and intonation. A set of notes would have the benefit of forcing the presenter to put the case in his own words:

Marcia Smith – 66, rheumatoid arthritis
House – rising damp, falling masonry, cracked plaster, no central heating . . .

It is not uncommon to see presenters in full fling on air, surrounded by
scraps of paper with such hastily jotted notes, or ripped-off sections of
news computer printouts on forthcoming programme items. Usually the
most spontaneous and lively programmes are those presented by someone
well versed in the art of *ad libbing* and able to pick up the main points
from details – hastily fed by the programme producer through the visual
talkback and quickly read on the monitor while a jingle is playing –
relating to a telephone interviewee that the producer has managed to dig
up to comment on an emerging news story.

Presenter functions

IN Chapter 4 we referred to three basic functions of a radio presenter: to
be the personality of the station, to represent the interests of listeners and
to maintain a constant flow of output (p. 110), or in blunt terms, to talk
on behalf of the station, talk on behalf of the listener and to keep talking.

As the *personality of the station*, the presenter takes on board and
projects a corporate identity. From the point of view of most stations, the
presenter is as vital a part of their operation as the transmitter. In terms
of station branding, presenters are recruited on the basis that their voices
and their personalities convey the station's image in the best way possible
for a particular point in the schedule and a particular target audience.

Presenter-less, computerised, jukebox programmes (see p. 84) are of
course technically possible but arguably the arid, flawless sound would
eventually encourage listeners to retune in search of humanity.
Computerised programming and music selection runs the same risk as
heavily formatted and over-formularised live programmes – listeners
would find little to connect with and would tire of the experience. It is
especially vital for stations that broadcast, say, 70 per cent recorded
music, for a genuine human being to link that music. If the popular radio
text were a battle between presentation and content, presentation would
always be the winner. This is not to suggest that radio conveys empty
messages, but that the successful presenter, like any good public speaker,
is able to enhance the impact of that message.

The presenter expresses his identity as the personality of the station
through the seamless professionalism of a vocal performance, combined
with the smooth integration of elements specific to the programme –
jingles, music and packages or responses by guests and audience
applause. The performance itself weaves in such qualities as vocal inton-

ation, pace, register, vocabulary and dialect to reflect a particular station identity. The technical functions of driving the desk and lining up sources are subservient to the presenter's performance. They represent part of the 'professional' world of broadcasting, with its specialist skills and practices, to which the public as consumers have little access, despite tantalising glimpses afforded by presenters working on location or in satellite studios subject to the public gaze.

Variations in station style influence the nature of the presenter's brief. A presenter on BBC local radio is expected to convey local knowledge not only in the correct pronunciation of local place names but also in recognising the key concerns of listeners when talking to those in positions of responsibility. The news-orientated style of BBC local radio output highlights the obligation on presenters to appear fair and impartial while maintaining accuracy. The brief for an ILR station specialising in 'gold' music may be to keep talk to a minimum but maintain the station's character through back-to-back music. Here, an ability to segue records and mix jingles and advertisements together in a dynamic manner is as essential a quality as the presenter's voice in turning the station's style policy into a positive and enjoyable listening experience.

In representing the *personality of the listener*, the presenter operates as the primary point of contact between the listener and the station – ultimately between the listener and all other listeners brought together by the station. Rather than talk down to listeners, or impose values and attitudes that have no meaning for listeners, the presenter takes on a role that purports to reflect their interests. A system of values, concerns and perspectives are assumed to exist *already* within the 'community' or 'nation' of listeners and the station presents itself as a forum for – and reflection of – the taken-for-granted, 'natural' view of the world. Thus the performance of the presenter as the personality of that station simultaneously reflects the personality ascribed to the listener. He appears to articulate the listener's thoughts and responses and to represent the distinctions that the listener would draw between the serious and the light-hearted, the significant and the quirky, that which accords with a 'universal' sense of propriety and that which calls out for an emotional response. In framing interview questions, he may assume the identity of the moderate, politically neutral member of a value consensus, projecting the unassailable logic of 'common sense'.

The presenter's dual function of station and listener representative is characterised by McLeish's guidelines on radio interviewing:

> The interview must be what it appears to be – questions and answers for the benefit of the eavesdropping listener. The interviewer is after all acting on behalf of his listener and is asking the questions which the listener would went to ask. More than this, he is asking the questions which his listener *would ask if he knew as much about the background to the subject as the interviewer knows*. The interview is an opportunity to provide not only what the listener wants to know, *but also what he may need to know*.
>
> *McLeish 1978: 39–40, our emphases*

One might argue that this calls for major assumptions about what the listener would ask and needs to know and represents a simplistic view of the notion of 'public service' broadcasting. The act of representing the listener involves an attempt to connect with the listener's perspective of a topic or news event by applying textual devices that promote audience comprehension and relate that topic effectively to listener interests. The interview serves this purpose through its question-and-answer format; the questions break the topic down into assimilable component 'issues' and prompt a particular type of explanation from the interviewee to make these issues clear to the listener. Thus a 'devil's advocate' role adopted by a political interviewer is not an assumption that listeners are sympathetic to an opposing political viewpoint. It is a device that seeks to make the politician accountable to the public through encouraging explicit responses and attempting to counter the coaching that many politicians are given in the art of evasiveness.

The merging of station and listener personalities and interests through the performance of the presenter serves to reinforce not only the station's individual branding with its own defined target audience, but also the capacity of radio generally to construct, through ideological work, a 'common ground' from which listeners may engage in the radio experience. Radio seeks to represent a *pre-existing* listener 'personality' through the presenter's spontaneous performance and the listener's instantaneous inner response to that performance. As a consequence, the radio experience effectively masks the necessary action on the part of the listener to adopt a specific, consensual mode of reception in order that he may understand and fully relate to the values and terms of reference of the programme that he is tuned into.

As spontaneity is the key to the reproduction of the consensual experience of listening to the radio, the third function of the presenter, to maintain a *constant flow of output* is clearly crucial. The organisation and technical infrastructure of a radio station – as we have discussed in Chapter 3 – is geared to the over-riding priority to produce an unceasing and ever-developing output narrative. The presenter is located at the central control point for this unrelenting textual flow with a wide range of resources – carts, CDs, recorded packages, outside lines – to marshal and put on air. If the system breaks down, the result is 'dead air' – the very antithesis of the radio experience. The most important and most basic resource to maintain this experience is the human voice.

Goffman proposes the effect of spontaneous and fluent speech as the 'key contingency in radio announcing' (Goffman 1981: 198) and highlights three ways in which this effect is realised: the impression that the announcers 'have a personal belief in what they are saying', that they are talking naturally without reading from a script, and that the listener is in the physical presence of the speaker (Goffman 1981: 237–41). He argues:

> Because talk is learned, developed, and ordinarily practised in connection with the visual and audible response of immediately present recipients, a radio announcer must inevitably talk *as if* responsive others were before his eyes and ears ... announcers must conjure up in their mind's eye the notion of listeners, and act as though these phantoms were physically present to be addressed through gaze, body orientation, voice calibrated for distance, and the like.
>
> *Goffman 1981: 241*

While these characteristics of the presenter's performance are of importance, particularly in an analysis of radio text as an instance of social and symbolic interaction, an especially significant aspect of radio talk is that it is performed *not* as if speaker and listener were in visual contact, but as an *alternative* mode of address to face-to-face communication. Unless taking part in a phone-in, the listener cannot give a verbal response to what the presenter is saying. And with no visual reference, the listener does not normally know what is happening in the studio when the radio goes silent. Thus the performance of the presenter is necessarily geared to the continuous flow of sound. Arguably the most suitable panel game for radio is BBC Radio 4's *Just a Minute* in which contestants must talk without repetition, deviation or *hesitation*. More difficult to deal with are the ten-second pauses when *Brain of Britain* contestants search their memories in vain for the answer to the question – often interrupted by the quiz chairman, Robert Robinson's gentle 'I'll have to hurry you . . .'.

For the skilled presenter, a sustained narrative flow does not appear to be produced through any process driven by a style policy. The listener hears the performance as the presenter's natural way of behaving and interacting. The flow is only noticed when it is broken. Like the boom mike appearing within the frame of a television drama, it is the technical breakdown that alerts the listener to the 'artificiality' of the production process, when the correspondent is not on the end of a line, the cart does not fire or the tape plays at the wrong speed. Listeners familiar with the codes of radio are able to distinguish between dramatic silence and dead air. The former is a natural part of radio's narrative flow. The latter occurs when that flow is broken.

The link

WITHIN the standard programming format for local radio and national music radio – the continuous delivery of music, packages, interviews, competitions, voiced reports, etc. – the link is a fundamental broadcasting device. It forms a substantial part of what a radio presenter has to say when setting up and contextualising each of a series of programme items and effectively brings together the three basic presenter roles – to talk on behalf of the station, to talk on behalf of the listener and to keep talking. Not only does the link introduce programme items, it suggests, explicitly through the presenter's comments or implicitly by the inclusion of the items themselves, how they should be interpreted, experienced and appreciated by the listener.

The link is the basic product of the presenter's craft. It epitomises radio's essential nature – the experience of one person talking to another, telling a story and defining a relationship. In this sense, the link could be said to represent the radio experience in its purest form. In comparison, other talk items – packages, trails, voiced reports, advertisements – are more evidently constructed and hence constitute less of a direct personal listening experience. The link signifies the presenter's controlling and mediating position. It can direct the listener's attention to the next item, by either introducing it or 'trailing' it (announcing that the item is coming up soon), and reaffirms that, whatever else is happening, the key relationship established in the discourse of radio is that between the presenter and the listener.

Links can be quite long and detailed with the presenter making up any comment or observation that he finds appropriate. It is possible to identify a range of link types which are common to most popular radio stations although the interests of innovative broadcasting are not well served by the notion of presenters selecting from a menu of ready-formulated links. The most engaging link is that which is unique to the moment in which it is used – the presenter's own way of taking an audience from one item and into the next. Nevertheless, a consideration of common link types gives some indication of their function in creating a structure and direction to output and an orientation to that output for the listener.

Name checks

These confirm for listeners the name of the station and the presenter.

Station frequency checks

These are not as redundant as they may seem. Listeners may have tuned into the station by a random search of the dial, or the radio's RDS has automatically found the station. Repetition of the frequency helps to embed it into listeners' memories.

Timechecks

Timechecks are particularly important during morning and evening 'drive times'. Listeners who are commuting are likely to retune if regular timechecks are not given.

Public service announcements

PSAs may prove useful as links between two pieces of music or to change the tone and direction of output. They may cover any topic from the latest weather report or traffic flash to a 'what's on' listing, working towards a station's 'local' branding. Many stations maintain a 'what's on' diary and ensure that a daily list of information is within reach of the studio presenter.

Music information

The song or tune title, name of performer plus historical information (e.g. the year it made number one) is supplied on music computer printouts as well as by more obvious sources – album sleeves or CD booklets. Listeners often find it annoying when this information is not given out, especially when the piece of music is familiar but they cannot remember the details. Also, music is an integral part of output, not something to play while the presenter does the crossword. He should demonstrate an interest in and commitment to the music that is played.

Trails

These are announcements of items lined up for later in the programme, and of forthcoming programmes, features and special events that the station will be covering. They enhance a sense of planned continuity and reinforce the presenter's role as representative of the whole station rather than someone who does not know what is happening other than in his own show. They also form part of radio's basic challenge to listeners not to switch off in case they miss out on something important or interesting. Trails may be recorded on cart and played at key points in the flow of a live programme, or they may be spoken by a presenter to provide 'signposts' in the narrative development of the programme – 'after the news, American football comes to Wembley'; or to signal that there will be more music after the next speech item – 'and in the next half-hour, music from Cliff, Sade and The Beatles . . .'.

Cues

Cues are anything that a presenter may say to introduce the next item – a record, competition or whatever. A cue for a recorded package is usually the most carefully planned of links, written by whoever made the package for the presenter to read out before running the package. It can be any length from a single sentence to a full minute of speech, but its final words in particular are often crucial to the sense of the package – for example, '. . . and he asked the Home Secretary whether he agreed with the Archbishop's views' would be followed immediately by the Home Secretary's response. Double cues – i.e. spoken by the presenter and then repeated in the recording itself: 'Do you agree with the Archbishop's views, Home Secretary?' – betray a lack of preparation and organisation by the station team.

Back announcements

'Back annos' are announcements to listeners of what they have just heard – the title and artiste's name after a piece of music, the name of a correspondent who has just given a live report. Back annos for recorded packages are also provided on cue sheets. The final three or four words of the package itself are written down as an 'out cue' for the presenter to follow. Back annos may take a very simple form such as a name check of the last voice heard on the package and stations have been known to ban their use on the basis that anything in the radio text that looks back at what has been said is redundant communication. Many stations use them, however, to promote interest in further development of the story – 'and the Archbishop will be giving his response later today'. Their value lies in orientating the listener within the narrative of the text and providing a sense of continuity. A back anno can double as a cue for the next item – 'The Home Secretary talking to Mike Lapel earlier today. The Archbishop backed up his claims at a news conference during his visit to Wormwood Scrubs. Our reporter Penny Tensory was there . . .'.

Recorded links

Jingles, recorded trails or advertisements are also effective means of signposting and punctuating the flow of items in a programme while reinforcing a particular output style. Virgin 1215 regularly interrupts its half-hour 'music marathons' with station ident jingles, as genuine thirty-minute stretches of non-stop music would reduce listeners' opportunity to locate and identify the station on the tuning dial.

Handovers

These often take the form of banter between two presenters, when one is about to take over from the other. They reinforce the station's character and singular brand image and often involve trailing items in the new presenter's show.

Silence

This is a rarely used link. A few seconds of silence can prove very effective if following an emotional and thought-provoking voice item or an expertly performed piece of music. The difficulty with silence is whether listeners recognise that it is intentional and many stations therefore choose to 'keep the needle wagging' on the output volume meter.

Presenter's own comments

Most significant of all in demonstrating the impact of the presenter's own personality on the text, these do more than link two components of a programme together; they add interest and colour to output, regulate a programme's pace and timing and shape output to maintain its overall link with the audience. The more confident or loquacious presenter may opt to say anything that comes to his mind at the time – humorous comments about people and events in the news, for example – without any advance preparation. The obvious dangers here are (a) the comment does not work in the way it was intended to, and (b) it has not been fully thought through and leads to listeners' complaints, if not litigation. Some presenters have been known to discuss personal issues on air – their divorce or their experience at the special clinic. Depending on the personality of the presenter and the context in which he is speaking, such baring of the soul on air can be either radical and compulsive listening, or an embarrassment to the station.

In view of the link's vital role in creating and reproducing the radio experience, it is ironic that its significance lies in its apparent spontaneity. Spoken links are often unrehearsed, *ad lib* products of the presenter's personality, based on his capacity to respond instantly to the content of items included in his show. In comparison, news summaries and music running orders are derived from expensive, time-consuming processes of checking facts and setting up a computer programme. Yet every word of the link matters precisely because – unlike the news summary or the piece of music – it is constructed as an instance of interpersonal communication, involving the listener directly. Whatever the purpose of the link, the presenter confirms the tone and style of the programme and station through pace, emotion, humour and intellectual level. Even the choice of the few words used in a link can reflect assumptions held by the station of listeners' values, educational background and existing knowledge of, and interest in, current events.

As far as stations are concerned, links should therefore be treated with considerable care rather than as throwaway comments, precisely because they are mostly unscripted and off the cuff, or at least sound as if they are. A presenter who has transferred to a big city station from one serving a largely rural community could unwittingly create the impression that he – and consequently the station – is not familiar with the seemingly trivial, everyday aspects of urban life by continually referring to issues more significant to people living in villages or working on farms. Thus, preparation for links should involve considering their likely impact on listeners. Presenters should at least check that they know what they are talking about; a quick read-through of the press cutting or 'what's on' listing before opening the microphone fader enables them to think of appropriate responses or even spot opportunities to link the information with the next piece of music.

The frequency, variety and duration of links are sometimes subject to strict house styles – referred to as 'formatting' – which have been drawn up to reinforce the station's branding and the character of its overall sound. A format may determine, for example, a particular way of introducing a news bulletin, using a specific 'news in' jingle combined with the presenter's own voice providing a station name and frequency check. Presenters may be confined to a format that forbids links of longer than fifty seconds between pieces of music, or be told that every link must begin with a station name check or include the name of one of the towns or cities in the editorial area. Similarly, the frequency of timechecks and station ident jingles may be prescribed in detail through formatting. Talk stations may insist on links with depth containing substantial useful information – 'what's on' details or trails for forthcoming features. Gold and AOR music stations may insist that presenters provide full details on each old record played – if not when it charted and for how long, at least its title and the name of the artiste.

Arguably such detailed instructions on links not only reinforce a station's brand identity but also provide a structure for less experienced presenters to work in, ensuring they have something worthwhile to say without getting into difficulties with their own unprepared remarks. This may guarantee a balance and variety of content in the radio text but can nevertheless lead to a dry, formula-ridden style of output. Often the experienced and competent presenter is able to judge when to take the opportunity to let personality shine through. The rationale behind formatting is to lift the overall level of performance but its success in reinforcing the station–listener rapport depends on the ability of presenters to allow their own humanity to come across the airwaves.

Through the appropriate use of links, the presenter's presence should be strong enough to create a bond of trust between himself and the listener. Within the radio text, a presenter occupies a higher position in a hierarchy of trust than other radio voices – the more dispassionate newsreader or the correspondent with more specialist knowledge. Through this bond, an effective presenter can use a good link to rescue a bad feature, whereas a poor link could destroy the impact of the best of features and the finest of tunes.

The personality

THE qualities that individual stations seek in their presenters vary according to the nature of the service and the brand image that each station sets out to achieve. Common to all stations, however, is the establishment and maintenance of a rapport between presenter and listener. While the presenter embodies the dual function of representing the station and the audience, the notion of an ideal presenter whose performance optimises the market appeal of a station implies a perfection far removed from humanity. The most accomplished application of presentation techniques can never replace the ability of the person to convey a positive and *distinctive* personality. The aphorism applies – 'good' presenters are born, not made.

A variety of character types have proved popular with local radio listeners, ranging from the 'no nonsense' presenters who 'tell it like it is', sometimes with little apparent regard for the feelings of hapless phone-in participants, to the humorous, offbeat and 'crazy' presenters who might think nothing of telephoning the Prime Minister while on air to find out what he is having for breakfast. Both of these presenting styles may be suitable for 'tabloid' radio (sometimes referred to unkindly as 'yob radio') with the focus on human-interest issues and topics such as sex, crime, film stars, pop stars and trivia, covered by quizzes, phone-ins, 'talky bits', comments on press cuttings, listeners' letters or faxes plus dialogues with co-presenters, astrologers, agony aunts, celebrities or other personalities.

Alternatively, stations may opt for a more 'serious', reasoned or 'intelligent' presenting style in which the authority of presenters rests in their knowledge of topics ranging from the complexities of economic policy-making to the equally complex considerations of a cricket team captain on pitch conditions, team composition and whether to bat first. Programme formats more suitable for this approach include live interviews, dialogue with specialist correspondents, the incorporation of recorded packages containing more interviews mixed with reporters' commentary, or panel discussions either in a studio or before an audience.

All of these 'character types' emphasise the presenter's craft of 'performing'. The 'purity' of the communication between presenter and listener rests in the capacity of a human voice, its pace, tonal qualities and language register, to construct the essence of a direct relationship between them. An interactionist perspective of the practice of any form of interpersonal communication highlights the extent to which it constitutes role-play by the participants. This aspect of presenters' communication skills is more evident when they are observed at work in the studio, wired into the machine of radio, talking into a microphone, listening through headphones. Presentation is a performing art, one that is all the more convincing when presenters are able to give part of themselves in the performance.

An essential quality of the radio experience itself is that it draws on the faith of the listener in the veracity of the communication. The entire discourse is based on the assumption that the listener shares in the perspectives and values that are implicit in the nature of the communication. Nevertheless the radio experience is only partially constructed by the presenter; the listener contributes through making the transition from the idiosyncratic world of the individual to the structured, 'common sense' world of the consensus. If the listener loses that faith, the radio experience becomes a jumble of meaningless noises.

The listener is encouraged to participate, to have faith, by the presenter's credibility. The presenter represents the listener, shares the listener's priorities, asks the questions that the listener would like to hear answered. A local talk radio presenter recognises and articulates residents' concern over the location of a new supermarket in a 'green belt' area and is able to convey a strong sense of local awareness, instantly spotting the implications of new developments of the story as they break on air. Arguably, the presenter 'constructs the issue' and makes the listener believe that the story is significant, simply by articulating it and exposing it to the social realm of the radio discourse. Whatever the interpretation of the presenter's opinion-leadership role, it is clear that his credibility rests on a knowledge of local issues, events, traditions and feelings.

Credibility is an equally important quality of the presenter on music radio. Knowledge of the music itself and the personalities and stories behind it, the ability to identify and discuss the trends, fashions and revivals that are reflected in the new releases, the communication skills to turn a constant 'that was . . . this is' announcement into interesting radio are all contributory factors to listeners' belief in the presenter as someone genuinely relating to them rather than simply spinning records.

In all forms of radio output, the presenting role is a positive one. An essential 'human' quality of presenters is the ability to smile, to convey that smile in the voice and to infect the audience with that smile. Even the most news-orientated reporter should be able to recognise the ironic, trivial and comical and be able to convey these moods at the appropriate time. Apart from the oppressive days dominated by a 'bad news' story – the outbreak of war, the major disaster – popular radio presenters seek to promote a 'feelgood' factor and to make their audiences feel entertained as well as better informed.

Multiple voice presentation

TWO alternative formats to the single presenter controlling the programme are the use of co-presenters and the so-called 'zoo format'.

Co-presentation

'Double-heading' is more common to talk radio than music services and can provide interest and variety in programmes that are strictly formatted. The two main hazards in co-presenting are: the presenters have such a rapport with each other that the listener feels excluded, and the presenters 'trip over' each other verbally by inadvertently interrupting each other or overlapping their speech so that the listener cannot make out what they are saying. Formatting and careful preparation with rehearsal help to overcome these problems but this opens up a third danger – overpreparation. The apparently scripted dialogue between co-presenters sounds even more false and contrived than the single presenter reading a prepared announcement.

Methods of co-presenting vary. One approach could set the presenters up as a kind of double-act:

> PRESENTER A: Good evening. This is Jenny Bright . . .
> PRESENTER B: . . . and John Spark . . .
> PRESENTER A: . . . once again testing your general knowledge with Telephone Trivia . . .
> PRESENTER B: . . . and on tonight's show, we discover . . .

BBC Radio 4's *Today* programme and its drive time news programme *PM* both apply this 'equal status' approach with two presenters taking turns to read cues and scripts or conduct interviews. This facilitates the programmes' 'rolling news' approach by enabling one presenter to prepare the next item while the other is addressing the listeners. Such an approach could also be used in programmes involving interviews or phone-ins, in which the presenters have opposing views and fire questions which reflect their differing perspectives. It would be unlikely for a radio station's own presenters to be publicly associated with, say, specific political viewpoints, but some politicians are themselves trained and competent broadcasters and could participate in such programmes. Opposing perspectives may also be represented by a male and female presenter.

A programme introduction may indicate a co-presenting relationship in which one presenter adopts a primary 'anchor' role while the other's function is to provide a specialist contribution, albeit from a secondary or subordinate position:

> PRESENTER A: Good evening and stand by your phones. This is Jenny Bright once again testing your general knowledge with Telephone Trivia . . .
> (sig. music)
> PRESENTER A: . . . and joining me as always with a multitude of mind-bending brainteasers, John Spark . . .
> PRESENTER B: Good evening and on tonight's show, we discover . . .

Arguably, this status differentiation offers greater potential for a natural and spontaneous flow in programme output for the very practical reason that only one person is able to operate the studio desk. That person effectively controls the proceedings through opening and closing microphone faders and introducing music, packages and other audio sources with split-second precision, maintaining the pace and narrative development of the programme.

There is in fact no need for both speakers to be in the same location for co-presentation to work. The main presenter could occupy the controlling seat in the studio while his colleague operates from a radio car or even uses a backpack to make regular interventions throughout the programme, each one from a different location. This is popular with local talk radio, as the presenter 'out in the field' is genuinely interacting with people whose domestic and working lives are intrinsically bound up with the issues and affairs of the editorial area, turning the everyday and mundane into interesting radio – dropping into local shopping centres, hairdressing salons, parks, bus stations, any location suitable for communing with 'real' people. Co-presenters may also work together with one located in a satellite studio, such that two diverse editorial areas are represented and pulled together. It is possible in these circumstances to set up a visual link between presenters through a closed circuit television system to enable them to work more effectively together.

It is not always possible to put any two presenters together in a studio and expect them to produce an effective dual performance, no matter how experienced either of them might be as broadcasters. Successful co-presentation depends on the participants' ability to interact while simultaneously addressing the listener. This in turn relies on an empathy between the speakers enabling them to 'spark off' each other to produce bright and, for the listener, captivating dialogue; this is after all one of the reasons for using two voices instead of one. Presenters should also be sufficiently familiar with each other's style of speech to recognise non-verbal cues indicating that one is about to allow the other to speak, wants to interrupt, or is about to throw in an off-the-cuff joke. With these conditions in place, there is still the possibility that the two voices, for reasons of tonal quality or delivery style, just do not sound 'right' together.

Zoo format

This involves more than two voices and is increasingly common in local and national radio in the UK. One well-known example of this was BBC Radio 1's *Steve Wright in the Afternoon*. The programme was focused on one 'lead' voice which gave way regularly to other contributors identified by name, or interacted lightheartedly with a host of anonymous voices. In some cases, a programme may be structured through input by regular contributors and interviews with a range of guests sitting together in the studio – an example of this approach is Radio 4's *Loose Ends* hosted by Ned Sherrin.

The advantages and hazards are the same as those of co-presented shows. When they work successfully, zoo-format programmes can provide lively and interesting radio but this depends very much on the ability of contributors to respond to each other, to identify and take up opportunities for witty, *ad lib* remarks, but not 'crowd each other out' or attempt to over-dominate the proceedings. The danger of creating a barrier to the listener's involvement is considerable and part of the key presenter's responsibility is to spot the implicit observations and in-jokes and attempt to make them comprehensible to the listener without inter-rupting the spontaneity of the programme. Another is to make sure that everybody does not try to speak at the same time.

Telling the story

A CRUCIAL distinction between the presenter and other speakers from the station team – newsreaders, reporters and announcers – is that while the former should appear to speak naturally and spontaneously, the latter have less of a credibility problem when reading out material. The tone and syntax of news stories, reports and announcements are evidence of a more obviously constructed form of radio speech although this does not take away the responsibility of any of these 'storytelling' speakers to *give* a performance through the expressive use of their voice and a well-paced delivery. A rule-of-thumb guide to pace is that the reader speaks an average of three words per second and a well-prepared report from a correspondent located at the scene of a news event can cover the essential aspects of the story with some descriptive detail to 'colour' the story in approximately 120 words or forty seconds. There are stylistic variations, however; announcements on BBC World Service are usually delivered at a slower pace than they would be on, say, Virgin 1215.

Scripted speech forms the basis of most news dissemination on radio. The entire news-gathering operation of organisations such as IRN and GNS essentially involves identifying, filtering and selecting data that can be packaged into a story, or development of an existing story, through being written up as a narrative that can be read out. In this form, the 'package' may be distributed within an organisation, or sold to other media organisations, and circulated as a ready-made audio piece sent down the line. Or it may be produced locally by a station's own programme staff drawing from their own news diary and range of sources and contacts.

Occasionally, a news story 'breaks' on air – a spokesperson of an organisation makes a statement during a live interview that indicates a major development in an existing story or a strong reaction to an earlier event; or a comment during live radio coverage of Prime Minister's Question Time is significant in view of current Government policy. It may, however, take a process of packaging and turning such an 'event' into a story before it is perceived by listeners as 'news'. In whatever way the news event is identified and 'gathered in', listeners first become aware of it in the simplest form of report – the *copy story*. The backbone of the news bulletin consists of a series of copy stories which have been either written by the station's own news team – sometimes the person reading the news – or received as ready-written items from services such as GNS or IRN.

The *voiced report* or *voice piece*[1] offers more depth and colour in journalistic terms to any specific story, is prepared by a reporter or specialist correspondent and is usually recorded on cart and inserted into a bulletin after the cue has been read out. In radio terms, it breaks up the bulletin by introducing a different voice; it lends authority to the station's news service and credibility to the story itself by providing the voice of an expert reporter or someone who was at or near the scene of the event in question. This 'status' accorded to the reporter arises from custom and convention and is often signalled by the newsreader's nomination of that reporter – '... our Midlands Correspondent, Bob Simkinson ...', '... our Chief Political Correspondent, John Sergeant ...' – although the text itself provides the listener with no evidence that the reporter is any more qualified than the newsreader, or for that matter the continuity announcer, to give an authoritative report, other than through what he says or from a difference in sound quality to suggest that the report is coming from a better 'vantage point' for the story than the studio itself. The practice of nomination is again subject to variation in style; some stations, such as Radio 1, enhance pace by *not* introducing reporters by name.

The *package* or *wrap* (see pp. 166–70) does offer more evidence of the reporter's privileged position or expertise in the subject area through combining his direct and scripted address to the listener with (apparently) unscripted interview extracts to support the story being told. Sometimes sound effects or ambient noise are edited or mixed into the recording to highlight the report's actuality status. Reports of this nature tend to be longer than voice pieces – three or four minutes although dramatic stories or in-depth items for specialist interest programmes could run for much longer.[2] Packages are therefore included in mainstream programming rather than news bulletins and are supplied to the programme presenter on reel-to-reel tape or cart complete with *cue sheet*.[3] This provides all the information needed by the presenter to incorporate the item into the flow of the programme:

- a title

- date and time that the package was prepared

- date and time of the intended broadcast

- name of reporter

- the cue itself, to be read out by the presenter

- the end words of the package

- the duration of the package (sometimes a total duration of cue plus package is also given)

- additional information – is the voice on the package recorded in top studio quality, on location or from a telephone line? Are there variations in level that the presenter or operator needs to compensate for (by 'riding the levels') when the recording is being broadcast? Is there a moment of 'dead air' (for example, a pause in an interviewee's response) which has been left in for effect and, if so, how many seconds into the recording does it occur?

Whatever the format of the scripted report, the nature of the communication is essentially the same – a speaker is telling a story by relating the facts (who said what? who did what?) objectively, dispassionately but with a sense of drama and immediacy. The reported event is usually one that has happened only recently; it is the job of the reporter to pass on the news and leave other voices to comment. Thus Elsinore Sound AM, had it existed, may well have carried this report:

In a statement last night, Prince Hamlet – nephew of King Claudius – said that the question for him is whether to be or not to be. Is it nobler, he asked, to suffer the slings and arrows of outrageous fortune or to take arms against a sea of troubles? He went on to question whether death would put an end to the thousand natural shocks that flesh is heir to. It could be just like sleep, he suggested, a chance to dream – although the rub, as he saw it, was what kind of dreams would a person have once they've shuffled off this mortal coil?

He proposed that the reason we grunt and sweat under a weary life, and put up with the whips and scorns of time, is our dread of what happens after death, which he described as an undiscover'd country, from whose bourn no traveller returns. Would we rather bear the ills we have, he asked, than fly to others that we don't know about? He commented that if this is the case, it's our conscience that makes us cowards.

Sometimes it is appropriate for the reporter to include description of the setting in which the reported event took place, especially if this adds to the story or indicates changes to the surroundings which have arisen as a result of the event. It is also necessary on occasion for the reporter to contextualise briefly or give explanatory detail so that the story makes sense. If the purpose of the programme maker is to provide a basic account of what happened without supplementary description, he may well select and apply the conventional formats of the copy story or the voice piece, but he is not constrained to this purpose or to these options. The principal determining factor should not be 'we've always done it this way' but an on-the-spot judgement by the programme maker of what is the best way of telling *this* particular story to *this* particular audience.

One form of reporting which does rely heavily on description – and is *un*scripted – is the *commentary*. This is most frequently used in live sports coverage although a reporter may be called on to give a commentary of any event from Trooping the Colour to a demonstration march through a town centre. Commentaries may be as long as a day's cricket match or fill a short forty-second break in a news bulletin where the reported event is taking place at the same time as the broadcast.

More than any form of radio broadcasting, the commentary is the technique that aims to re-create in the minds of listeners the 'pictures' that would be available to television viewers. This is not to say that commentary has to compensate for a 'weakness' of radio within a culture of visual information. Effective commentary not only 'paints' a picture, but also applies words to convey the emotion and drama of a scene and to highlight its significance. Combined with the background actuality sound, the voice conveys immediacy and signifies the reporter's (and therefore the listener's) prime, on-the-spot position. The news value of an event described on live radio may be apparent through the reporter's own reaction – the exhilaration of a British gold medal in the Olympic Games, the mild surprise of an England test match victory, the sense of hopelessness as thousands of refugees wait for permission to cross the border, or the anger at the indifference of an army general to the discovery of more burnt-out households in Bosnia.

While they are essentially live radio, most commentaries require advance preparation to enable the reporter to contextualise the event being described. Thus live coverage of a demo requires information on the number of marchers, names of their leaders, their route, their progress so far, details of their history and, of pragmatic value to listeners who are likely to be in or near the location, details of traffic diversions and public access.

With this information at hand, the reporter selects a perspective from which to report the event. He may describe the people at the front of the march and then 'pan' back along the procession, verbally depicting the banners, buildings and police presence at selected 'drop in' points of the column of people. Or he may choose a fixed point and describe people as they walk past it. A large enough event may justify the use of two reporters occupying different vantage points and handing over to each other. The choice of perspective is important in providing the most effective vantage point and conveying the greatest sense of drama *and* involvement. The sound of a reporter speaking live from an overhead helicopter may be dramatic in its own right, but without a perspective of the individual marchers, their moods and facial expressions, the reporter is not providing the full story.

Live commentary alternates between general description and explanation to focus on specific and illustrative detail. It not only communicates the visual – colours and shapes – but can also call on our other senses by evoking smells, sounds (not all sounds are clear or self-evidently meaningful to the listener) and the overall atmosphere of an event: exciting, threatening, uplifting, ominous, or whatever. Sometimes the most significant aspect of an event is conveyed by its own sound and the commentator may judge it appropriate to say nothing but allow the listener to absorb the atmosphere of the occasion itself through actuality.

A hierarchy of voices

THE term 'presenter' is applied generically to all who talk on air while controlling output of a radio station throughout a programme. The presenter is the key person who holds a particular programme together, introducing records, providing the cues for recorded packages, conducting live interviews, giving timechecks and so on. In popular radio's format of a rolling and live audio narrative, mainstream programmes tend to be identified by the name of their presenters, whose personalities constitute the main character and focal point of the output.

Talk presenters draw a strict distinction between their own role and that of *disc jockeys* who are just one type of presenter, controlling an output that is predominantly music. *Newsreaders* are not regarded as presenters; their role within the radio text lies in the area of 'informed' announcer or contributor. It is a role that reflects the status of 'news' as a seemingly neutral and objective account of world events. Traditionally, newsreaders have no involvement in that material beyond writing some of it and placing the items in order, unlike presenters whose use of language and overall mode of address reflects the person who is concerned with news issues and who reacts analytically and emotionally to news events. Again it is worth stressing that the difference in delivery between presenter and newsreader varies from station to station, and that style policy may call for a more unified sound incorporating a less formal delivery of news.

An explanation of the radio text solely as the consumable end-result of a production process sets out a view of the presenter as a fundamental ingredient of the product. Presenters personify their station's brand image and personality and engage listeners through language register, intonation, pace of delivery and accent, as much as through what they have to say. As the voice of the station, they constantly reaffirm listeners' need to consume this product, and reassure them that this is the best brand of product for them to consume. Taken in isolation, this perspective of the presenting role is reduced to the functional and instrumental business of marketing. However, the presenter's position in a broader cultural context indicates radio's place within the fabric of listeners' experience as consumers of popular cultural forms.

The voice of radio articulates and provides the terms of reference for our day-to-day, minute-by-minute thoughts and perceptions. It fills the space we work in, relax in, drive in, wake up in and – free of a physical, visual reference point – is as intangible as our own private thoughts. It is capable of structuring our thoughts, of untangling the constant flow of perceptual events that make up our 'raw' experience and of instantaneously making sense of these events – their significance and position within an overall 'scheme of things' – not simply in terms of how they *look* (the shocking television image of the war child wounded by shrapnel), but in terms of how we think and feel about them.

Hence the presenter occupies a position within a cultural map, in terms of authority, credibility and resonance with listener's own experience and identity. Kumar discusses the development of the roles occupied by the BBC's announcers and presenters since the pronouncement in 1924 of its first Director General, John Reith, that announcers should be thought of as 'men of culture, experience and knowledge' (Briggs 1961: 292, cited in Kumar 1977: 240), and their contribution of 'many voices' to the 'one mouth' of the BBC (Briggs 1961: 123, cited in Kumar 1977: 240). He identifies three 'strata' of 'professional presentation' that have built up in the BBC's history – announcers and continuity men, newsreaders, and 'the presenters, "link-men", chairmen, "anchor-men" of the regular programmes' (Kumar 1977: 241–2). These roles represent a hierarchy in terms of audience address. The earliest stratum reflects a formal, overtly institutional role; the later one is more flexible –

> a reliable, familiar broadcasting personality with whom the audience can identify, and whose authority, derived from his professional skills, enables him to direct and control anyone from an aggressive and aggrieved trade unionist to an eccentric lighthouse keeper from the Scilly Isles on a bad telephone.
>
> *Kumar 1977: 245*

A further distinction may be drawn between the voices of members of the radio station itself, i.e. the speakers who reflect the position and status of that station, and the voices of those outside the station who represent other institutions, whether spokespeople for specific organisations, sample representatives of the 'general' public, or indeed speakers noted for their individual and perhaps outspoken or humorous comments on specific issues. The former, according to Hartley in his study of broadcast news, are coded as 'institutional' voices while the latter are 'accessed' voices. The institutional voices are 'those of the newsreaders, correspondents and (with certain exceptions) the reporters on location [which] deny their constructed, provisional status – the things they say are said as if they were completely transparent' (Hartley 1982: 110). Accessed voices 'are all subordinate to the overall structure of a story as presented by the professional broadcasters' (Hartley 1982: 109).

These codes are important to the text of radio because they work towards the impression of 'objectivity' that a station seeks in its coverage of news, both through bulletins, in which the 'institutional' readings of items are occasionally interrupted by 'accessed' newsclips, and through in-depth discussions of news issues in which the presenter, as 'institutional voice' mediates the 'access' that listeners have to interviewees. This differentiation of the status of voices is referred to by Fiske as a 'discursive hierarchy'. In a news bulletin, the newsreader dominates this hierarchy through speaking 'the objective discourse of "the truth" ', while nominated reporters 'need individual signatures so that their "truths" appear subjective . . . and therefore lower in the discursive hierarchy than the "truth" of the newsreader'. In this formulation, the voices of people from outside the broadcasting organisation, 'the eye-witness, the involved spokesperson . . .' are voices that 'appear to speak the real, and that therefore need to be brought under discursive control' (Fiske 1987: 288).

The irony of this hierarchy is that the 'accessed' voice of the spokesperson, expert or member of the public, while subordinate to the presenter's 'institutional' voice, actually works towards the credibility of the overall text of radio. Listeners are not only told of 'what happened' in the news by the station itself; they are also told 'how and why it happened' by speakers who are in a better position to speak in these terms and thus lend authority to the station's overall coverage of the event in question.

It is nevertheless through the presenter's central position within the discourse of the radio programme that the listener gains an orientation to the events, issues and personalities that are represented in the text. The presenter is effectively enabled to embody and reinforce a system of values upon which the programme is based – the system that determines, for example, what is and is not in the interests of listeners. The values represented by studio guests may not coincide with those represented by the station; perhaps the guest represents the 'values' of bureaucracy, party politics, a specific commercial enterprise, or a 'deviant' sub-culture. However, while the presence of the studio guest has the potential to undermine the values inscribed in the programme, it is through the presenter's mediating role that these values remain dominant. The presenter has the authority to set the terms of the discussion, phrase the questions[4] and introduce and wind up the dialogue.[5] It is an authority that skilled interviewees may question – indeed, leading members of political parties are trained in techniques which challenge the presenter's control of the broadcast discussion or interview – but it is one which may be exercised ultimately by the presenter's physical control over the material means of broadcasting. If an interviewee 'breaks the rules' of the interview by speaking for too long, being abusive or in any way acting inappropriately for an 'accessed' voice, the presenter can reach for the fader and say goodbye.[6]

Activities and points for discussion

1 Think of an event that you have recently witnessed. Make an audio recording of you describing this event in a telephone call to a colleague. If you are unable to record the telephone call, sit back-to-back with your colleague and record your description. It is important that you do not use *visual* devices to support your description.

Now work with your colleague to devise a way of describing this event on radio. This may take the form of a news bulletin or part of the routine of a programme presenter. Record your description.

Compare the two recordings and pick out any differences in vocal style, vocabulary or expression. What is it about the second recording that makes it essentially 'radio', as opposed to the first recording? Also, compare your 'radio' performance with a genuine news bulletin or presenter routine recorded from a radio programme. What devices in speech and expression does the newsreader/presenter use in describing something on air? How many of these devices have you consciously or unconsciously incorporated in your own 'radio' recording?

2 Record a selection of radio news bulletins. Play back and transcribe on paper the wording of stories read out by the newsreader. For each story, count the number of sentences. For each sentence, count the number of words. Calculate the average number of sentences per news item and the average number of words per sentence.

Compare these average scores for bulletins on BBC Radio 1, your local ILR station and BBC Radio 4. Is there any correlation between these scores and the overall output style of each station?

Select a number of news items from your local newspaper and write up a script for each to be included as copy stories in a news bulletin on any of these stations. Aim to maintain the average scores that you have calculated.

Now record your bulletin. Play it back to colleagues and discuss as a group how effectively each story has been told. Is there enough information given to understand the story? Is the story interesting and dramatically described? Is the news event described in simple language? Does it need additional audio material? And does it 'read' well? Stories may look fine on paper but sound awkward when read out.

3 Record a selection of packages from a local talk radio station. Play these back and transcribe them word-for-word on paper. Analyse each package according to the WHAT formula, i.e. identify which words

- state *W*hat has happened – the basic 'facts' of the reported event

- state *H*ow it happened – the necessary contextual information to make sense of the story

- function to *A*mplify the basic 'facts' by adding colour or description to paint a fuller picture

- function to *T*ie up any loose ends in the listener's understanding of the story by rounding it off with a solid conclusion.[7]

An alternative method of analysis is to identify how each package answers the six 'W' questions: *W*ho, *W*hat, *W*here, *W*hen, *W*hy and Ho*w*?

Ensure that any copy you write for your own audio packages can withstand both forms of analysis.

4 Form a group of three or four. Each writes a script for a forty-second voice piece (how many words is this likely to be?) on any topic of your choice – a local event, an item from a newspaper, or whatever.

150

The scripts are then passed on in a circle so that each person in the group is able to edit someone else's script.

When editing, look out for

- sentences or phrases which would sound clumsy or awkward when read out

- complex words – jargon, officialese or specialist scientific or academic terms

- complicated sentence structure – overuse of dependent clauses (parts of the sentence starting with 'which', 'that', 'who', etc.), or simply too many words conveying too many ideas at once

- overuse of clichés[8]

- ambiguities or otherwise unclear descriptions

- over-dramatic writing and exaggeration

- colloquialisms appropriate for everyday conversation but not for objective news reporting (e.g. there were loads of people there; the Principal sounded pretty cheesed off)

- unattributed statements, i.e. statements which are clearly based on opinion, albeit informed opinion, but not on widely recognised fact (e.g. 'the Government's move will prove unpopular with students' should be qualified with something like 'according to the National Union of Students' President')[9]

- offensive, sexist or racist wording, even if unintentional.

Pass the stories round again for further editing. Continue until group members have their own stories back again. Discuss the thinking behind the editing decisions that were made. Read out or record the final versions of the stories and evaluate their effectiveness.

An alternative to this exercise is to start with a script for a one-minute copy story and reduce it by ten seconds each time it is passed round for editing without losing the essence of the original story.

5 Using a portable tape recorder (a basic cassette recorder will do), record a running commentary of any appropriate event – a sports match, a walk by the reporter through the countryside, a vintage car rally, a tour of an exhibition, or a craftsperson at work. Think in advance about the different aspects of the event that you may wish to describe and the duration of the commentary (try anything from one to five minutes). Where appropriate, allow actuality sound to add to the story or bring in other *vox pop* voices. Do not dry up or switch off the

recorder before the allotted timespan. Imagine this is going out live –
keep the performance going and keep it interesting.

A challenging alternative to this exercise would be to give a radio
commentary of a game of table tennis!

6 A role-play exercise for two people – you are co-presenting a radio
programme and you have ninety seconds in which to conduct an *interesting* dialogue before you play the record that will lead you into the next
news bulletin. Talk. Keep the patter going. Keep it interesting. Try this
out in a larger group with members taking turns to co-present while the
rest of the group observe and time the performance. Observers may
keep a tally of

- number of hesitations
- number of times speakers overlap
- balance of input by each speaker.

7 You work for an advertising agency and you are involved in a television campaign to maintain and enhance consumer interest in a well-
known product (for the sake of this exercise, you choose which one).
You decide that the television commercial needs a voice-over, spoken
by a popular radio personality. Conduct a survey to establish listeners'
views of the style, character and personality of different radio presenters – you might even ask respondents to listen to tape recorded
extracts of different presenters in full swing. Find out whether your
respondents consider different voices to be friendly, authoritative,
patronising, sexy, intelligent, youthful, and so on. From your survey
results, make a decision on which presenter's voice would be the most
appropriate for positive branding of the product being advertised. Give
a detailed account of your reasons.

8 As a group, conduct a co-ordinated listening campaign on a BBC
local radio station, an ILR station, a community station (if available)
and a national music station for a pre-determined period of, say, two
hours. As you listen, make a written record of *all* links that are used.
Compare notes. To what extent does the scope of links and their application reflect differences in station branding? Is there evidence of formatting?

6 Production techniques

....

Storytelling devices

F ROM the basic link to the edited and mixed package, the voice of the individual presenter or reporter seeks to achieve radio's function of telling a story or describing a situation whilst *connecting* with the listener – relating to her experience and perspective. Having considered the roles and functions of those whose voices engage the listener in this process, we shall now concentrate on the range of techniques available to these speakers to transform their individual stories into a structured entity, identifiable within the radio experience as a programme. In this chapter, we consider such techniques in terms of their individual contributions to the radio experience; in the following chapter we discuss how they fit together to create the programme as a whole.

A starting point for a broadcaster to identify which techniques to apply in telling a particular story is to determine the essential point of that story. Its 'bottom line' is definable in a succinct statement that sums up the story's impact on the listener's knowledge or experience: for example, homelessness is on the increase, there's a cat show in a local village hall, there was a great concert last night in the arts centre. From this it is possible to decide on qualities inherent to that story which may be effectively 'put across' in the production process: to what extent is the story likely to appeal to the station's target audience? Is there an unusual 'hook' or angle to the story that increases its interest factor? Is there potential for interesting audio effects or incorporation of music?

Considerations of this nature underpin decisions on how an item – news story, personality feature, review of a recent event, or whatever – should be 'treated'. In journalistic terms, the treatment of a news story refers to the way that story is presented, the angle that is selected or, as Hartley explains, the 'definitions' of the topic made by the news organisation and the 'voices' that are 'accessed': 'Typically, the "accessed" voices belong to representatives of "both" sides of a dispute, and to an "expert" commentator' (Hartley 1982: 42; see also pp. 148–9). The practical outcome of the news-based approach that is shaping BBC local radio (see pp. 47–8) is the application of the techniques and technology of news production to all forms of broadcast speech.

'Talk' items on popular radio – the individual word-pictures, dialogues and mini-debates that constitute speech output – range from the spontaneous phone-in chat to the carefully planned package. However, to a greater or lesser extent, all 'talk' items are themselves products of a planned 'industrial' process, based on an organisational system and infrastructure – as we have already described in Chapter 3 – designed to maintain a regular, up-to-date supply of such items. The complex, ever-flowing, ever-developing, constantly metamorphosing world of events is reduced to a sequence of discrete stories, individually packaged in both a literal and metaphorical sense. Literal because the story is subject to a production technique or set of techniques constructing it in the form of a fixed duration 'item'; it is then cued, presented and rounded off with a back anno (see p. 136). It is available to the presenter in packaged form, complete with identifying title or computer file name. Metaphorical because our understanding of the world in which we live is itself structured by the social phenomenon of language[1] and the defining of things, events and issues, in terms of their position within this structure and of their apparent distinctiveness from other things, events and issues. Each story told focuses our attention on a particular sequence of specific events, it highlights those events as significant (for example, 'news' as opposed to 'non-news', 'local' as opposed to 'national', etc.) and relates them in a narrative form that accords with the chronological structure of our own life experience.

Radio represents a unique combination of six characteristics, affecting the means of exposition available to it. Some of these are inherent in its nature as an audio medium; others have become apparent through the role that radio plays in people's lives.

1 Radio is about *immediacy*. This has a clear influence on the selection and treatment of news and factual stories. Radio's technology and infrastructure enable it to report events quickly and provide live on-the-spot coverage. Reports from the scene of a major accident or the hastily convened meeting to call a lightning strike can make exciting listening whilst fulfilling radio's public service function.

2 Radio is about *people*. Its focus on the spoken word and the sound of the human voice directs it constantly towards the 'human' angle of any story. Events and processes reported and discussed on radio are made more explicable and interesting through the observations and reactions of people – specialist news correspondents, people affected by events or people whose actions cause the events.

3 Radio is *simple*. It provides a linear sequence of sound events with no other information simultaneously transmitted. This creates production challenges when a complicated story is to be told. The history of the Balkan crisis, for example, could be easier to understand with access to a map. This forces radio to seek the most simple explanation and illustrates effectively how the lack of visual data can constitute a strength; as radio reporters and correspondents apply their journalistic skills to tell the story simply, so listeners gain a deeper understanding.

4 Radio is *targeted*. As we have discussed in Chapter 2, radio tailors its output to a target audience. This means it tells stories that are likely to interest a defined listener group, that relate to their experience and that draw on shared terms of reference. The use of lengthy *vox pop* teenage voices may involve styles of expression that relate easily to young listeners but are not readily understood by listeners aged 40-plus. However, social history items or radio drama set in the early 1950s may prove nostalgic for listeners who remember rationing, conscription and the Coronation but would clearly be unsuitable for Radio 1.

5 Radio needs an *endless supply of features*. Individual programme teams invest considerable time and energy into producing features – anything from a short wrap to a full programme – but can never satisfy radio's hunger for more. Even as a production item, the immediacy of a feature dissipates as soon as it is exposed to airwaves; once the story is made public it rarely has value in being told again other than as a piece of archive material. Thus, radio not only seeks a constant supply of stories that can be told as features, it also puts pressure on broadcasters to apply techniques in such a way that features are produced quickly with minimum use of resources. An adverse effect of this is a 'production line' of features and links following a tried and tested formula. Creativity and innovation in radio calls on the broadcaster to identify the elements that make up a feature and to apply and juxtapose these in the most effective way for telling that particular story.

6 Radio shows its greatest inherent strength as a medium when it *engages the imagination*. It calls on the listener's active participation in constructing an experience of sights, smells and sensations evoked by the pure medium of sound. The appeal and effectiveness of a radio situation comedy, historical drama or an extended news report is derived partly from a willingness by the listener to believe in the authenticity of the scenario which is being represented and then to draw on her own knowledge and imagination to create the total radio experience inside her own mind.

In the previous chapter, we identified a number of storytelling vehicles – the copy story, voice piece, package and live commentary. Other pieces of the mosaic – the interview, the pre-recorded package, trail, PSA or commercial, the live debate and phone-in discussion, the competition and the bulletin – are techniques which take us further beyond the 'single voice to microphone' model of the essential radio experience to more complex forms of output that provide shape and colour to that experience. As well as discussing each of these techniques in this chapter, we consider the applications of production devices in radio fiction – and the ways in which 'fictional' devices may also enhance 'factual' radio – before suggesting that all production techniques are geared towards establishing a tangible point of contact – the 'edge' – between the radio text and the listener.

The overall output style of the station, the context in which items will be placed and the more pragmatic concerns of costs and available resources are factors taken into account in the determination of which techniques may be applied. Nevertheless, the essence of *creative* radio is a form of representation that is captivating, striking, illuminating and capable of connecting to the emotional as well as the rational perspectives of listeners. Thus a perceptive producer in radio identifies an impact which she wishes to achieve through the telling of a story and, as far as time and resources will allow her to do so, selects and applies whatever techniques and devices are necessary to achieve it.

Interviews

A RADIO broadcaster working in isolation considers production techniques in terms of how to ensure the best overall sound. This means not only how to obtain optimum sound quality from the available technology, and the best voice quality from her performance and pace of delivery, but also how to enhance the desired mood and atmosphere and produce the best impact through the creative juxtaposing and mixing of available audio material. More often than not, however, the business of producing live or recorded radio involves input from other people, particularly those outside the station team itself, and therefore the broadcaster also has to think in terms of how to gain their co-operation and use their voices to best effect. She could be dealing with professional spokespeople trained in media techniques and public relations or members of the public as *vox pop* interviewees, phone-in participators or eyewitnesses to a news story. Their voices may be incorporated in a variety of ways but in all cases the broadcaster attempts to apply production techniques which maximise the impact of the story that they have to tell.

Presenters talk to people on air through informal chats, more formal interviews or in the context of the highly formalised structure of, say, a quiz show or public debate. The *interview* is a standard part of the radio experience through which the listener is given access by a presenter or

14 **On location – on air**: all the interviewee hears are the reporter's questions while the reporter, equipped with headphones, receives cue and the producer's comments or advice on questions to ask via talkback. Standing outside, next to the radio car, creates more atmosphere with the omnidirectional microphone picking up background noise. If the weather is less pleasant, the effect can still be achieved simply by conducting the interview inside the car with the windows open.

reporter to the voices of news story protagonists, representatives of organisations, 'experts' whose opinion and analysis will facilitate the listener's understanding of events and issues, and members of the public offering a wide range of stories, viewpoints, opinions and eye-witness accounts. Depending on the 'status' conferred by the presenter on the interviewee, the tone of the dialogue could be anything from a friendly discussion, in which both speakers appear to share similar perspectives on the topic in question, to a combative cross-examination, in which the interviewer challenges the position represented by the interviewee.

McLeish identifies three types of interview – the informational, interpretive and emotional – although he acknowledges that particular interviews may involve more than one of these categories (McLeish 1978: 40–1). Within this framework, the function of the interview ranges from providing the listener with 'the facts' to indicating the interviewee's reaction to a situation, based on either informed analysis or immediate and personal feelings.

The two way

An informal one-to-one interview between a presenter and a fellow broadcaster – usually a news reporter or specialist correspondent – is referred to as a *two way* or a *question and answer* (or Q and A).[2] As the interlocutors are members of the same organisation, the dialogue takes the form more of a consultation in which the interviewee's statements and opinions are not challenged or questioned. The discussion follows the rules of interviewing only insofar as one person asks questions and the other responds. The presenter's questions are planned in advance by the reporter along with the cue for the item. The purpose of the entire exercise is to provide a familiar narrative structure that explains, clarifies or provides colour to an issue or event. Listeners may well recognise two ways as staged events but 'go along' with the performance in the interests of gaining enlightenment on the topic being discussed. The staging may also incorporate the use of a newsclip to illustrate one of the answers given by the reporter.

The two way is often used as an alternative to a package containing interviews with the people involved in the story. There may simply be too many interviewees needed to make sense of the story, leaving the reporter little time to put the package together or – if time were available – creating difficulties anyway in incorporating so many voices without 'losing' the listener. Or potential interviewees may be simply unwilling to talk on air, even if they are prepared to give a statement or comment – attributed or unattributed – to the reporter.

This device can aid listener understanding by providing context and background to a reported event. It can also provide variety with a sense of the dramatic in the way that issues and events are discussed on radio. A story on house prices in the region rallying after falling for twenty consecutive months could be presented with a degree of dynamism through a two way, demonstrating the extent that the station will go to in providing a detailed local picture – '... this lunchtime I've spoken to fifteen estate agents in the area and they all say ...'. Similarly, a well-defined picture can be painted of a mass public rally through the reporter's own observation, or the atmosphere conveyed of an election count in which the trends and implications are highlighted as they arise. The BBC especially have built up a cohort of national and regional expert correspondents in a range of areas – local and national government, politics, transport, legal matters, the media, and so on. As reporters, they specialise in these fields and as trained broadcasters they are able to take part in interview formats to communicate their analyses of events succinctly with clear 'radio' voices and in a language appropriate to the station's audience – probably more effectively than, say, the expert from the local university.

The benefits of the two way as a narrative device should be weighed against the danger of its overuse. Listeners may feel alienated by a station that fills the airwaves with media people talking to media people. The role-play undertaken by both participants in the dialogue requires them to make explicit the processes and implications behind the event or topic in question and to enable the listener to share in an informed perspective. However, this can also be achieved by 'expert' interviewees from outside the radio organisation if they are proficient speakers on air, with the added bonus of the presenter being able to challenge their 'expertise' without undermining the journalistic function of the station and thus provide a suggestion of the inquisitorial to add spice to the dialogue.

Programme guests

The circumstances in which guests are included in a programme vary enormously. Many guests are well versed in the processes and techniques of making contributions on air: politicians, press officers, professional spokespeople, pop stars, authors, etc. all of whom regard appearances on national and local radio as part of their normal day's work. Radio stations also keep a 'stock' of regular guests – 'outsiders' who have good voice techniques and personalities and are called in, sometimes at a specified time slot each week, to give a short talk on air or to take part in a discussion with the presenter on a particular topic. On local radio, such guests may include a local church leader commenting on the week's news events from a religious perspective or a representative from the local police calling for listeners' help with unsolved crimes in the editorial area. The station may also draw on a range of institutions to supply speakers on various topics. Not only do universities and colleges of higher education supply 'expert' speakers, but also such 'recognised' organisations as the local chambers of commerce, trade unions, citizens advice bureaux, community groups, film societies, youth clubs, sports clubs, etc.

The interest and dynamism that a variety of voices can offer a programme is the usual justification for using studio guests. The presence of a guest enables the presenter to establish an alternative mode of address from that of speaking directly to the listener. That is not to say that the listener becomes excluded; the presenter's function of speaking on behalf of the listener becomes paramount and her comments or questions are articulated as representative of the listener's concerns and interests. This in turn reflects the position of the radio station itself within the listening community. The presence of programme guests effectively reinforces the station's role as a forum within that community and a focus for the issues and values that hold that particular community together. The guest may be asked to explain an issue or topic from the perspective of an expert or eye-witness. She may be challenged, asked to be accountable or to defend a viewpoint. Or she may be set up as an exemplar of model citizenship, a 'victim' of bureaucratic ineptitude, or a 'typical' member of the listening community 'treated' to an 'inside look' at local radio (perhaps as a result of winning a phone-in competition) and being given a chance to be heard by family and friends tuning in.

The nature of the interaction between presenter and guest – and the position or role afforded to the guest – is established by the presenter through specific ways of providing the listener with access to the dialogue. The introduction given by the presenter to the dialogue provides clear clues for the listener. For example:

> It's Thursday evening – that means that Katie Wall is here to tell us what's happening on the jazz scene. What hot sounds have you got for us this week, Kate?

– the regular presenter is about to provide considerable space to the regular 'expert' and play a minimal intermediary role whilst the guest shares her information and knowledge with the listeners. Or:

> As you heard on the news, another increase in the local crime figures. I'm joined by Labour councillor Adam Brate. Councillor Brate, surely Councillor Lily Gilder's got a point when she says this town is getting like Dodge City?

– the presenter establishes the perspective that will be provided by the guest on a specific topical issue – in this case, a political perspective – and structures the discussion through questioning and to some extent challenging the views expressed by the guest from a 'neutral', 'common sense' or 'devil's advocate' standpoint. In a further example:

Now when you go shopping, do you ever stop to think about the messages you give out about yourself through the things you buy? According to psychologist Professor Sarah Brawl we're more concerned with self-image than we are with value for money when we visit the supermarket. Welcome to the studio, Professor Brawl. Surely in times of recession people buy what they can afford?

– the presenter takes on a 'common sense' perspective to challenge the 'academic' viewpoint and establishes a friendly but combative discourse.

Programme and presentation styles themselves influence the terms in which guests are introduced and treated. This can vary from ' . . . and Sharon Dippity is here now to tell us about it – welcome to the studio, Sharon' to ' . . . and Mia Kulper is here now to respond to those criticisms. Miss Kulper, does your company accept responsibility for this situation?' The first of these examples includes a 'courtesy welcome' which is appropriate for interviews with celebrities, people deemed to be high-status members of a community or members of the public with a story to tell, but may well be dispensed with in more confrontational interviews or in fast-paced news magazine programmes.

The dialogue between guest and presenter conforms to a number of conventions or rules, specific to the discourse of radio, which determine for example whose turn it is to speak, how speakers should be addressed and what type of question may legitimately be asked. Underpinning the particular meaning of the dialogue's content is a universal set of meanings concerning the function and rationale of the dialogue as part of the radio experience. The very act of providing access to a studio guest conveys its own message to the listener: the dialogue is presented as a reflection or commentary on a known issue or event; it is an exercise of accountability to the listening public by a person in a position of power; or it is a demonstration of the station's own function of providing a public forum for debate and discussion.

Such meanings, while not in themselves expressly articulated, are apparent through auditory codes which regularly govern the presentation of a dialogue on air. The basic components of the radio text – words, music, sound effects and silence – are organised, juxtaposed and presented in specific and meaningful ways. Listeners learn these codes as surely as they learn the 'code' of the alphabet, and their reception of radio output is based on an expectation of the 'correct' mode of radio presentation – a knowledge of these codes. Thus the auditory codes, upon which radio dialogue is based, are apparent through such factors as voice intonation, the absence of music or sound effects, the length of time allocated to the dialogue and the mode of address adopted by the presenter when talking to the guest.

In providing access to the voice of a programme guest, the radio station is in a position to control and mediate that access. If the guest were appearing on television, she would be seen responding to the interviewer, not directly to the viewer. The codes of television interviewing are such that the presence of the interviewer is clearly signalled; even if the interviewer is not on screen, the interviewee is usually framed so that she does not directly address the camera. Radio has many equivalents to these visual codes, highlighting the position of the presenter as one *providing* and *mediating* access to the programme guest. Differences in sound quality between the voices of presenter and guest may be apparent if the guest is located in, say, a radio car or at the end of a telephone line – an effective mediating strategy in itself despite radio's constant striving towards better audio quality. The presenter's actual performance provides indication of speaker roles, which 'rules' of dialogue are being applied and hence which definition of the issue in question should be treated as dominant. Mediating strategies applied here include: interrupting the guest's responses to questions and repeating a question to a guest on the grounds that it was not satisfactorily answered the first time.

While the two way interview between presenter and reporter constitutes a staged interaction in which both participants share an agreement on the 'rules', interviews and discussions with 'outsiders' are more unpredictable and often reflect differing motivations by the speakers. For example, the studio guest may be less concerned with the station's position as an objective commentator and more interested in 'plugging' her latest book. Or she may be openly critical of media coverage of the viewpoint that she represents. The responsibility of establishing the 'stage directions', whilst maintaining the appearance of a spontaneous, 'natural' conversation or discussion, rests with the voice of the station – the presenter or interviewer.

A comparison of transcriptions of a discussion on air and a conversation between two people away from a microphone would reveal the staging strategies applied in the former. Radio discussions take place within a time limit – anything from two or three minutes to the length of an hour-long programme. They are therefore structured and controlled by one person – the presenter – who has worked out in advance which points she wishes to cover and at what stage of the discussion she wants to bring in a second or third guest. The presenter's own contributions are usually interrogative and the style and wording of her questions are designed to enhance the clarity, dynamism and explicitness of the guests' responses and overall discussion.

McLeish indicates how questions are asked from the presenter's position of 'informed naivety' (1978: 44) to fulfil a number of specific informational functions: to establish facts (for example, who? when? where?), to gain an interpretation of facts (what? how?), to establish a reason for something (why?), or to seek a confirmation or denial (are you . . .?, is it . . .?, will they . . .?, do you . . .?) (ibid.). When conducting interviews on air, broadcasters aim to build up the specific 'blocks' of information (facts or reactions) elicited from these questions to lead the listener to an overall conclusion or to enhance the listener's enlightenment of a situation or the interviewee's character. Hence formal interview questions – as opposed to those asked during chats or discussions on air – usually call for a specific and singular answer: 'What was the main purpose of the Queen's visit?' 'What was the gist of the Prime Minister's statement?' 'What was the most significant development in today's discussions?'

The interviewer's control of the dialogue is exercised through the amount of leeway she *does* provide to the interviewee. In a *political interview*, she may provide scope for detailed and explicit responses through posing open questions, before 'steering' the interviewee towards the 'pen' by picking out and seeking expansion on those parts of the responses that seem most significant, then attempting to 'close the gate' with the specific 'yes or no?' question that, according to some broadcasters, politicians are congenitally unable to answer. Or she may conduct a *profile interview* in which an insight into the personality of the interviewee herself is constructed through questions following a chronological development – eliciting details of the interviewee's childhood, education and formative events, leading to her present day views on favourite people and occupations, tastes in music and interior decor, and so on.[3]

Obviously, part of the rationale behind the framing of interview questions is to enable the listener to develop a clear understanding of the event, issue or personality that forms the subject of the interview. Questions may seek elucidation of fact, acting as prompts for eye-witness accounts for example, or they may provoke responses that are more revealing in terms of how they are given rather than what they say. Furthermore, an interviewer can determine the pace and style of output through the type of questions asked – for example, calling for explicit responses to open questions before suddenly throwing in the crucial question that calls for a straight 'yes or no' answer.

Multiple voice interviews

If two or more programme guests are being interviewed simultaneously, the presenter controls the development of the discussion for the listeners, and the guests themselves, by nominating the person she wants to answer a particular question, preferably before the question itself is asked. Focused interviews with more than one guest are often structured to highlight contrasting viewpoints, perhaps between party political speakers or between management and union representatives. These may be confrontational in nature with the interviewer acting as mediator or referee, admonishing speakers if they 'break the rules', for example by asking questions instead of answering or talking directly to their 'opponents' instead of via the interviewer herself. Or they may be reflective, light-hearted or 'free for all' with the interviewer playing an unobtrusive role apart from the occasional prompt to keep up the momentum of the discussion.

Variations of the multiple voice interview include:

163

Separation of respondents

Respondents are interviewed in succession by the same person, or by different interviewers, and given no opportunity to talk directly to each other on air.

'Round-table' discussions

Interviewees and interviewer engage in a less structured, more spontaneous conversation; the interviewer may be better known to listeners as a critic, journalist, actor, academic, anything other than a professional broadcaster and may thus share a similar perspective to that of her interlocutors.

'Intellectual zoo-format' discussions

These are similar to the 'round-table' discussion except that a linking role is played by the programme presenter accompanied by regular celebrity interviewers talking to one-off celebrity interviewees; the former have undertaken the necessary research on the latter and lead the discussion at their allotted times during the programme although anyone else seated round the table may interject; examples of this format are BBC Radio 4's *Midweek* and *Loose Ends* programmes.

'Panel interviews'

Regular programme guests form a panel and – under the guidance of a presenter – interview or interrogate individual programme guests; an example of this format is Radio 4's *The Moral Maze*.

Managing studio guests

Local talk radio's continuous flow of packages, chats and features interspersed with music calls for a regular supply of competent speakers able and willing to contribute, preferably live and in the same studio as the presenter. The topics for discussion are often recently emerging issues or news stories; therefore the programme plan may be finalised only minutes before the programme goes on air and could even be altered during transmission. The production team strives to ensure that all source material is lined up when it is needed and that output appears to be spontaneous while meeting specific timed deadlines for weather and traffic reports, on-the-hour news, etc. This often means calling in interviewees at short notice (two hours or less), putting them in front of a microphone only minutes before their 'item' is broadcast, conducting the interview for three or four minutes only, and then thanking them while the next record is being played.

This is par for the course for experienced, 'professional' guests who can dash through the interview before moving on themselves to the next appointment – perhaps another interview on the same topic for a rival station. However, local radio is often orientated towards local voices – members of the listening community who may be less experienced at broadcasting and therefore need a little more tender loving care if they are to perform effectively. It is not uncommon for a normally eloquent speaker to 'dry up' or talk gibberish when faced with the alien environment of a studio, or for the guest to be overconfident and blasé about the fact that she is speaking to thousands of listeners and thus sounding unduly arrogant or pompous on air.

Therefore, the business of controlling a programme also requires the production team – and the presenter in particular – to 'manage' studio guests and coax an optimum and credible performance from them. This involves convincing guests that they do not need scripts, that questions and answers should not be rehearsed and that listeners will be interested in their immediate responses and reactions to points raised in the questions.

Broadcasters conducting interviews with inexperienced programme guests, whether live or recorded, recognise the value of developing some rapport with the guest before the interview gets under way by holding a friendly chat, running through the general points to be covered in the interview and acclimatising them to a situation in which they can feel relaxed. The presenter of a live 'continuous flow' programme may not have as much opportunity to settle in a studio guest, other than a few quick words while a record is playing and in between setting up the next jingles and packages. In these circumstances, a few encouraging words from the programme producer may be called for to prepare the guest.

The 'pre-chat' is of practical value, not only in relaxing the guest but also in getting her used to talking into a microphone. This enables the presenter to quickly check the audio level of her voice and to ensure that there are no unwanted noises – rattling jewellery, rustling pages of notes – to distract the listener from the focal points of the item: the voice of the guest and what she has to say.

Production items

MOST popular radio is live. Immediacy is a key factor in the successful interaction between radio and its audience. It enables the medium to produce an instantaneous link between the listener and a world of ever-changing events and to position her within a community of fellow listeners. Nevertheless, live radio twenty-four hours a day tends to develop a sameness in mode and function with a succession of presenters taking turns to weave together a raw 'here and now' style of audio text. Live radio is more likely to maximise its impact and dynamism as part of a multi-textured listening experience which also allows space for the planned, produced, self-contained 'finished items' with their own stories to tell and their own creative methods of expression.

Packages

Pre-recorded material, produced in the station itself, can take a number of forms, ranging from the thirty-second trail to the ninety-minute radio drama. The most frequently produced items are packages – usually, but not necessarily, two to five minutes in length, providing an alternative texture of sound within the live programme format. While they tend to be more 'glossy' and more evidently 'produced', packages give broadcasters the opportunity to control and design output that will most likely enhance audience appeal or stimulate imagination. A package can fill a fixed-time slot with exciting and captivating audio material and can be reused, for example in a programme that looks back over the highlights of the previous week's broadcasts.

Some items are more suited to packages than live coverage. Stories that involve several differing viewpoints may be more effectively controlled in a package. A local radio item on, say, the building of a new road through a former nature reserve to divert lorries from a residential area would call for voices of householders, local industry spokespeople, conservationists and a representative of the local authority's planning department. Thus the story may be handled by a package that brings in all but the last speaker who could be interviewed live off the back of the recording to respond to the points that have been raised.

A standard format for a package is the juxtaposing of the reporter's narrative account, directly addressing the listener, with actuality material, almost invariably including edited extracts of dialogue – informal chats or formal interviews – between the reporter and other speakers. By combining speech, sound effects, ambient noise and, where appropriate, music, the package tells its story through a clearly marked narrative development. There are many variations in possible narrative structures although either of the following two approaches are common to most compact packages:

- Describe a general situation; then highlight specific features which add colour and depth before 'rounding off' by summing up the general picture (general → specific → general)

- Describe a specific situation to intrigue the listener; then provide the general information that is vital to contextualise, explain and demystify the specific; then 'round off' by returning to the specific, now that it 'makes sense' (specific → general → specific).

The following is an example of how a 'general → specific → general' structure might be planned.

PLAN FOR DISABLED DRIVING FEATURE

CUE – invites listener to imagine hurtling a brand new Ford Mondeo round a rally course, then trying out the skid pan. Hundreds of disabled drivers are doing this today. Our reporter Penny Farthing had a go.

MUSIC – theme to BBC's *Top Gear* for fifteen seconds, then fade
  under . . .

AUDIO – PF's commentary (twenty seconds) with rally under way
  in background. Describes event, location, purpose. Introduces
  competitor

AUDIO – competitor describes importance of event

SFX – gear change noise

AUDIO – judge describes challenges of part of the course that tests
  manoeuvrability

LINK – PF identifies judge, then states that she had a go on skid
  pan with judge sitting in car with her

AUDIO – car skidding

AUDIO – judge comments on PF's driving ability

SFX – applause

AUDIO – short interview with winner of competition

MUSIC – fade up theme from *Top Gear.*

By working out as much of the plan as possible before visiting the
location, the reporter is able to record most of the material in the order
it will finally be used. This reduces the amount of time it takes to edit
the recording and prepare it for the package. Furthermore, the limited
supply of tape and power for a portable recorder (see p. 105) makes it
inadvisable to record anything that makes a noise in the hope that it might
be used.

On returning to the station, the reporter transfers the actuality material
– interviews, wildtrack (background sound), etc. – onto separate carts and
prepares a more detailed running order. This provides a set of instructions
for her to follow when she goes into the studio to mix together the
actuality material with music and special effects on CD plus her own
voice for the link. It itemises each piece of audio, its duration and – if it
includes speech – the final words heard ('out' words) before the next
piece of audio is mixed in. The running order for this example may look
like this:

MUSIC – CD. Band 11
Dur: 1'45". . . fade after 22"

CART *1/commentary
Out: . . . who's from Sheridan
Dur: 20"

CART *2/competitor
Out: . . . it's very easy
Dur: 46"

SFX – CD. Band 13
Dur: 5″

CART *3/judge
Out: . . . take your time
Dur: 10″

LIVE LINK: Sid Dewis who's the senior judge on this part of the competition. He says that by the time competitors get to the skid pan, they're sufficiently confident with the car to go straight out and have a practice spin. Sid was less sure of my ability . . .

CART *4/wildtrack (skids)
Dur: 15″

CART *5/more judge
Out: . . . more practice
Dur: 45″

SFX – CD. Band 9
Dur: 5″

CART *6/winner
Out: . . . next year
Dur: 46″

MUSIC – CD. Band 11
Dur: 1′45″ . . . leave up to 30″ to go under back anno.

In this instance, the reporter will have transferred six items of actuality onto carts, numbered in sequence. Each of these carries a voice recorded on location – either her own or an interviewee's – apart from cart 4 which contains the sound of wheels skidding. Additional material is available on compact disc – the theme tune and the sound effects of gears changing and applause – and the only material recorded in the studio itself is the live link.

The reporter would also prepare a cue sheet (see p. 144) to instruct the presenter on how to cue and back anno the item:

DISABLED DRIVERS
BROADCAST: DRIVETIME, MON 3 MARCH
REPORTER: PENNY FARTHING
7¹/₂IPS

CUE:

. . . I should imagine there's something immensely SATISFYING about hurtling through the forest at TOPLEY'S MOUNT near Sheridan in a NEW FORD MONDEO . . . well aware that you don't have to pay for any damage to the car! I also think it would be rather FUN to then test your skills on the skid pan there. Well, three hundred disabled driver are doing JUST THAT today. PENNY FARTHING has been to Topleys Mount and compiled this report . . .

TAPE
IN: (Music 22″ then . . .) I'm standing here . . .
OUT: (Music ends 5′ 40″)
     (Speech ends 3′ 55″) . . . again next year
TOTAL: 5′ 40″

BACK ANNO:
Penny Farthing at the Disabled Drivers' Competition at Topley's Mount. And our congratulations to Harry Caine from Sheridan on that victory.

Here, the complete item from cue to back announcement is set out in the order in which the presenter would need to refer to it. The first block of information identifies the package, broadcast time, name of reporter and playback speed of the tape. The cue to be read by the presenter is set out with stress words highlighted. Following this, a brief description of the beginning and end of the recording includes 'in words', 'out words', duration up to the end of recorded speech and total duration. In this case, the difference between 'speech ends' and 'music ends' times enables the presenter to give the back announcement over the music.

Packages structured along the lines of specific → general → specific often cover stories that are quirky, unusual and with potential for humour or, in journalistic terms, human-interest. One example would be an item on an alleged curse on an ancient right of way crossing land scheduled for development:

PLAN FOR HAUNTED FOOTPATH FEATURE

CUE – Seems there's an industrial dispute on a local building site. Workmen have all downed tools. More money? No, reason anything but materialistic. They claim land is cursed – anyone who disturbs it due for a sticky end. Our reporter Graham Lynn went to find out more.

MUSIC – theme to *The Twilight Zone*, fade under . . .

AUDIO – Foreman (Ian Dolent) describes how two workmen were taken ill within twenty-four hours of digging up footpath. A third broke his arm.

LINK – GL identifies foreman on a building site at Doornail Park. Except – not much building going on at the moment. Workmen demanding site owners to call in an exorcist. Could there really be a curse?

AUDIO – Local historian (Anna Kronus) begins tale of secret passage . . .

LINK – GL briefly identifies historian . . .

AUDIO – Historian describes how passage was escape route from local monastery, discovered and blocked up by soldiers in 1536 when Henry VIII ordered dissolution of monasteries. Believed three monks trapped inside and perished.

SFX – 'horror' sting . . .

AUDIO – short interview with site owner's agent – will contact a priest if that's what it takes to restart work.

MUSIC – fade up theme from *The Exorcist* for five seconds then down again under . . .

AUDIO – GL commentary – standing on footpath, got a pickaxe, shall I put curse to the test? Perhaps not.

SFX – ghostly laughter.

In this item, initial reference to the curse promotes intrigue and invites further concentrated listening to explain the oddity. The local historian's comments provide the necessary contextual information while the interview with the agent effectively resolves the story. Nevertheless, the narrative returns to the specific with the presenter threatening to challenge the curse, to maintain the atmosphere of suspense and sceptical humour.

Seamless editing

Packages are effectively mini-documentaries. Whether the duration of the recorded item is five or thirty minutes, the background research, production techniques and considerations of narrative structure are essentially the same. The overall shape and development of the item is planned first. Then the audio material is collected before the final stage of production – mixing and editing the material to turn the plan into reality and ensure a smooth textual flow. Longer documentaries may incorporate a wider range of production devices – for example, formal interviews, *vox pops*, studio discussions and more detailed clips – which facilitate greater depth and analysis of the story. Nevertheless, they share with packages the function of introducing actuality material to demonstrate that the reporter *went* to the location and *spoke* to the people concerned. The listener is immersed in the story rather than told it from a dispassionate distance as an item on a news bulletin.

Sound effects, music clips and background noise contribute towards the telling of the story as much as the spoken word. Experienced reporters on location listen out for opportunities to record specific sounds related to the story as well as general ambient noise for wildtrack to re-create the 'atmosphere' of the location. As with words and phrases, however, certain sounds may detract from the creative impact of the item by being clichéd: for example, the sound of wedding bells to launch an item on marriage, or the use of *Chariots of Fire* for any feature with an athletic theme.

Similarly, narrative structures themselves may become overused and predictable. Because many packages tell their story most effectively through a clip-link-clip-clip-link approach, any opportunity to adopt an alternative structure is likely to make the package more salient. The item may be self-explanatory without the use of links, inviting the listener to eavesdrop on 100 per cent actuality material, for example of a mock battle being fought or a fractious dress-rehearsal at the local operatic society. It may simply fade in and out of interview clips, denoting a longer conversation between reporter and interviewee, for example while they are walking round a museum, or investigating wild life habitats along a local canal.

Whatever structure is applied and whatever material is edited together, the criterion of successful communication is that nobody notices the joins. From a professional broadcaster's point of view, evidence of editing reduces the impact of the recording and distracts the listener from the message that it is intended to convey. It betrays the act of manipulation that has occurred; the recording reveals its own process of production and is identified instead as an artificial construction.

Typical indicators that an audio text has been edited include:

Inadequate gaps between words and phrases

A phrase has been removed by the editor leaving no realistic 'breathing space' for the speaker in the edited version. A supply of wildtrack is useful to 'create' any necessary gaps in speech.

Discontinuity in background sound

Reporters should be aware of specific rather than continuous sounds while recording. Specific sounds might be a clock striking, an aircraft overhead or a passing ice cream van, as opposed to continuous sounds such as waterfalls, seagulls or general traffic noises. Sudden changes in background sound betray the editing process.

Variations in audio level

Sound-checking and keeping an eye on level should be second nature for the reporter and changes of location or variation in interviewees' voices may cause her to adjust recording level during the assignment. While it is possible to compensate for this when dubbing material in the studio, the process of editing is evident if sudden changes occur in background noise, say, during an interview.

Syntax errors

If part of a recorded statement is taken out, what is left should remain meaningful and grammatically correct, or at least feasible for speech. Editors have been known to relocate phrases, or even individual words, to 'make sense' of a clip that has been necessarily edited, perhaps to remove distracting background noise. It takes considerable precision and some luck to edit together successfully a statement that has been reconstituted by a rearrangement of utterances without the tell-tale clipped words or unnatural pauses. The exercise could also be construed as unethical; even if the overall meaning of the statement remains unchanged, alterations in nuance may constitute an unfair representation of the speaker.

Arguably, listeners are aware that the apparent spontaneity of a recorded package is indeed an effect produced through a process of artificial construction, but are willing to suspend this awareness and participate as co-conspirators in the deception of immediacy that recorded radio text sets up. Thus considerable effort on the part of the broadcaster is put into the maintenance of the illusion that a package is a true and instantaneous representation of the event or issue that is the subject of the report.

Recorded announcements

The shortest and most compact 'production items' at the presenter's disposal are the short recorded announcements on cartridge tape which fulfil a range of functions in live radio:

- *trails* (or *trailers*) – announcements of forthcoming programmes, features, promotional or special events involving the radio station

- *public service announcements* (*PSAs*), sometimes referred to as social action broadcasting (SAB) trails – consumer information, job vacancies, where to obtain help for specific problems, news of events or exhibitions, entertainments 'what's on' announcements, etc.

- *commercials*.

All such items are relatively short – usually between fifteen and fifty seconds' duration – and self-contained, requiring no cue or back anno from the presenter. They are voiced by someone other than the presenter: in the case of programme announcements, usually by the person whose programme is being trailed. The most frequent format for the recorded announcement is a script delivered in crisp, succinct English and in an enthusiastic tone, often over a music bed. Archive material, clips and sound effects may also be incorporated. Alternative formats include:

- a two- or multi-voice presentation addressed directly at the listener

- a mini-drama or dialogue 'overheard' by the listener
- an audio montage of archive material with a brief explanatory announcement placed at the end
- a song or jingle in which the information is provided in the lyrics.

Trails and PSAs are normally recorded in the station itself, unlike commercials which – like jingles – are usually prepared in a production house containing a more fully equipped recording studio. While designing commercials primarily to meet specifications of clients, production houses also work to a brief that reflects the style and sound of the stations on which the commercials will be played.

For the presenter in the middle of a live broadcast, the recorded announcement may seem a useful device to fill forty seconds while she is setting up the next main item. Like all components of output, however, it plays an essential part in building and reinforcing a total sound and, for the listener, a particular texture of radio experience. Trails, PSAs and commercials are similar in nature to packages; they are production items carrying a human voice, telling a story or imparting information in a way that stimulates listener imagination and maintains radio's challenge to the listener *not* to switch off (see p. 135). The impact of the story or announcement is enhanced through careful positioning of the recording within the overall text of the programme. A trail or commercial can act as a 'gear change' in moving the text onwards – a slow interview could be followed by a medium-paced trail to bring the programme up a notch before a lively and dynamic sounding item is introduced. Inappropriate placing of a recorded announcement could lose the intended impact of the message it is conveying – a brash trail enthusing on a fun-packed programme to be broadcast later in the day could sound insensitive immediately after an in-depth interview with someone who has been made homeless; a commercial for the video release of an action-packed war movie could appear tasteless after a gentle and moving love song, or after an interview with a war refugee.

Recorded announcements can also prove less effective through too much – or not enough – repetition or simply by being played at the wrong time. Possibly, very few mid-afternoon listeners would be interested in knowing about the late-night rock show. Stations that regularly incorporate trails and commercials in their output seek to maximise their impact by planning a 'trails traffic' schedule, informing presenters which announcements should be played when. The schedule ensures that all trails get played throughout the week and prevents a harassed presenter from picking out a trail at random for a programme that was broadcast earlier that day!

Sometimes, a co-ordinated campaign of recorded announcements is worked out along similar lines to a planned advertising campaign. For example, a station may offer advice for young people who have just received their GCSE results. An hour-long programme on this, broadcast at a fixed time, could lose many potential listeners who are not able to tune in at that time, and lose several more who cannot sustain an interest throughout the full length of the programme. An alternative approach to disseminate the advice would be through a series of PSAs blended into the flow of the day's output and repeated to maximise the number of listeners reached. Their presence as an integral part of programming illustrates the 'drip–drip–drip' effect of popular radio's continuous flow structure – each announcement is absorbed by the listener as it is repeated and as it develops from information given earlier. Individually, the announcements tell their own stories: a special advice line offered by a local careers service; the pros and cons of re-sits; benefits available (or lack of them) for those choosing to leave school; opportunities for further education; and so on, until a full campaign of information is built up. The mini-features, each lasting no more than forty seconds, could include testimony from speakers who have been through the process and provide dynamic and interesting listening to a larger audience than a single detailed programme.

Debates, discussions and phone-ins

PROGRAMMES in which people take part in discussions are ironically not confined to talk radio. Major news stories, long-running ethical issues (capital punishment, blood sports, etc.), or matters which are trivial, entertaining, amusing or intriguing, all provide material for discussion on air, either in formal and structured programmes in which speakers are controlled and nominated by a chairperson or in informal zoo-format (see p. 142) or phone-in programmes. Arguably, the discussion constitutes the essential 'excitement' of live radio – considerably more so than the single presenter or DJ format – partly because it is not scripted and nobody, not even the presenter, knows what is coming next, and partly because it provides listener access to people behaving spontaneously, reacting to other people and in *real time*. A politician on Radio 4's *Any Questions?* may have a stock of answers ready for points that can be reasonably expected to arise, but participants in live discussion are generally providing instant and raw reponses to other people's comments, rather than 'official' statements previously prepared by public relations experts.

Such dramatic immediacy contributes to the appeal of the *radio debate*. Individual speakers may be known for the views they represent, but their interaction with each other often proves enlightening, for example for listeners whose access to candidates in an election campaign may be otherwise restricted to a series of sound-bites on news programmes. Debates also enable listeners to gain a more comprehensive awareness of topical issues and arguments which are not necessarily self-apparent from the distanced and objective discourse of news reporting. Debates provide an opportunity to 'take stock' and consider the development of a situation to date from the differing perspectives of those who have clearly defined 'positions' on the issue in question. This offers potential for interesting and captivating radio if the topic is complex and relevant to many people – for example, should people take the law into their own hands to combat rising crime? Should a school opt out of local authority control? Should a system of proportional representation be used in general elections?

Radio debates may be conducted on location as an outside broadcast programme and in front of an audience. Or they may take place in a talks studio as a 'round-table' discussion, possibly with input or questions from listeners phoning in. A debate need not constitute the sole item of a programme but could be incorporated as a 'rolling debate' in a presenter-led, continuous flow broadcast, based on a central topic but covering different aspects throughout the programme with contributions brought in from speakers in the studio or on a line. Alternatively, the debate may be highly structured, with participants speaking for and against a specific motion or acting as counsels and witnesses in a mock court case – for example, a scientific debate in which the concept of global warming is 'in the dock' with speakers arguing that it is a genuine threat or that it is built up out of proportion to discredit scientific progress.

While speakers in the radio debate are invited for their expertise, interest in the topic, political or moral viewpoint or ability to communicate effectively on air, those taking part in the *phone-in discussion* may not have any of these qualities. Listeners are invited to telephone in to a radio station for several reasons – to take part in competitions or 'ring and buy' sessions,[4] vote in 'fun polls', make appeals for volunteers, commodities or information, pass on greetings and messages to friends and family listening in, accept 'wacky' challenges made by presenters, and so on – although the radio discussion calls on their ability to articulate a point succinctly and convincingly and to follow up with interesting responses to questions or counter-points raised by the presenter. Sustained listener involvement forms one vital element of the phone-in; the other is a presenter who is knowledgeable on the topic under discussion and has the personality to develop and maintain an interesting dialogue with the caller plus the ability to recognise and introduce alternative arguments.

The phone-in discussion may be a radio station's way of providing a forum for members of the public to air their differing views, a chance for listeners to argue with a guest (e.g. a Government minister) on a controversial issue, or an opportunity for listeners to consult an expert on anything from managing their tax affairs to getting rid of dandruff. Some stations even further their public service role by providing an off-air telephone line for listeners who wish to seek confidential advice on a specific problem related to the theme of a programme.

Topics for discussion need not be serious or generated by current news items. People's own life stories or schoolday memories, falling in love, visits abroad, or opinions on favourite television programmes, other people's driving, fashion, or whatever, are all grist to the mill of phone-ins which can become the regional, national or international equivalent of the conversation over dinner or in the pub. There may be more than one theme for discussion with the presenter suggesting a 'menu' of possible topics, individual callers introducing their own issues and others calling in to respond to points raised earlier. Whatever form it takes, the phone-in constitutes access radio in which listeners can to some extent determine the content and direction of the programme.

The station does, however, maintain strategies of control. Callers are vetted initially by the programme producer who determines whether their contribution will provide a 'good listen', add to the development of the discussion and not land the station into difficulties of litigation or complaints about bad taste or language.[5] The producer informs the presenter via a visual talkback (see p. 120) of callers lined up – their names, where they are calling from, what they have to say and their line number – allowing the presenter to judge which speaker would be the most appropriate to choose next.

Once the caller is on air, it is the presenter's responsibility to direct the development of the topic through her responses and questions. There are occasions when the presenter has a professional obligation as a broadcaster and representative of the station to challenge views expressed by the caller, especially if these views are racist, sexist, specific to one religious or moral viewpoint, party political or in any way controversial.

While performances in the radio debate tend to be formal – involving carefully phrased comments and, if a studio audience is present, the use of rhetorical devices and intonation to stimulate applause – some phone-in discussions can become personal and emotional. This is encouraged by some presenters on the grounds that it produces lively and dramatic radio, although the practice invites the risk of an incomprehensible and pointless shouting match that does little but fill the airwaves with bad feeling. Presenter styles range from the 'nice' person who recognises the validity of every view expressed to the 'nasty' person who challenges and insults the participants or cuts them off prematurely at the slightest provocation. Ironically, the latter approach is popular if handled with care, with listeners phoning in to take part in a verbal combat.

Competitions

Listener participation in the radio text frequently takes the form of the phone-in competition; indeed for music radio this represents one of the main sources of speech. Therefore, it is worth the investment of the programme maker's time to ensure that this production device has been carefully prepared. The incorporation of competitions in output provides evidence of a station's perception of its listeners and the nature of the relationship that it seeks to establish with them. Phone-in competitions in particular form part of an interactive radio experience, not only for competitors themselves but for all listeners who consider the questions or problems set as if they were competitors.

Competitions often involve an invitation for listeners to phone in with the answer to a simple question to win a copy of a book, CD or video, free tickets for a concert, or a prize in some way related to a promoted item. They may be linked to an interview or feature on an author or recording artist promoting her latest work. Promotional competitions may pose questions with obvious answers or those which listeners can only guess at. The latter may encourage listeners to participate anyway if a choice of possible answers is given. Listeners may give their answers on air and take part in a quick chat with the presenter, but the primary value of this exercise is usually its potential to enhance public attitude towards a product and to mobilise public response to the station's own output. The popularity of competitions seems to arise more from the opportunity for listeners to take part and interact with the presenter than from the value of the prizes themselves. Radio stations have offered prizes ranging from a new car to a packet of tea bags; if the competition itself offers a stimulating challenge, listeners will still take part.

The rationale behind the design of competitions is to provide texture and variety to the radio experience and establish a framework for interesting dialogue between speakers that will engage and involve the audience. Competition formats range from general knowledge and trivia quizzes – either for one phone-in contestant or two in 'combat' with each other as part of a 'knockout' tournament – to on-air verbal 'parlour games' in which listeners' skills in quick thinking are tested. A 'rolling' competition format may provide a spine for a substantial part of a programme, perhaps with different callers taking part after each record, enhancing dramatic tension by attempting to improve on previous scores or aiming for more demanding targets.

Whatever form they take, competitions celebrate radio's capacity to develop a tangible relationship with listeners rather than adopt a distanced position from which to play music and make announcements. Listeners enjoy the satisfaction of being able to work out the answers and the potential of themselves becoming involved in the text. In the context of popular radio, the strength of competitions lies in the structure they provide for often captivating broadcasting. Participants respond as 'real' people who are put into a sometimes stressful position of being tested, having to dredge their memories or use their minds to work out problems, perhaps against the clock.

Competitions do not have to be difficult or complicated to work; even the most basic general knowledge quiz can transform background listening into a text that fully engages the listener. What is important from the perspective of the station itself is that preparation for the competition takes account of its contribution to the station's overall style of output and the extent to which it can promote and reinforce a bonding between the station and its audience.

Bulletins

BULLETIN information is the outcome of radio's primary public service function – to keep listeners informed of those events and developments of particular interest and relevance to them. The emphasis is on reporting these events, not discussing or analysing them. Bulletins convey data in the form of individual stories often honed down to their basic elements and told dispassionately; there is space elsewhere in the schedule for presenters and correspondents to weigh up the implications of the information reported. Most bulletins are scheduled for broadcast at fixed times of the day and other output has to fit round them. Listeners often time their domestic or travelling routines according to what they can hear on the radio.

Information most commonly conveyed in bulletin form is news, travel information and weather. On some stations and at certain times of the day there are also sports bulletins, updates on the stock market and specialist weather information such as shipping forecasts, weather forecasts for farmers and pollen counts. Separate bulletins may be broadcast for local and national news, the latter supplied to the station by a networked live bulletin service (see p. 82). Or the station may combine local and national news in a single bulletin compiled by its own news team but incorporating newsclips and reports from other sources. A station may also compile specialist bulletins to promote itself within an editorial area – for example, news on the half-hour focused on a particular town. Or it may incorporate bulletins within an overall programming theme – for example, hourly updates on a major meeting or conference, or regular reports on a topic such as homelessness or pollution.

Bulletins are broadcast live, often from a contributions studio in which the announcer is able to control the incorporation of newsclips and other recorded material. Listeners recognise the features that distinguish the bulletin from other forms of radio text, in particular the authoritative tones of the announcer and the concise and up-to-date nature of the information given. Audience familiarity with the bulletin format enables programme makers to apply it to other purposes, such as public service announcements. Recorded 'mock' bulletins are sometimes prepared to give 'updates' on a theme for a day's output, e.g. homelessness, health awareness, the environment. Special broadcasting campaigns such as the BBC's *Children in Need* may also use bulletins throughout the day to report on fundraising events and progress.

The status of information conveyed in bulletins is signalled in various ways – the duration of bulletins, their frequency, the precision of their timing and the 'build up'. News and travel bulletins are usually introduced with a 'news in' or 'travel in' jingle, functioning as a 'fanfare' preceding an important announcement. Depending on the station's output style and the length of the bulletin, music beds may also be used. These provide a 'busy', dynamic backing to the shorter summary of headlines or news of traffic 'black spots'.

News bulletins

These take one of three forms: the hourly summary, the major summary and the news headlines. The latter are the most succinct, providing the 'bare bones' of the current main news stories within a slot as short as two minutes. Hourly summaries in continuous flow schedules usually take up to five minutes' airtime and include a wider range of stories, some with illustrative material to support the story, such as voice pieces or actuality recordings. Major summaries are broadcast at key times, usually at breakfast, lunch and early evening. These may run for five minutes or longer; BBC Radio 4 runs thirty-minute bulletins at 6pm and midnight.

Hourly and major summaries in particular represent a variation in a station's mode of delivery. The interactive chat and bright discussion formats of continuous flow output or of individual magazine programmes contrast with the more formal enunciative performance of the news-reader. Such differences in style provide a more interesting texture to a station's overall sound – and signpost for the listener the passing of time and progress through a structured programme schedule. Nevertheless, news bulletins form an integral part of the station's product and thus tend to reinforce its output style rather than interrupt its textual development. Variables within the bulletin itself that may reflect on a station's overall brand image are:

- the newsreader's pace of delivery

- the number of stories covered and the amount of time given to each one

- the type of story covered, the order of priority given to stories and the inclusion of humorous or human-interest 'and finally' stories

- related to this – the mixture and juxtaposing of local and national stories

- the mixture of production techniques – copy, newsclips, voice pieces, wraps or packages

- language style – the extent to which language of news bulletins reflects an 'official', authoritative perspective or a more colloquial 'street-level' viewpoint, a distinction characterised by the terms 'quality' and 'tabloid'

- newsreader personality – as indicated by the age and accent of the newsreader's voice

- the relationship established between the bulletin and the rest of pro-gramming.

This latter point effectively illustrates the station's treatment and contain-ment of news discourse within its overall text. While the conventional method of news bulletin delivery – the objective and impartial account of recent events – is coded by the separation of the newsreader from the rest of the programme team[6] – the distance of that separation is influenced by the extent to which the news bulletin is intregrated into the overall content of radio text. It may be treated as a necessary interruption to the flow of music and DJ patter – it fulfils the station's public service function but has little bearing on programme content. Or it may contribute considerably to the textual development, whereby the presenter comments on news stories or refers back to them when cueing packages.

In the continuous 'flow programming' format of popular and local radio, a sense of the presenter and newsreader working for the same team is sometimes promoted in the format for introducing the bulletin. A formal news bulletin at the key time of 5pm, for example, may be opened as follows:

PRESENTER: It's five o'clock . . .

(News jingle starts, then fades)

PRESENTER: (over jingle) . . . and today's news headlines – Mount Etna is set to erupt say scientists as Italy prepares itself for a major national disaster, the police strike threat should be taken seriously says Archbishop of Canterbury, and at last a cure for the common cold. Here with the details and the rest of the day's stories is Ray Porter . . .

(jingle fades out – newsreader starts).

Even though the jingle functions as a boundary mechanism between the conversational text of the presenter's progamme and the enunciative style of the bulletin, the voice of the presenter is heard on the same side of the jingle as that of the newsreader. This produces a smooth handover rather than a clean break in the flow of output. The effect is also achieved by the presenter naming the newsreader after the jingle without giving the headlines. Similarly a brief and less formal 'handover' exchange between newsreader and presenter may occur at the end of the bulletin.

Travel bulletins

These are as important as news in reinforcing a local radio station's brand image and providing a service within a defined editorial area. Travel information is of functional value to listeners while the references to local places, routes and travel centres for road, rail, sea and air serve to express the station's local identity and public service role. Place name checks contribute to the station's process of bonding with a listening community, articulating a familiarity with the area. Therefore, travel news needs to be immediate and accurate, conveying sufficient detail and local knowledge to be of value. It would be of little use to listeners if the location of a reported traffic jam, for example, were not recognised because its name has been mispronounced by the announcer.

Stations draw on a range of professional sources to provide travel news. The AA Roadwatch service is linked with BBC and many ILR stations, providing specialist travel announcers contributing from remote studios at regional headquarters. Stations gain more localised information from the transportation and highways departments of local authorities and have access to traffic control centres, complete with television cameras monitoring traffic flow in the area, if these are available. Further information on potential delays through roadworks is circulated by water, telephone, gas and electricity companies. The police advise if they are to escort abnormal loads through the area. Travel companies themselves advise on delays and cancellations.

15 *Travel news:* up-to-date information on travel is an important service for radio. One useful source of news on local traffic conditions is access to fixed cameras at potential problem spots. Here, the travel reporter is able to broadcast bulletins from a local authority traffic control unit where she can also receive travel news from other sources via fax and phone. Through an agreement between the authority and the radio station, the unit is equipped with a microphone and means of receiving cue and talkback.

The information gleaned from here is combined with details received from public utilities and the public itself to provide a local picture that the station's own presenters can broadcast in addition to bulletins provided by specialist regional services such as AA Roadwatch.

Listeners also contribute to the station's intelligence on travel, highlighting radio's interactive role within a community keeping itself informed. Response from listeners with car radios and phones is generally strong when presenters ask them to advise of hazards or delays. Stations also recruit traffic watchers – individuals who live near junctions notorious for traffic hold-ups who receive a token fee and report in if there are any problems. Probably the best known 'traffic watcher' and one that illustrates the extent that a station will go to in providing accurate and up-to-date travel information is Capital FM's 'Flying Eye' – a reporter in an aeroplane flying over London and gaining the best view possible of conditions on the roads.

Travel information when delivered is prioritised. The newest information is usually given first, or that which affects the largest number of travellers. Further down the bulletin come reminders of ongoing roadworks or delays and finally announcements of no delays if that is the situation for local public transport services. Vital to the functional role of travel information is the announcer's ability to deliver it clearly. Motorway or main road directions are expressed in terms of compass points (north-bound, south-bound) or of destination (towards London, towards Manchester). Ring roads and orbital routes are expressed as clockwise or anticlockwise. Wherever possible, place names and landmarks are given to back up junction numbers or A and B road numbers. Advice within the profession is KISS (keep it simple, stupid!).

Weather forecasts

In common with travel news, weather information is often provided by specialist reporters at fixed time slots, although the programme format may require presenters themselves to give brief weather summaries at particular points (e.g. after the first record after the news) during peak listening times. And like travel news, the station's provision of weather forecasts constitutes one of the main reasons why listeners switch on their radios in the first place.

Applying the KISS formula, weather information can be broken down to five variables: hot/cold, dry/wet, still/windy, clear/misty, and level of airborne substances – pollen or pollution. Audience profile and output style influence different stations' approach to weather forecasting. Short, functional forecasts address each of these variables succinctly and answer two questions – what will the weather do in the next twenty-four hours and what is the outlook? More detailed forecasts discuss the current weather situation across the editorial area and provide technical reference to fronts, anticyclones and air pressure changes. Some stations also apply their own house style to describing temperature, based on their judgement of whether listeners prefer Celsius or Fahrenheit.

Weather information is received in the form of printed bulletins supplied by the Meteorological Office. These should be rewritten in the appropriate style for the station's own announcer to read out. The Met. Office can also provide its own announcers to read the forecast live via landline and give more detailed explanation of climatic conditions. Local stations often make additional use of 'weather watchers' – keen listeners located across the editorial area who agree to inform the station of temperature readings and local conditions.

Local radio demonstrates its community value most effectively when the weather deteriorates. Listeners turn to their radios whenever the conditions are extreme to find out the effects on travel and likelihood of school closures and cancellations of events. Many stations therefore have procedures in place to enable them to respond quickly to floods and snowstorms by receiving and broadcasting this type of information (see pp. 227–9).

Fact or fiction?

AS a means of telling a story, the production techniques that we have considered so far constitute methods of representing the 'real world' of issues and events through combinations of the spoken word and actuality. Many of these techniques have become established through convention and the reinforcement of audio codes that separate out and categorise items as 'serious news', 'human-interest stories', 'personality profiles', 'magazine programmes' and so on. The presence and juxtaposition of elements within the radio text serve to articulate such codes to indicate, for example, the status of the central voice (presenter? newsreader? announcer?), the nature of dialogue taking place (informal chat? formal interview?), the importance of the issue being dealt with (does the item include music or sound effects? or newsclips or ambient noise?), and so on. These coded elements are fundamental to radio's act of reconstructing a *real* world through the application of production devices. Listeners are able to interpret the resultant text through their recognition of and familiarity with these codes.

The codes through which listeners interpret radio's portrayal of the 'real' world are *journalistic*. The audio text overall purports to *reflect* the world but in fact applies codes to *construct* a representation of the world within the terms of the radio experience. Listeners have learned to recognise the voice of the newsreader or reporter through its intonation, pace, vocabulary and authoritative, dispassionate mode of address. They know when an interview is taking place, even if they only hear a brief clip conveying one answer to an unheard question – the vocal behaviour of interviewees is distinctive and unique. And listeners identify the setting of a verbal delivery or exchange – a studio, a location, a telephone line – by the overall sound of the output. These are just a few of the wide range of audio codes that signify a text as framed within the conventions of radio journalism.

An alternative (or additional) coded system exists for the *non-journalistic* audio text. This tells listeners that what they are hearing is *fiction* – a different form of construction to that of the journalistic text although, arguably, one that is equally capable of connecting listeners to the 'real' world via the radio experience.[7] It can relate, in the listener's imagination, to the known sensations of sight, smell, taste, etc. Further to this, radio fiction can create experiences that are unfamiliar to the listener – taking part in a famous battle in history, or travelling on a spaceship powered by improbability drive, as in *The Hitchhiker's Guide to the Galaxy*. Codes are applied that are understood by listeners and that relate to their existing knowledge of (a) 'real' experience and (b) radio experience. Drawing on this knowledge, listeners are able to construct in their minds the experience represented in the fictional item.

The important proviso therefore to radio's capacity to create any scenario in time and space is the listener's awareness of how radio's fictional codes work. Radio fiction – drama, comedy, readings or whatever – connects with listeners through its reference to a coded and *learned* framework of representation. Through this, listeners develop an understanding of the rules of narrative, the incorporation of sound effects, the differentiation between words that are 'spoken' and words that are 'thought' by one protagonist, and so on.

In his discussion of radio drama as a form of 'stage interaction', Goffman refers to conventions in radio which 'provide functional equivalents of what could not otherwise be transmitted' (Goffman 1980: 164) – sights, smells, textures, tastes, the simultaneous stimulation of *all* the senses for the witness of a 'real life' scene and, in Goffman's terms, the 'multiple-channel effect' whereby that witness repeatedly shifts focus from one channel to the next to gain a full picture of what is happening. One convention or strategy which signals, if not replicates this effect is the use of volume control and microphone positioning (see pp. 122–3) to suggest distance and the listener's orientation to the action. Another is the articulation of a protagonist's thoughts to indicate feelings or response to a situation, either as a form of soliloquy – 'Hello, what's this? – (gasp) – a pool of blood!' – or through a narration by a voice signalled as the storyteller – possibly even the protoganist as an older person looking back on the event. A further convention in radio drama, Goffman suggests, is to provide 'verbal accompaniment' to make sense of otherwise isolated sounds – 'Well, Pete (sound of key turning), let them try to open that lock' (Goffman 1980: 164).

These conventions illustrate the coded experience of radio fiction. Goffman also highlights how different meanings arise within the radio experience through the context in which sound events occur. Music, for example, in radio drama may represent background 'musak' as heard by the protagonists. Or it may provide a 'bridge' between scenes, or function to emphasise the dramatic action during the scene – 'a sort of aural version of subtitles' (Goffman 1980: 165).

As with journalistic radio texts, the production techniques of radio fiction reflect the organisational structure of radio stations, the technical and human resources at their disposal and the audiences they are trying to reach. These considerations determine, for example, which narrative devices are most appropriate for particular time slots and particular output styles – a one-off extended radio play running for ninety minutes, a single voice reading for ten minutes, a radio soap, a series of half-hour mini-dramas, and so on. Whether the script is one of the 10,000 originals received annually by the BBC's Radio Drama Department,[8] an adaptation of an existing play or novel, or an item for a sitcom series or established soap, its first pre-requisite is that its narrative development fits into a format that has already been devised to create the optimum listening experience for a defined audience.

The organisation of fictional narrative to fit into a schedule and enhance audience involvement is illustrated in Horstmann's discussion of Radio 4's popular soap *The Archers:*

> Each episode . . . lasts fifteen minutes . . . usually contains five scenes, and not more than seven characters. The plotting is the longest and most demanding part of the process. Some writers actually do this on graph paper, ensuring that storylines peak in the right places in the week to keep listeners tuned in . . .
>
> Each . . . episode needs to be planned for a good mix . . . An echo-y barn interior might follow a breezy scene on Lakey Hill; a cosy slow-moving chat among the old folk of Ambridge might be followed by a snappy, funny scene with younger characters; an emotional scene might need a comic scene to pick the audience up again. Each scene needs to 'thicken' at its ending, and in some way signpost the listeners on: the momentum of a soap is always onwards.
>
> *Horstmann 1991: 37*

The techniques of radio drama are sometimes applied to reinforce local branding or to promote a specific theme or message within a radio station's public service remit. A joint project between a radio station and a local health authority could lead to a series of mini-dramas which encourage listeners to be more health-conscious. Similarly, the use of radio actors may prove more effective in a feature on employment – for example, demonstrating how to behave in a job interview – rather than a presenter talking about it with a personnel manager.

Drama provides a powerful means of highlighting sensitive issues such as domestic violence, rape or drug-taking, to complement – or provide an alternative to – interviews with victims, police and social workers. Techniques that may be employed to strong effect include the monologue – an actress portraying a character telling her own story, or reciting it from a 'diary' – or a scripted dialogue, such as a mock interview. The same principle applies here as it does to the presenter link: the programme maker has a choice of storytelling techniques and weighs up which will be the most effective for each individual story – package, live interview, PSA or mini-drama?

Some stations provide a showcase for material by local would-be professional writers of not only plays but also prose and poetry. This material can be of high quality, provide an alternative to the more familiar chat-and-music radio format and connect with listeners through its relevance to local events and people, issues, concerns and the overall character of the editorial area.

The edge

T
O construe the range of production techniques available to radio as
devices for conveying information, atmosphere or impact does not
tell the full story. The selection and application of these devices
by programme makers take place within a 'professional' context – a framework of knowledge and attitudes shared by experienced broadcasters
which provides an unspoken, internalised rationale to their activities and
decisions on how an audio text should be put together.

A vital element of this professionalism is an orientation towards the
audience beyond that knowledge gleaned from meticulous listener
surveys or market research. It involves a deep-seated appreciation of the
fabric of listeners' day-to-day living experience and the part that radio
plays in relating to and structuring that experience. The radio experience
depends not only on listeners being literally tuned in to the output, but on
the programme makers being figuratively 'tuned in' to their audience.

Effective radio simultaneously reflects and reinforces the patterns and
rhythms that provide a framework for listeners' cultural experience. It
achieves this through an element in its output that is crucial but difficult to
define – an 'edge' that represents and resonates with the unspoken values
and routines that lie at the core of this experience. The edge constitutes all
aspects of the radio text that reveal its empathy with listeners, not just in a
universal sense of 'knowing' an audience, but in a very particular day-to-
day sense, expressed through a chronological pattern of output that
synchronises with the pattern of life experience for the listener. It is the
means whereby radio shows solidarity with the listener in the business of
functioning as a member of a society or culture.

The edge can be identified and developed in three ways: through the news
routine, the topicality of trends and issues, and the topicality of the season.

The news routine

Whether a station's news output comprises regular two-minute summaries
or extended bulletins as part of a relentless diet of talk radio, it is likely to
operate within a strict routine of news broadcasting. A common pattern is
a series of fixed and regular, relatively formal announcements of world
events throughout the day. These function effectively as waymarks which,
while not necessarily breaking the overall flow of a station's daily output,
are usually distinctive enough in style and delivery to provide a contrast
with the rest of that output and hence a form of structured listening.

The routine of news not only punctuates the radio text and structures
the radio experience – it provides tangible points of reference for the
listener in her own experience of a daily routine. The instant that the
minute hand reaches the top of the dial signals a mood and an anticipation
of audience receptiveness to this formal delivery of information through
which the rest of the world intrudes into the otherwise one-to-one

interaction between broadcaster and listener. Through the positioning of the bulletin at various fixed-time slots, the radio experience touches a real sense of structured and ordered activity for the listener. This is usually work activity that involves engagement in certain tasks at specific times – getting ready for work, commuting, taking a break for lunch, completing a range of domestic chores, adjusting back to a domestic routine at the end of a working day, and so on.

The content of news stories contributes further to radio's edge in connecting with listeners. Daily experience of news consumption tends to follow a pattern in which listeners wake up to emerging stories which establish the day's 'terms of reference' of topical and key issues, learn of developments at lunchtime and reflect on these developments as reports and analyses of the day's events are consolidated during the evening 'drive time' news broadcasts. This process is punctuated throughout the day by the breaking of new stories at those points in the schedule fixed for news bulletins when listeners are most receptive to the news discourse.

Whatever the programme schedule, news provides a relatively consistent routine. The edge to radio's text is apparent through a listening schedule structured by news and through an expectation by listeners of the nature of broadcast information – and its mode of delivery – at different points of their own daily routines.

Topicality of trends

To be in tune with its listeners, the radio station should recognise and reflect the short-term fashions and values that act as a cement of common identity for its audience group. A station risks creating an alienating distance between itself and its listeners if it does not offer a response to emerging issues that is consonant with their perspectives and attitudes. The most successful point of connection between the radio text and a targeted listener group is evident through the station's awareness and appreciation of the up-to-date trends and fads that are current and predominant within the social and cultural experience of its audience.

At any given point in time, certain styles of music, certain movies and celebrities, certain commodities are 'in vogue', talked about and established as cultural icons, reflecting the crucial '*now*' element of listeners' collective experience as consumers. These icons may be carefully nurtured through public relations campaigns and the 'placing' of products, or concepts related to these products, within media texts. Or they may achieve prominence through notoriety, unwelcome publicity and chance public reaction to news items. Whether a person, product or issue is seen in a good or bad light, the radio station maintains its edge through recognition that 'everybody is talking about it' – at least 'everybody' within its defined audience – and loses that edge only if it appears to be out of touch with its listeners' preoccupations.

The topical edge is further sustained through the station's ability to

187

identify which news stories and issues have the greatest potential to intrigue or concern its audience, whether these address the latest comings and goings of the royal family as reported in the popular press or a major controversy on the condition of local schools. Longer-term interests and attitudes, characteristic of the age we live in, also help to establish radio's point of contact with that which is meaningful to the lives of individual listeners. The inclusion of a regular environmental news bulletin on Radio 1's *Steve Wright in the Afternoon* reflected the growth of 'green' consciousness throughout the 1980s. At the same time the 'City' news bulletins on Radio 4's *Today* programme have acknowledged greater participation by its listeners in a 'share-owning democracy'.

It should be stressed, however, that the edge to the radio experience is not just a reflection of listeners' interests but an involvement in their activities and lifestyles, a recognition for example that people also read newspapers and watch television. It was demonstrated by the first station to ask listeners to send in messages by fax, or to use their mobile telephones to inform the station of a traffic jam.

Topicality of the season

Radio strengthens its connection with listeners' life experiences through its reflection and reinforcement of the cyclical patterns of the year and its participation in the activities and preoccupations of listeners that are specific to the season. Obvious ways in which radio establishes its edge in this respect are through its address of both the spiritual and commercial values of Christmas with its inclusion of items that focus on children and family life, its recognition of listener values and routines during Easter and other religious festivals, and its reference to specific days of the year that are significant to the lives of particular groups of listeners within its editorial area – 1 March (St David's Day), 17 March (St Patrick's Day), or variable dates such as the Jewish New Year, Shrove Tuesday or the first day of Ramadan. Occasions that inspire specific items and promotions for many popular local radio stations include Valentine's Day, Mother's Day and April Fools' Day.

Programme themes, production items and entire schedules are also adjusted to maintain radio's seasonal edge. The start of the tourist season in some areas may mean an increase in travel bulletins and 'what's on' news. Exam periods and revision periods represent a distinctive phase of the lives of young listeners and their families and often provide the theme for topical packages, phone-ins or studio discussions. The announcement of exam results similarly may spark off a series of social action items on career options or opportunities for continued education, live interviews, features, panel discussions and so on.

The topical edge of radio is further enhanced through its recognition of the 'social' season of events that are embedded in national culture as highlights of the time of year. Output ranging from the basic presenter link to the full-length production feature may relate to key national sports events – the Boat Race in March, the Grand National in April, Wimbledon, the start of the football season – or to significant annual occasions such as the Chelsea Flower Show in May or the Last Night of the Proms in September.

The existence of a well-detailed news and events diary is obviously a pre-requisite for a radio station's seasonally topical output. However, unless a station is totally dedicated to back-to-back music or is in any other way wholly specialist in its appeal, it is not sufficient simply to announce events without demonstrating a more intrinsic response to the patterns of the year in terms of output style and structure. Radio enhances its meaning to its target audience by establishing itself as part of the fabric of their lives and cultural experiences, rather than as a distant and pale reflection. The radio experience's synthesis with listeners' life experience is created not only through the content of output and its topical relevance (important as this is) but also the shared emotions, values and atmospheres that give particular colour to listeners' life experience at different times of the year.

Putting the pieces together

FROM our discussion in this chapter so far, it could be suggested that radio constructs an edge to its output by holding up a mirror to a changing pageant of fashions, trends and the year's events and personalities. Within this context of continuous change, however, a radio station also aims to maintain its own consistency with listeners, such that it remains a constant point of reference in their lives and a familiar institution within their cultural (and physical) environment.

The danger of this is that a station could appear to sit on the sidelines with the listener to watch the pageant go by, whereas the listener is more likely to be actively involved simply by *living* the culture, accepting its values and priorities and consuming its commodities. Radio's point of contact with its audience is not only through the recognition of the icons and symbols of the 'here and now', but also through its own role within the tangible cultural experience of its listeners. Its output is itself a cultural commodity; the style and identity of a particular radio station relates to and reinforces the identity of those who tune into it. Radio therefore should be part of the dynamism of an ever-changing cultural climate.

To achieve this, its output would need to be provocative rather than reflective, proactive rather than reactive. The business of producing a text that connects with listeners within the shifts and flows of cultural experience calls for an internal dynamism – an approach by programme makers that never falls back on the rationale of 'we've always done it like that' and that treats formats and formulae as points of reference rather than overbearing production precepts. Innovative radio is not a question of stealing a march on competitors; radio has to be innovative to keep that connection with listeners *and* constantly move to maintain an orientation to their own dynamic cultural experience. Innovation is the key to radio's ability both to feed and feed off that experience.

Rather than check the rulebook, programme makers should approach each story that they have to tell as a call upon their own judgement as to the best way to tell it. Each production technique has its own communicative strengths and weaknesses; each is definable in terms of the codes of representation that listeners have learned to recognise; each thus sparks off its own set of listener expectations. The creative programme maker recognises that there is never a universally right or wrong selection and application of production technique in the telling of a story. Her judgement is based on her analysis of the 'here and now' of cultural experience and where that positions her, the station and its audience. Her objective is to create the optimum impact and add to the overall value of the life experience of listeners.

The activity of making programmes is not one of picking out and building up the tried and tested production techniques but of starting out each time with a blank piece of paper and working out how to achieve that impact on *this* particular audience at *this* particular point in history.

Activities and points for discussion

1 Imagine that you are able to put *one* question only to a famous person of your choice and that the person *must* give a truthful answer. What would you ask? Discuss this as a group with each group member stating at least one famous person and one question. The purpose of this is to work towards a technique of fast-paced interviewing that gets straight to the point.

2 Select a suitable topic which may be covered by a single voice piece of two minutes' duration on a radio station serving your campus or locality. Establish the key points of the narrative that you wish to put across to the audience of that station, then write a script that will achieve this and record the item.

Now refer back to your list of key points and, with a colleague, prepare and record a two way dialogue, in which one of you takes on the role of a specialist correspondent or reporter with direct access to, or interest in, the topic you have selected. Play back both recordings and discuss with a group the extent to which each of these recordings provides an interesting and dynamic account. Does the dialogue of the two way sound natural or contrived? If the latter, what aspects of the performance could be improved?

3 Record a selection of packages from a local radio station and write a list of the individual elements that have been juxtaposed to build up the story – audio, voice links, music and special effects. In each case, identify the structure for narrative development and look for common devices for 'telling the story' – for example, starting with an 'odd' specific point to stimulate listener interest in a wider, more general topic, and returning to that point at the end of the package.

How 'transferable' are these narrative devices? Can any story be told, for example, through a 'general → specific → general' or 'specific → general → specific' structure? Try it out: identify a 'story' for a campus or local station and plan a package such that it will fit either of these structures.

4 Tune in to a radio programme in which recorded packages form a significant part of its content. Make a written record of all items of music, special effects or natural sound (wildtrack) that are incorporated in the packages. For each of these items, identify the function of the sound; how does it help to develop the story or relate to the experience or understanding of the listener? To what extent would you consider any of these sounds to be clichéd?

Select examples at random from the following lists of topics and approaches. (Don't cheat – write each word on a separate piece of paper, mix them up in a 'topic' bag and 'approach' bag and draw them out. Add any other topics and approaches you may think of.) Consider how you would represent and convey the atmosphere of the selected topic to reflect the selected approach if you were putting together a production item for a radio programme. In particular, state what sounds you would incorporate in the production item to suggest immediately the topic and approach to the listener without ambiguity.

Topic

holidays
sumo wrestling
gardening
DIY
supermarket shopping
travelling by ferry
hang gliding
market trading
the popular press
spiders
time travel
schoolday memories
working as a secretary
open day at a local brewery

Approach

  humorous package – aimed at 18–25 age group
  humorous package – aimed at 40-plus age group
  topical and local news feature
  account by reporter who 'has a go' or becomes directly involved in
      the topic
  a short story read over the air with appropriate audio effects
  a trail for a programme that will focus on the selected topic
  a commercial or public service announcement

5 As a group, assume the role of a production team for a popular mid-morning talk programme on local radio. Today you are planning for the 1 April edition. Characteristic features of the programme include: plenty of opportunities for listeners to phone in to chat on the air or take part in simple promotional competitions; a regular succession of studio guests, ranging from people with an interesting story to tell (explorers, people with unusual jobs, people who have made remark-able achievements, etc.) to 'experts' offering advice on healthy living, petcare, legal issues, financial issues and so on; and the occasional 'surprise' phone call by the presenter to an unsuspecting listener who is celebrating a birthday or anniversary.

In previous years, the programme has developed a reputation for pulling the occasional 'April Fool' stunt, usually through a phone call to a listener. This year you feel the audience will be anticipating this and that something different is needed – an elaborate and convincing hoax that is maintained throughout the programme and encourages listeners to unwittingly but actively *participate*, perhaps by phoning in.

Conduct a brainstorming session to agree on a possible hoax and then plan in detail how it would be perpetrated. Take into account the technical facilities that would be available at a well-resourced radio station and be conscious of the need to maintain the appropriate radio experience and to connect with the programme's audience by relating to their interests, values and lifestyles. Then present your idea verbally and succinctly as if to the station's Managing Editor.

7 The programme

....

The programme schedule

WHETHER part of a long-running series, a segment of the day's flow of output or a one-off extended production item, the programme represents a discrete organisational unit within the radio station and the pulling together of the various techniques in presentation and production that we have so far considered. It is also one facet of the station's overall product. The very purpose and identity of the programme represents the station's view of what should constitute the radio experience for its particular audience at that particular time. Therefore, to begin this stage of our discussion, we look at how the programme fits into the overall pattern of output before focusing on how it is built up from its individual production and performance components.

In terms of the management of the station, the position and identity of the programme lies at a point of intersection between two internal organisational structures – the departmental structure of the station itself, reflecting the allocation of staff responsibilities, access to technical resources and the station's position within a wider network, and the textual structure of the station's output, expressed as the programme schedule. The schedule varies from station to station and, like the internal organisation and thinking behind the deployment of staff, relates back to the fundamental issue of branding.

For some stations, the programme schedule may be defined primarily as which presenter is occupying the 'hot seat' of the studio at which time of day, based on the station's view of who provides the best 'morning' personality, 'afternoon' personality, and so on. Or the schedule may reflect the station's strong orientation to journalism and locate key, news-based programmes at those times of the day when listening figures peak – breakfast time, lunchtime and early evening drive time.

The organisation of programme staffing in some stations may reflect that the programmes themselves are relatively similar in structure and content – for example, a single presenter voice and a large quantity of music on CD – and less labour-intensive to organise and produce. Those production staff who are needed to support the presenter could therefore be relatively flexible in terms of who is to work on which programme, as the nature of their contribution would be much the same. Other programmes may have their own unique character and distinctive structure, requiring a 'dedicated' production team familiar with the special problems and processes involved in putting it together. A third category of programmes are those which are located nearer to the periphery of the station's organisational structure, catering for a specialist audience and transmitted at non-peak times. Personnel involved here may have a more tenuous relationship with the rest of the station – perhaps as part-time or guest broadcasters, working in liaison with a senior member of the production staff.

Both the schedule and the internal organisation of the station reflect the listening patterns of the audience that is targeted. Naturally individual stations will attempt to influence those patterns as part of their drive to maximise their own listening figures through marketing, advertising and public relations campaigns. However, a station's viability depends largely on an awareness of the existing patterns of work and leisure activities of its audience and a process of branding whereby the station's output constitutes a 'natural' part of its listeners' lifestyles while relating to their values and perspectives.

Listening patterns themselves are largely governed by the structures of economic and domestic activity. The largest potential audience for any radio station is in the morning between 7.30 and 9.30am. During this time, individual listeners tend to tune in for short periods of, say, thirty minutes. The radio experience here is usually secondary, whereby listener concentration on output varies while people are engaged in their routine start-of-day activities. The text provides a reference point through timechecks, travel news and weather reports as much as it shapes and colours listeners' experience as consumers of news, music and talk. Even those stations which would otherwise feature documentaries, quizzes or radio drama do not schedule these pre-produced recorded programmes during this period.

For many stations, the general rule for listening figures is that they reduce as the day progresses after the initial early morning surge, perhaps peaking slightly at lunchtime and more so between the hours of 4.30–6.30pm when a significant number of listeners are tuned in on car radios. Other stations, for example specialist music stations for young listeners, may follow a reverse pattern and achieve their highest audience figures in the evening. Or stations may aim for the best of both worlds and adjust their output throughout the day to appeal to different audiences whose numbers peak at different times. Stations are also aware of variations in listener patterns during weekends. Perhaps not surprisingly, the build-up to the morning peak happens later on Saturdays than it does on weekdays.

Early morning audiences do not only rely on timechecks to provide a monitor of progress through their domestic routines. The regular, fixed-time inclusion of specific items provides a constant orientation for the listener engaged in these activities. This illustrates an approach that stations adopt not only to planning one programme but also to scheduling all of their programmes – once a plan has become established, stations aim as much as possible to keep it consistent. Even the UK service that reaches (arguably) the most sophisticated audience, Radio 4, has a bedrock of programmes upon which the audience can rely to be transmitted at fixed-times – the news-based *Today*, *The World at One*, *PM* and *The World Tonight*, the 'magazine' format *Woman's Hour* and *Kaleidoscope* and the never-ending saga of *The Archers*. For the Radio 4 listener, these represent a solid foundation for the structured experience and routines of a listening day with clear entry- and exit-points.

This form of scheduling is referred to as *sequence programming*. Listeners tend to know *when* particular programmes are to be transmitted and often organise their day's routines around these times. Audiences may change quite dramatically from one programme to the next. The thing that they have in common is that they relate to and maintain their loyalty to *that* station, even though they are usually discriminating about which particular programmes they listen to. Consistency in scheduling is clearly vital in these circumstances. A change of transmission time for one programme can have the effect of seriously upsetting the daily domestic and social routines of a substantial number of listeners.

Sequence programming is most widely used by BBC Radio 4 and the World Service. Most other stations – popular music and local talk radio – employ a structure referred to as *strip programming*. That is, they choose to maximise their target audience by broadcasting a seamless flow of live output. Each programme tends to run for two, three or even four hours and contains its own continuous delivery of short items of speech and/or music before making a smooth handover to the next programme, often very similar in format, although not in content. Entry- and exit-points for listeners are more haphazard and less dependent on the start and finish times of individual programmes although there are many examples of programmes that have themselves built up particularly strong listener commitment, or of programme items that listeners tune in especially to catch.

Strip programme scheduling is less problematic than sequence programming in terms of consistency of programme times, although audiences still appreciate a reliable and dependable sound and that they will engage in a certain type of radio experience whenever they switch on in the mornings or early evenings. Scheduling becomes an important consideration for stations whose output varies in style and/or content throughout a day. If output is 80 per cent music-based on the same playlist and style policy, scheduling is a relatively straightforward matter of selecting the most suitable daytime and late evening presenters and placing any specialist music or talk programmes that the station might carry into the mid-evening slots or during the weekend.

Weekend programming

F OR millions of potential listeners, weekends still represent a change in day-to-day routines, different social and family environments, and a focus on the consumption of leisure – in spite of recent cultural changes such as the dramatic increase in seven-day week shopping, the growing proportion of people working in the six- and sometimes seven-day week service sector and the scheduling of popular sporting events across the week. The extent to which weekend schedules of radio stations differ from their weekday output depends upon the nature of listeners' engagement with that output. There is a tendency – but with many individual exceptions – for weekend programming on talk radio to be very different from weekday schedules, while there is less of a distinction between the two for music radio.

Music output is less governed by the ebbs and flows of listener activity. School term times, holiday times, weekends and weekdays may have their influence on the selection of specific items of music – anything from Bing Crosby's *White Christmas* to Alice Cooper's *School's Out* – but stations whose branding is based on the style of music they play are likely to broadcast a similar overall sound during weekends as they do on weekdays. Indeed, this is their strength; listeners who tune into an effectively targeted music station know that they will hear what they want to hear, no matter what day of the week it is. Apart from minor differences – for example the use of 'weekend' themed jingles or an alternation in the schedule of news bulletins – the expectation of the market is similar to that of someone turning on a tap for water.

As talk stations attempt to reflect in detail the day-to-day pattern of life for their listeners, their approach in programming involves balancing a need to maintain a distinctive but consistent sound that reinforces a brand image, against a priority to connect with listeners by relating to the different texture of the weekend experience. This means generally addressing different content areas for weekend programming while maintaining a similar style in presentation.

Examples of content areas that are more readily associated with weekend lifestyles are: shopping, sport and leisure, religious worship, family visits, DIY, socialising. These areas are generally regarded as more difficult to relate to a programme schedule than those associated with weekdays – local council activity, courtroom activity, parliament, activities in financial institutions, schools, colleges, and so on. Such institutions can be relied on to operate within a routine during weekdays and to supply regular topic material and self-contained stories for radio programmes, often at fixed-times of the day. The weekday also follows a common structure for many listeners with clearly defined times for activities such as commuting, having lunch and children coming home from school.

There are fewer discernable trends or patterns of routine during weekends. Activities are more idiosyncratic and less dependent on an institutional structure of events. For example, many people still travel to work, but not in sufficient numbers to warrant concerted commuter-orientated output. The two predominant features of weekend broadcasting are sport and, to a lesser extent, religion. Sports fixtures are by no means confined to the traditional Saturday afternoon. Nevertheless, this is the time when most local talk radio stations – and many music stations – offer a selective coverage of the most popular sports events in the editorial area plus a round-up of the day's results. Programmes with a religious or moral theme are sometimes included in the Sunday morning schedules of talk stations.

The most significant feature of the weekend for many listeners is its opportunity to organise leisure time and to consume leisure-orientated products – anything from days out, visits to restaurants and pubs and trips to the cinema to computer games, Sunday dinner and home videos. Many of these commodities are linked to family time together, which in turn suggests a different pace of life in a different social environment from many listeners' weekday experience. The challenge for radio is to reflect this distinctive atmosphere in programme style and content, even if it is difficult to determine and reflect the patterns of weekend activity in programme scheduling. For music radio, this challenge is addressed through the selection of music to reflect the experience and lifestyle of the weekend, as well as through presenter links and commercials. Talk radio has other strategies at its disposal – for example, emphasis on competitions, especially those that involve children and put their voices on air, or the use of OBs as a means of enhancing the station's visibility and highlighting radio's interactive capacity.

The difficulties of weekend scheduling are compounded by staffing arrangements. Clearly, it is not possible for the main presenters of a station to maintain a seven-day week profile on air. A higher proportion of weekend broadcasters are part-timers who are not only conducting the difficult job of relating to less clearly defined lifestyles of listeners, but doing so with fewer people in the station building to provide feed-back or support. The existence of a different schedule with different voices and personalities produces an unavoidable break in the continuity of the station's output. This may give rise to problems for station branding through the reinforcement of a consistent and recognisable sound, although weekend schedules can also represent a welcome break for listeners who believe in keeping the weekend distinctive. And for stations who are willing to allow space for a new generation of broad-casters to develop their skills and experience, the weekend does provide an opportunity for trainees and student broadcasters to gain access to the airwaves.

Sport

E VEN on many music-dominated stations, sport provides the theme for a substantial amount of output, especially for local services. To recognise the rationale behind local sport coverage and its relatively high profile, we would need to go back to the fundamental point about local branding.

Clearly a focus on local teams and sporting events simultaneously reflects and reinforces the identity of a station's editorial area, although it is not enough simply to broadcast local names and talk about fixtures in that area. A sense of local identity does not arise for listeners through knowing where the boundary is drawn on the map, but instead relates to the less tangible but more significant sense of personal identity. Today, one high street or shopping centre looks very much like another; many once-local businesses have been swallowed up by national and multi-national concerns; many regionally specific industries – for example mining and steel-manufacturing – have virtually disappeared. Nevertheless, notions of the geographic community and an interest in events and issues related to local areas, accessible to listeners on a day-to-day basis, are still prevalent. Listeners are able to relate to local radio output through sharing an orientation to, and familiarity with the area it covers. Sport in particular offers a focal point for this relationship.

This is still only part of the story behind the significance of sport within the radio experience. When it began broadcasting on 27 August 1990, BBC Radio 5 tapped into a widespread interest in sport on a national level.[1] While it provided varied forms of output from children's programmes, radio drama and education to presenter-led shows and phone-ins, it was through its sport coverage that Radio 5 established a strong reputation, with a Sony Gold Award for its coverage of the 1992 Olympics. This illustrates a wider point about radio's recent renaissance as a medium (see p. 10); the appeal of so-called 'spectator' sport is by no means confined to television. As football clubs jostle for positions in their leagues throughout the season, or as national hopes focus on the possibility of one England bowler wreaking devastation on a visiting test side, sport provides a continuing fascination through its constantly developing stories and individual dramas (sometimes in the board room as well as on the field) which are as effectively conveyed by radio as they are by television. In fact, radio coverage makes it possible to monitor the progress of a key match, or a series of matches, as a background to other activity. Even spectators at the venues themselves can tune into a clearly delivered and well-informed commentary while watching.

Radio listeners gain not only a detailed description of sporting events but also a chance to absorb the atmosphere and excitement through the voice of the commentator. Sport provides the broadcaster with the rare opportunity to be biased. Even the commitment by BBC broadcasters to be accurate, balanced and impartial becomes academic when the local football team is winning the FA Cup final.

Sports coverage gives a strong indication of the extent to which a local radio station sets out to perform as an integral part of a listening community. The station demonstrates its involvement in, and affinity with, local feelings and attitudes through the attention it gives to the performance of local sporting heroes and its reflection of the priorities given to different types of sport within the area it serves. A diet of football, rugby, athletics and cricket is not enough to reinforce local branding, for example, if a station ignores the success of a local speedway star, or for that matter the overall popularity of a particular sport in the area it serves, such as angling or hockey. As with news, it is also vital to successful local branding that all parts of the editorial area are evenly represented in local team coverage.

Local radio's interest in sport does not end when the final whistle is blown. Part of a station's involvement with its audience stems from a recognition of the highs and lows of people's feeling about a local or national team's performance. It is not unknown for industrial productivity to increase in an area when the local football team is doing well and part of the connection that radio makes with its listeners is through its reflection of local euphoria or disappointment at the result of a key match.

Sports broadcasting is made up of four programme types – bulletins, studio-based programmes, live coverage of an event and the sports round-up. Each of these draws on specific resource areas and production techniques although a combination of two or more of these may be used for any specific programme as the station sees fit. The inclusion in the schedules of regular extended sports programmes, whether studio-based or live coverage, reflects the station's overall programming brief and the number of staff made available for sports reporting. Stations which place strong emphasis on local branding allocate resources and staffing – perhaps a sports editor supervising a team of reporters – for more comprehensive sports coverage than stations whose output caters primarily for listeners' tastes in music.

Sports bulletins

These are prepared in a similar way to news bulletins. BBC local radio stations make use of material provided nationally by the BBC's sports desk; similarly, ILR stations access IRN for national sports stories. This is augmented with local information to produce a sequence of copy stories for single voice presentation with the occasional clip of an interview or commentary, or even a brief live link-up with an interviewee. Traditionally, sports bulletins are tagged to weekday core news bulletins at 7am, 8am, 1pm, 5pm and 6pm, or included as a separate item with a separate voice within those bulletins. Alternatively, sports bulletins may be allocated their own fixed times – say, thirty minutes past the hour – as a separate contribution to, or integrated part of a mainstream presenter-led programme. Some stations schedule in additional bulletins or updates throughout the day to cover ongoing events such as racing, golf and cricket. Sports bulletins can be as short as forty-five seconds or as long as five minutes, depending on the strength of the day's sporting news and the significance that the station attaches to it.

Studio-based programmes

Extended studio-based programmes range from 100 per cent sport to a mixture of sport and music – in some cases with greater emphasis on the latter. Organised in a similar way to the weekday presenter-led show, extended sports programmes, with or without music, are usually scheduled for weekend afternoons and geared up to provide latest information on local sporting action, half-time and final football and rugby results, latest cricket scores, regular brief reports from one or more of the main events in the editorial area, and packages. These may contain background to main sporting stories, personality interviews or features on minority sports, new sporting venues, training facilities and so on.

Clearly, extended sports programmes that contain a high proportion of talk material are complex to organise and dependent on a co-ordinated production team. Four or five reporters may be located strategically across the editorial area with radio cars or mobile phones, while the studio presenter may be supported by one or two assistants, receiving telephone calls and reports, and making calls to contacts at local clubs not covered by the reporters to get updates on results and highlights.

The broadcast can put the production team under considerable pressure – a reporter at a key Rugby Union match, for example, may be called on at short notice to give a summary on the air of the game so far. He could be required to provide reports for more than one station and even record a brief voice piece for television. On the basis that people who can meet such demands can handle any situation, local radio sports reporting is a common starting point for developing a career in broadcasting.

A radio station may identify a sufficient segment of the audience to focus its production resources into a specialist programme on one particular sport in the editorial area. Angling is an increasingly popular topic and also viable for programming during the early hours of the weekend during the season.

An alternative studio-based format is the sports phone-in, providing an excellent opportunity for local radio to fulfil three important functions – reinforce local branding, engage listeners in interactive radio and provide dynamic and captivating live dialogue that relates directly to the emotions, loyalties and deep-seated opinions of listeners. Most football fans know what players *should* have done or what decisions the referee *should* have made; the phone-in provides an ideal forum to give these views public expression.

Live coverage of sports events

Within the brief of many local stations, live coverage of key mid-week football matches, or weekend county cricket matches may take priority in the schedules over regular programming. This can occur at short notice if, for example, the fixture was previously postponed and thus force station management to decide if the 'cost' of disrupting the schedule – taking programmes off that other listeners were expecting to hear – is acceptable for maintaining the station's overall status within the listening community.

The broadcast organisations and the sports club concerned agree a fee in advance for the station's right to commentate and there is sometimes a condition that the station cannot advertise in advance its live coverage of a particular match, as this may affect ticket sales. There are circumstances when the club will ask for commentary to be provided – if, for example, only a limited number of tickets is available.

If the scale and importance of the sports event warrants the investment, a station may install a team of correspondents to cover a range of functions – describe the action itself, provide background and statistical information, or conduct interviews and provide commentary from locations within the venue away from the fixed commentators' area. Stations often employ sporting celebrities to work as part of the team and to provide their expert perspective.

Sports round-ups and results

At some point in the Saturday afternoon schedule, between 5.00 and 6.30pm, all BBC local radio and a large proportion of independent music stations provide a run-down of the day's sporting events in their area and nationally. Some stations link into a national network for this service, while others serving more urban and densely populated areas with more local teams and fixtures supply their own summary of the day's action.

The programme may take the form of an extended bulletin with a higher proportion of voice pieces to describe key events in the area. However, sport provides not only a continuous supply of stories and features – and radio has an unabatable appetite for these – but also a constantly updated mass of such data as results, league positions, starting prices, records (world, national and personal) and so on. It is for programme makers to consider the extent to which their sports programming should include a comprehensive results service, but there is a strong argument that the experience of 'radio' becomes transformed to that of a public address system if too much airtime is given to the sound of a voice dispassionately reading out the scores. The best medium for charts, tables, lists and statistics is the newspaper. Radio's strength is its immediacy and ability to allow one human being – the reporter – to convey the drama and sense of occasion of selected sporting events to the listener.

More scope for innovation

Sport and people's attitudes towards it form a very strong thread in the fabric of cultural experience. Interests in different sports are fuelled by

201

motivations which include the altruistic – an interest in the fortunes of individual sports personalities; the patriotic – supporting the national side and of course the local team; and the pragmatic – an interest in winning the football pools. As a broad topic, sport arouses passions and creates causes for genuinely felt exaltation or disappointment. Clearly, many stations ignore sport at their own peril.

However, innovative programme makers seeking to produce distinctive sports coverage constantly need to review assumptions and values, arguably entrenched in tradition, to ensure that their output is making the best use of resources to connect with the target audience. For example:

Is football the most important sport within the editorial area?

Stations serving towns and cities with teams in the national leagues should reflect listener interests in those teams, especially when they are playing away from the area. Nevertheless, programme makers should weigh up the value of a programme full of football match reports against analysis of, say, a major athletics or swimming event in the area.

Is sport a male preserve?

The simple answer is no, although (sadly like many other areas in radio)[2] the balance of male and female voices on local and national radio reporting on sport events would suggest a dominance of the male perspective. This issue is also pertinent for choices made by radio stations of which sporting events to cover. Women's football, cricket and rugby are still more likely to be featured as novelty human-interest items than as subjects for serious match reports; hence a potential for interesting and exciting radio is lost.

Where does sport rank in listeners' thoughts on the important things in life?

Media sports coverage has been justifiably parodied for its frequent sense of self-importance, lack of subtlety and overuse of clichés. Bluntly, there are two reasons why local radio sports coverage can provide the ideal atmosphere for these problems to thrive: (a) sport is a popular training ground for aspiring, but inexperienced, broadcasters, and (b) local radio is more likely to employ local reporters who are less than objective about the fortunes of local teams. This latter point may not be a problem for local radio, which is meant to reflect and relate to the feelings and attitudes of its listeners, but reporters still need to keep a sense of proportion – a tragedy is someone dying in a road accident, not a rugby team losing a cup final.

Is the station's approach to sports coverage making use of radio's full potential?

Decisions on which sporting events to cover may enhance a station's visibility and open up untapped 'segments in the market'. Sports which may seem to have a minority appeal nationally may have a strong local following, if only a local station takes the trouble to investigate and consider the 'risk' in covering it. The same point applies to youth and schools leagues with their potential audiences of family and friends.

The nature of the coverage itself is also worth constant review. A radio commentary is not the next best thing to being at the event itself – it is an alternative way of experiencing the event. This is illustrated by the BBC's celebrated history of test cricket coverage with commentators offering arguably little less than an epic poem of five days' duration. People do not have to like (or even understand) cricket to appreciate the coverage. They just need to enjoy life.

Programme planning

Structure

The structure of a radio programme may be planned to varying degrees of precision. Live extended programmes, in which content largely reflects a news agenda, work to an outline framework of planned and predicted items. The programme structure in the spaces between is flexible, with decisions by the producer on which items should go on air sometimes reached seconds before they actually do go on air. As much advance preparation as possible is undertaken for programmes which carry breaking news stories to minimise the pressures on the presenter and production team while on air. The team works to a provisional plan which sets out:

Fixed-time items

These are items which the programme *must* include at specific times because they are networked or form part of the station's own commitment to its listeners to provide accurately timed news bulletins, travel reports, weather updates, etc. Commercials come under this category as it is important to the station's credibility with advertisers that the commercials schedule is adhered to.

Items with flexible start times and duration

Although sometimes flexible only within a minute or two, these comprise interviews, phone-in competitions and any item over which the presenter can exert reasonable control and bring to a quick close if necessary. Some live interviews, however, are effectively fixed-time items – the interviewees may be tied to a tight schedule of appearances on a number of radio and television programmes covering the same story.

Fixed-duration items

These may be anything pre-recorded from a package to a CD track. Such items could run at any time of the programme but would commit the programme for a fixed period of time once started. Early fading out of a music item may be less problematic than that of a package (unless it consists of a song with a punch line at the end) but many stations discourage this in their style policies. Otherwise, the item is perceived primarily as a space-filler rather than an element fully integrated into the rest of the programme with its own appeal to the target audience.[3]

In the heat of the live broadcast, there is no guarantee that material prepared in advance will be used, and, if it is, at what stage of the programme it will be included. Nevertheless, items such as packages, trails and public service announcements are on hand complete with cue sheets where required and can always be brought forward if, for example, technical difficulties prevent a live telephone interview or a studio guest is held up in the traffic.

Programmes that are less tightly structured, such as phone-ins, may follow whatever theme or line of argument that presents itself as the most significant in the course of the discussion. Their only restrictions are the precise start and finish times and possible fixed-time interruptions for travel reports, commercials or any other commitment that the station has overall beyond the programme itself.

A more detailed level of preparation is applied to live programmes which carry a substantial amount of specially recorded material linked together by a presenter. Such programmes may cater for specific audience interests (e.g. specialist music, movies, the arts, in-depth political analysis) but, because they are live, need to be able to cope with the unexpected news or weather flash or the over-running interview. Programmes which fulfil particular functions best achieved without constant up-to-the-minute updates on news developments – consumer programmes, live coverage of sports events, extended interviews, OBs etc. – may also incorporate fixed-duration items to create a more structured listening experience, obliging programme makers to think ahead so that these items can fit in with other fixed-time commitments.

Where advance preparation to a reasonable level of detail is possible, the determination of a programme's structure serves a purpose beyond that of making sure everything fits. It enables the production team to consider the programme as a unified and coherent listening experience rather than a collection of discrete and disconnected items, and it provides a contextual mood or character to orientate the listener to each of its component parts.

Such coherence is achievable in talk programmes through the application of organisational devices such as:

- a structured zoo format (p. 142) in which contributions from regular participants are interspersed with interviews with one-off guests

- a series of *vox pop* and character interviews on location as the presenter follows a particular route through a town, street, building, etc.

- a montage of clips from recorded interviews, dialogues and actuality, edited to follow a narrative established and signposted by presenter links

- the imposition of a thematic structure by the presenter of a round-table discussion. A new aspect of the topic under discussion is introduced at pre-determined times to build in this structure. This approach also provides shape to an extended one-to-one interview.

Music programmes can also be designed according to a pattern of events, themes and moods within the programme to provide shape and orientation for the listener. Devices here include:

- the incorporation of regular, fixed-time features – a rolling competition, a listeners' letters spot, a feature spot for a particular type of record (comedy, musical, popular classical, song by this week's featured artist, etc.)

- regular trailing of items occurring later in the programme, as a means of signposting and suggesting that the textual flow follows a particular route

- the selection and sequencing of music tracks to control the mood and atmosphere of the programme – perhaps beginning with an up-tempo, 'happy' song and building up a sequence to provide musical contrasts and continuity. It is possible to programme the station's music computer to select material on this basis (see p. 51)

- the use of trails, jingles and sound effects on cart to establish and reinforce the mood direction of a programme, say, from party to romantic to zany, and so on

- the selection of a theme to run through an entire programme, for example cars and taxis – the programme may include tracks such as The Cars' *Drive* or Joni Mitchell's *Big Yellow Taxi* interspersed with, say, a package on test-driving the new Jaguar or a live telephone interview with a New York taxi driver.

The recorded programme

Programmes that are planned to even greater precision are those which are recorded. It is possible to script such programmes fully and plan their structure to the nearest second if necessary. The main requirement for recorded programmes, such as radio drama productions or special documentary features, is that they run for a pre-determined length of time and that the duration is known. An episode of a radio 'soap opera' may run for fifteen minutes but, if transmission begins late because of a previous broadcast over-running, it would be possible to shorten that time by fading the closing signature tune early – provided it is known how long the signature tune in the recording would last if it were left to run to its full extent.

Other recorded programmes may be largely unscripted – for example, studio discussions or panels of experts answering questions put by members of a studio audience – but further 'preparation' is possible before they go on air; they may be edited to fit into a time slot with the option of prefacing with scripted studio commentary.

Ironically, producers of recorded programmes may consider that the use of a detailed script works against the interests of lively, spontaneous broadcasting. The charged atmosphere in a studio of working 'live' and against the clock can lead to a fresher sounding and more dynamic product, even if such an atmosphere is created artificially by recording within a self-imposed time limit.

The structure of a recorded programme is not easily adapted to accommodate or respond to the 'here and now' information that arises during the time of the actual broadcast, although it is possible to create an impression to the listener that a recorded programme is live. The audio tape carrying the programme is banded (see p. 100) at points where it would normally include, say, a live travel report. Thus, if the start-time of the recorded programme cannot be fixed (perhaps it follows a live news bulletin which could run for anything between ten and twelve minutes), the material chosen to lead up to the banded section of the tape is that which can be faded out prematurely without losing the 'sense' of the programme. The most obvious disposable material is music. Premature fading could shorten the programme by minutes although more subtle adjustments to programme length can be made by fading out audience applause or atmospheric sound that leads up to a break in the programme.

If a recorded programme is to be interrupted by a fixed-time live travel report, the presenter also records separate 'travel in' and 'travel out' announcements on cart. This enables the operator in the studio during the broadcast to fade out the tape and fade in the live travel report at a precise moment.

The 'deception' that a 'live' programme is actually recorded is nevertheless not an easy one to sustain. Many elements of live dynamism are necessarily missing – timechecks, off-the-cuff remarks about the weather or recent events, banter during the handover with the travel announcer, or indeed a handover in which the name of the travel announcer is given, as this fact may not be known at the time of recording. The procedure runs the slight risk of creating an effect of insensitivity. The travel report may contain news of a very serious pile-up in the area, something that would normally warrant a brief comment by the presenter if the programme were live.

Another possible side-effect of the recorded programme is that it may be uncannily free of slips of the tongue by the presenter or guests. With the opportunity available to edit these out, the temptation may be difficult to resist although this risks producing a sanitised form of output that lacks a sense of human warmth. Programmes recorded in front of studio audiences are prone to a similar difficulty. Guests who know the programme is being recorded have on occasion been careless about making statements that are offensive, requiring the station to edit out the remarks. This is a task made more difficult by the presence of ambient noise from the location and audience. Sometimes a guest 'corpses' (giggles or laughs uncontrollably) or has difficulties in making a statement, requiring him to repeat it as if it were spoken spontaneously. This can produce audience laughter which would sound odd in the final transmission if the original statement were edited out.

In fact, one effect of the post-deregulation growth in UK radio is an increasing proportion of live programming. Not only is live radio more flexible and easier to schedule than a sequence of recorded programmes, it is also cheaper to produce. The three main formats of popular radio – recorded music, phone-ins and news-and-talk – depend on the 'here and now' factor which itself provides a distinctive edge and excitement to the radio experience. The edge is created through the instantaneous and spontaneous link that the programme makes between the listener and the world of events and social discourse. The excitement arises from the unpredictability of that discourse and the broadcaster's skill in adapting, improvising and responding to the 'now' situation. As listeners become increasingly acclimatised to the immediacy offered by live radio, the notion of the radio programme as a meticulously planned, scripted and structured event becomes more the exception than the rule.

The recorded item represents a different form of experience – a 'set piece' to divert, entertain, stimulate or inform the listener. In telling a story, it challenges its audience to stay tuned in and discover how the story resolves itself. Whether the recording is a single voice piece, such as Alistair Cooke's *Letter from America*, a consumer investigation piece on *Face the Facts*, or an eighty-five-minute Radio 4 *Playhouse* production, it draws the listener into its own terms of reference through a narrative structure designed to enhance listening pleasure. The structure determines audience access to events and protagonists through various techniques, including:

- the introduction of voices at specific points in the text to control the narrative direction

- the timing of revelations and dénouements to enhance dramatic effect

- the positioning of the audience in relation to the text through micro-phone technique (see pp. 122–3)

- alternating between description and actuality to construct a particular mode of understanding.

In live radio the structure is always provisional and can be changed through the decision of a producer in the course of the broadcast. The only permanent structural features are the fixed-time events which can constitute deadlines to add to the live programme's characteristic appeal – for example, the need to resolve a competition or achieve a conclusion in a debate before the next news bulletin. Often there is no singular point of resolution, just a curiosity shared with the presenter over the inter-viewee's next responses or the views of the next phone-in participant. The programme's live appeal is enhanced to the extent that structure is *apparently* absent with the presenter seemingly entering the realms of the unknown as soon as the microphone fader is open.

Time management

BROADCASTERS are slaves to time. During live programmes, in spite of any best-laid plans, the studio clock dominates the proceedings. When planning a programme, a presenter or producer would need to know the precise duration for some items and be able to make realistic estimates of timing for others. Items that can be precisely timed are those which are recorded, such as packages, trails, jingles, commercials and CD tracks. Programme items whose timings can only be estimated are those which are live – single or panel interviews, discussions with specialist correspondents, phone-in discussions and competitions, and so on. A reasonably precise estimate can be made of a scripted voice piece on the basis that speech is delivered at an average of three words per second (see p. 143). Programme makers have to gauge the minimum time it would take to fix the main points from, say, an inter-view, and to set that time as a target to complete the item.

The running order

Planning the running order of a live continuous flow programme involves making decisions on such matters as the preferred balance of different types of output, e.g. music and speech, the overall sound of the programme, the availability of resources, ranging from technology to willing interviewees, and the structured development of the programme – how specific items within the programme relate to each other to create a total listening experience.

These considerations reflect the overall programme style and the ground rules which are constant to all editions of the programme, no matter what variances there may be in individual programme content. Hence, style and branding provide the terms of reference for planning a specific programme. The running order itself is based on consideration of three questions:

How much significance or weight should be given to specific items to be included in the programme?

An item could appear to be flippantly covered if insufficient time is allocated to it. An overlong item could appear laboured and accorded more importance than is due. Its significance is indicated not only by its duration, but also its position within the overall structure of the programme. A frequently used device in radio is to 'keep the audience hanging on' for an item of relatively high significance or interest-value. A presenter may trail such an item at the beginning of the programme (' . . . and coming up later, a 50 per cent reduction in the price of petrol – could it really happen?') but the length of time that the listener should wait before the item is actually heard depends on factors such as the total length of the programme and the time of day it is broadcast.

How will items work in relation to each other within the overall programme structure?

Items may be characterised as light, serious, politically orientated, specialist interest or human interest and judgement is needed on how to balance these characteristics such that one half of a programme is not unduly sombre, flippant, biased to one political viewpoint or focused on one theme to the point of obsession. The mode in which the content of items is conveyed should also be taken into account in planning the running order. For example, should two items be run consecutively if they both include *vox pop* pieces? There are practical considerations also for the presenter: a recorded item of sufficient length may provide a useful space for the presenter to settle in studio guests taking part in a subsequent live interview.

At what specific time of the day should an item be run?

The shape and structure of the day's output of a station reflects a variety of moods and atmospheres associated with listener routines and activities. This pattern influences the selection and location of specific items for individual programmes. For example, evening 'drive time' hours on talk stations and, for that matter, some music stations are largely news-driven or judged to appeal to the widest interests. This is the time for analysis of the day's big stories and major interviews. The time of day of a particular item may also be governed by its theme or topic. Programme makers should be sensitive to topics which their listeners might regard as inappropriate to consider at particular times of day. For example, detailed medical descriptions may make uncomfortable listening for breakfast-time or Saturday morning audiences.

A further consideration for the timing of news items is whether they have been embargoed. An embargo, while not a legal constraint, constitutes a 'strong request' by the supplier of a news item – for example, a public relations agency that has produced a press release – that the item is not made public until the time and date stated. This is basically a device to control the flow of public information to suit the interests of the news source or create an optimum impact. A media organisation may choose to break an embargo if it considers that it is not justified, although this runs the risk of damaging a co-operative working relationship with the news source.

Fine tuning

Armed with knowledge of the likely position of items within a live programme and precise or estimated times of each item, a programme maker is able to maintain control over the structure of output. It is likely that adjustments will be needed to the running order and time allocation of some items while the programme is on air. Interviews may over-run, guests may arrive late, technical difficulties may affect lines from external sources, updates on news items may be fed through to the programme during the broadcast; these are just some of the circumstances that regularly upset the best-laid plans of a live programme. However, the producer is able to fall back on the overall programme plan when making these adjustments and to set targets for the timing of individual programme items.

If the presenter of a live programme is ahead of target, he can adjust the timing of items in a number of ways. Within the main body of a programme, spontaneous and improvised discussions – for example as a response to a package or piece of music that has just been played – may maintain the programme's pace for a few vital seconds, although the status of some voices included in a programme would be inappropriate for this form of informal chatting. A presenter could, for example, undermine his objective position by conversing informally with a studio guest representing a particular political viewpoint.

Presenters usually keep a file or set of notes handy on topics for improvised discussions. These may include bizarre statistics, anniversaries of events, birthdays of famous personalities, forthcoming local entertainments, sports fixtures and public meetings, or topics to be covered on programmes later in the day.

Techniques for precise timing adjustments are sometimes called for. A presenter or technical operator keeps a selection of 'station ident' jingles nearby. Each jingles cart is marked with the duration of the jingle; thus the presenter is able to make fine adjustments if necessary, within as little as four or five seconds. The following is a circumstance in which such fine tuning may be necessary.

Two local radio stations – A and B – each broadcast their own output up to 8.05pm. This includes a news summary given out by each station simultaneously, 8.00–8.05pm. At precisely 8.05, the stations link up such that both share Station B's output for the rest of the evening.

The presenter in Station A has handed over to that station's own newsroom at 8pm as usual. However he still has control – the signal carrying the news is still going through his desk. At 8.05 it will be that presenter's responsibility to open the fader that links Station A to Station B. This of course depends on the ability of Station A's and Station B's newsreaders to finish reading the news at precisely the same moment.

The presenter must listen to both news outputs at the same time. He may use 'split cans' such that Station A's output is heard through the left hand channel of the headphones and Station B's through the right. The presenter is listening out for a pre-arranged cue to be given by Station B's newsreader – for example, a time cue: 'It's five minutes past eight' (Figure 8 – see p. 212).

If Station A's newsreader finishes six seconds too early, the presenter must still wait for Station B's cue before making the changeover. To avoid six seconds of 'dead air', he may play a five-second 'station ident' jingle before linking with Station B (Figure 9).

If Station A's newsreader over-runs, the presenter has two options. One would be simply to fade out the newsreader, no matter what he is saying, and to bring in Station B at the point when the cue is given. This can work if the fade-out point occurs at the end of a sentence and only omits a timecheck or station identity announcement (Figure 10). Or the presenter may aim for a new point to link in with Station B. The cue may be followed by Station B playing a fifteen-second 'station ident' jingle. If Station A's newsreader has missed the cue by five seconds, the presenter could play a ten-second jingle and then make the link to Station B (Figure 11).

Backtiming

Programme structures and running orders are subject to non-negotiable fixed-time events over which the presenter and producer have no control. For them, part of the discipline of professional broadcasting is the priority of finishing the programme – or a section of a programme – at a precise moment prior to a network link-up or the pips of the Greenwich Time Signal (GTS). For programme output to impinge on the latter (for example, by missing out the first pip!) would appear to be almost sacrilegious in view of the traditional authority that this sound has for British listeners tuning in to a BBC news bulletin.

If a presenter knows the precise time (to the nearest second) that a recorded item should finish, and the precise duration (in minutes and seconds) of that item, he is able to calculate the exact point in the programme to start running that item. Backtiming in broadcasting is the

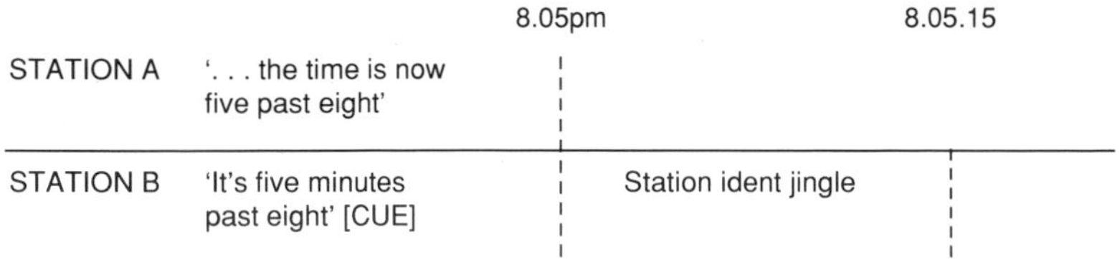

		8.05pm	8.05.15
STATION A	'. . . the time is now five past eight'		
STATION B	'It's five minutes past eight' [CUE]	Station ident jingle	

Figure 8   *Fine tuning: a time cue*

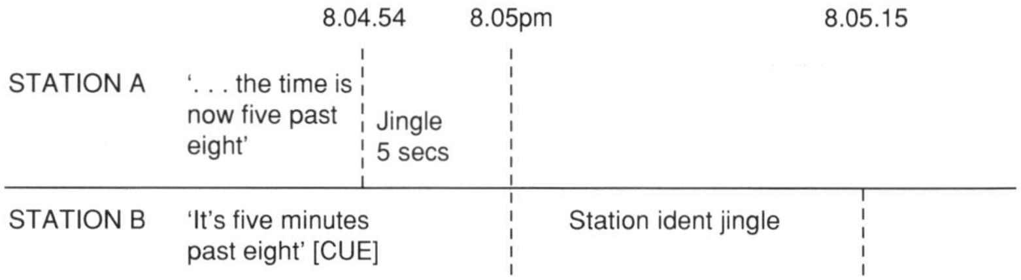

		8.04.54	8.05pm	8.05.15
STATION A	'. . . the time is now five past eight'	Jingle 5 secs		
STATION B	'It's five minutes past eight' [CUE]		Station ident jingle	

Figure 9   *Fine tuning: a five-second jingle*

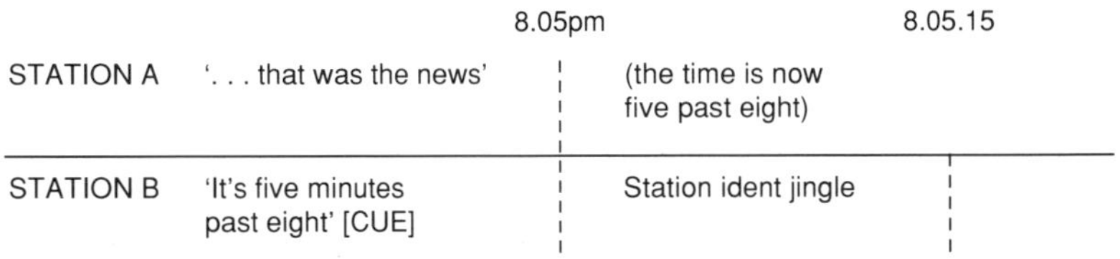

		8.05pm	8.05.15
STATION A	'. . . that was the news'	(the time is now five past eight)	
STATION B	'It's five minutes past eight' [CUE]	Station ident jingle	

Figure 10   *Fine tuning: the fade out*

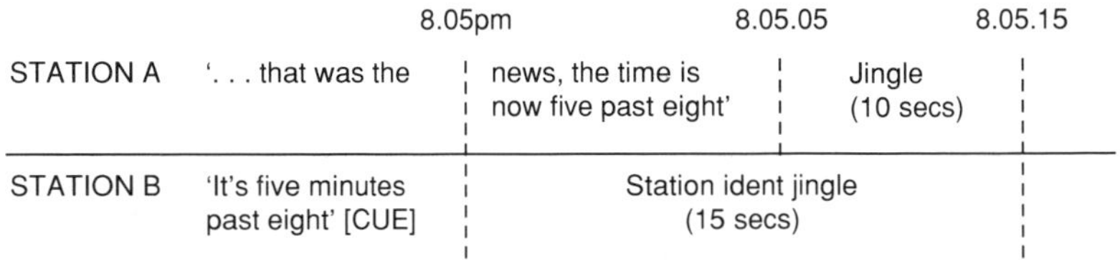

		8.05pm	8.05.05	8.05.15
STATION A	'. . . that was the	news, the time is now five past eight'	Jingle (10 secs)	
STATION B	'It's five minutes past eight' [CUE]	Station ident jingle (15 secs)		

Figure 11   *Fine tuning: the back-up handover point*

technique of ensuring that a package or CD track finishes at a precise moment in the programme and is necessary if that recorded item is preceding an event such as the GTS.

To enable a presenter to backtime, the precise duration of all recorded items – trails, jingles, wraps, packages – is marked on their labels.

Similarly, the times of all items of music to be broadcast are noted (although the times given on the covers or labels of albums and singles are not noted for their accuracy). Compact disc players or the jukebox VDU provide displays of total duration of a track, how much has been played so far, and how much of the track is remaining. The time displayed may include a long slow fade at the end of the track or audience applause which could be faded at an earlier point.

Studio reel-to-reel tape recorders also give a time display, although this only shows how much of the tape has been played and its accuracy depends on whether the counter was zeroed at the precise point where the recorded section of the tape first contacts the playback head of the machine. The time counter acts as a useful warning for the presenter to listen out for the final words on the tape, indicated as 'out words' on the cue sheet that accompanies the package. The 'out words' of a trail, public service announcement or commercial on cart are written on the label, along with a reference to any other audio effects that may end the item.

Special events programming

STRUCTURED and scheduled programming at least provide broadcasters with the security of routine. Additional challenges arise when pressures are abnormal and the usual weekday schedule gives way to the seemingly one-off radio event.

Special events in radio may take any number of forms and arguably it is their unique nature – their 'specialness' – that makes them difficult to categorise or fit into an existing framework of procedure. For our purposes, a 'special event' is defined as any event creating pressures on a radio station that are beyond the norm. Such events fall into two broad categories: those events which are predictable and those which are not.

The *predictable* special event is placed against a future date in the diary, a date that marks the culmination of a carefully planned schedule of activities, such that everybody in the station knows what to do when the day arrives. An obvious example is the charity radio campaign, which may be undertaken exclusively by the radio station or may form part of a wider, multi-media event, such as the BBC's *Children in Need* campaign. Other predictable events include royal visits, elections, public transport strikes (assuming that advance notice has been given), live broadcasts from major national events staged in the area (trade shows, sports meetings, conferences, etc.), OB events promoting the radio station itself and, of course, Christmas.

Special events which fit into the category of the *unpredictable* or spontaneous include major breaking news stories – a royal death, an abdication or the resignation of a prime minister – and events which have an immediate and significant impact on the day-to-day lives of listeners, such as a fall of heavy snow or a major incident in the area affecting work, shopping or travel routines. For a radio station to respond

213

effectively to spontaneous events, it is necessary to have a plan of action already worked out such that all personnel know what to do or at least to whom they should refer when the need arises.

Planning the predictable – the charity event

A RADIO station's campaign for the 'predicted' special event, such as the charity radiothon, can be summarised as a three-phase operation: (a) *planning* – organising staff and resources to ensure that everything is in the best possible position for the event and the broadcast to work; (b) *promoting* – generating excitement and public enthusiasm for the event through a build-up or 'count-down' on air, based on a campaign of trails and presenter links; and (c) *performing* – making it happen on the day. When fundraising is involved, a fourth phase is *paying off* – or literally paying out – distributing the money and recording material for next year's event on how it is being used. Broadcasting organisations normally invite bids for the money, to be considered by a formally and legally constituted committee.

The publicity and public relations values for a station to stage a major charity event – and to adjust output and schedule to focus on that event – are obvious. The station enhances its role as a pivotal and active institution within the community it serves and it demonstrably represents the community interests through its mobilisation of 'good nature' to help 'less fortunate' community members. It also enhances its own visibility through events – OBs, sponsored walks, stunts, public appearances of celebrities – and hence through other news media covering these events.

Broadcasters are aware of equally good reasons for not committing themselves to the risks and expenses that would arise from a special fundraising event on air. Stations that are targeted at narrow niche markets, for example, are not in the best position to generate the scale of response that a major station with popular appeal might expect. Even stations that do attract a reasonably high proportion of listeners within an editorial area will weigh up the likely benefits, in terms of maintaining that appeal or developing a potentially 'exploitable' market sector, against the risks of negative reaction from existing listeners and overall donor fatigue leading to disappointing results. As with every production technique and programme structure available to the station team, the decision to run with a co-ordinated charity broadcast event is based on a judgement that takes into account the station's market position, its working objectives and the extent to which the team believes that the risks can be minimised and are worth taking.

The main benefit of the charity event in the establishment and reinforcement of a positive radio experience is that it demonstrates in the most effective way the role of a radio station as a link between individual listeners and the 'here and now' of the world they inhabit. Devices such as the radiothon actively call on the participation of listeners and construct a positive association between the station and a 'caring' and proactive community (or nation) of listeners. They turn on its head the notion of listening to the radio as a passive experience of consumption and suggest instead that each listener is able to make a real impact on the outcome of the event. This is further enhanced through collaboration between the station and other local media or business organisations or, in the case of the BBC's *Children in Need* and *Comic Relief* appeals, the local station's role within a nationwide attempt by the entire Corporation to raise millions of pounds.

Listener response is encouraged through the 'special' nature of the event. The 'rules' of conventional broadcasting are subverted – special programmes are scheduled in, presenters come out of the studio and into the community, a complex OB network comes into operation and many listeners who contribute to the fundraising are rewarded with access to the airwaves. The point of connection between the radio text and the listener – the edge – lies in the drama of broadcasting, away from the schedule and into the unknown.

The 'planning' phase of a broadcast charity campaign involves all aspects of a radio station's operation. For BBC stations, *Children in Need* calls for co-ordinated activities in programming, news, engineering and staffing. In addition, ILR stations organising a concerted fundraising event involve their advertising departments and encourage advertisers to play a full role in the campaign, for example through sponsorship.

The choice of the date and the duration of the broadcast event can have a significant impact on its ultimate success. *Children in Need* is staged for one weekday only – a Friday in November before the Christmas promotion takes over the airwaves. The campaign in fact runs for considerably longer with donations accepted at radio stations, banks and building societies across the country throughout the year. Local radio events can run for an entire weekend, or even a week, with regular bulletins on fundraising progress, or packages on specific moneyraising ventures, inserted within the normal output schedule. Nevertheless the focus of one day in which to raise as much money as possible constitutes a 'challenge' that reinforces a community spirit of 'we can do it' and promotes a strong sense of achievement for everyone involved if the target is met. In fact the radio charity event offers one of the few opportunities to make a large number of listeners feel not just 'good' but elated as a result of being tuned in to a broadcast. The 'warm glow' shared by station staff and listeners when a target has been achieved can create a genuine moment of bonding between them.

Radio stations cannot hope to engage sufficient public interest in charity events from within the safety of a studio. The strategy of focusing the event into a reasonably short period of time necessitates an investment of time for careful preparation of the logistics and ensuring that all broadcasting equipment available to the station – as well as station personnel and helpers – are in place to maximise coverage of events and OBs across the editorial area. Crews in radio cars and vans, and individuals with portable recorders and backpacks are allocated areas and provided with lists of events that are known to be happening and are likely to produce interesting broadcast material. Furthermore, OB units are strategically placed to increase the station's chances of covering the unexpected, or arriving at one which is reaching its point of drama: the release of balloons into the air, the arrival of a bagpipes band, the toppling over of a pile of coins.

Charity events are very labour-intensive and, as with technical resources, decisions are needed on how to get optimum use out of human resources. As a rule, radio staff involved in major charity events find themselves doing jobs for which they have not been fully trained. Journalists become live presenters; studio presenters become roving correspondents or sponsored participants in the walk, run, bike-ride or any other event that might be staged to make the campaign visible. Student helpers, receptionists and station management will find themselves roped in to take on tasks they would not normally expect to do – driving off in a radio car at short notice to cover a sponsored horse-and-cart surfing event put on by the Young Farmers group, receiving a generous cheque from a local supermarket manager well versed in the arts of public relations and, most important of all, receiving the 'pledgeline' telephone calls.

The 'promotion' phase, leading up to the event, emphasises the unity and homogeneity of the station's output. Every programme and every presenter is involved in the campaign – promoting, trailing, discussing on phone-ins – to ensure that the station's full range of listeners are aware of the date, time, target, what they can do to help and how to pledge money. The event relies on public participation and well-planned promotion helps to reduce the risk of a public relations flop. If the campaign is based on a single event such as a sponsored walk following a set route, its success depends on people turning up to take part, spectate and give money, even in the rain. If the campaign involves stunts and fundraising events by the public – sponsored shaves, human jukeboxes, collection-tin rattlers on pub crawls – information on what is happening often only comes through during the final stages of preparation, when listeners finally become caught up in the atmosphere generated by advance publicity.

Mobilising and encouraging public involvement is essential not only to raise cash but to maintain powerful, lively and engaging output. This means all available OB units reporting on the fundraising events or keeping up with the participants of the single sponsored event. Their output is channelled through the studio with a presenter (or two) at base to co-ordinate the output. Once the 'performing' phase has been reached, the presenter's challenge is to keep up the interest for however long the broadcast takes when there is essentially only one story to tell – people are out there raising money.

For the sake of preventing disorientation for listeners, well-controlled presenter links provide structure in a broadcasting environment in which everything can seem to be going crazy. They include announcements – or cues for other people's announcements – of further donations in a step-by-step build-up to a clearly defined target. If fundraising stunts have been organised, their perpetrators line-up for their fifteen seconds of fame and their voices evoke a fast-moving montage of bizarre images as they describe what they did and how much they raised.

Moments of drama and tension are constructed through the placing of certain items at pre-announced times – a particularly extravagant stunt, the appearance of a VIP celebrity, or the final announcement of the total cash raised. Inclusion of such items, and the trailing of them, prevents the broadcast from drifting aimlessly along. Possibly, listeners are more tolerant of the 'craziness' of the event if they are regularly reassured that things go back to normal after a deadline. This deadline itself may heighten the dramatic impact of the campaign – will donations beat last year's total? Or will the campaign raise a milestone figure (thousand or million)? Throughout the event, presenters have regular access to a 'totaliser' – a computer monitor giving an up-to-date figure for money received or pledged so far. Thus a simple formula is in place for dramatic listening – the total increases as the deadline looms. Stations may even have special jingles prepared to accentuate the drama – fifty minutes to go! thirty minutes to go! – as the presenter announces the latest figure on the totaliser.

This provides an opportunity for stagecraft and manipulation which the skilled presenter would not resist to maximise the impact of the broadcast. Only he and the producer know exactly how much money is recorded on the totaliser and they would not be averse to holding back announcements of targets being reached or exceeded, or of particularly generous donations being made, until the last few minutes of the broadcast.

The radio team may be totally committed to the charity cause but listeners do not necessarily share this sense of involvement and tire quickly of continuous cheering, applause and announcements of how much cash has been raised. Other items are therefore incorporated alongside these announcements providing texture, contrast and direction to the output – recorded packages on how last year's money was spent, records and live music, interviews with beneficiaries, celebrities and local dignitaries involved in the campaign, and so on. The inclusion of professionally produced packages in the output not only allows presenters to sort out information for the next live link, but also reinforces the station's responsible approach. This is a point worth emphasising – after all, the station is collecting and looking after listeners' money.

While the 'paying off' phase depends on the performance during the broadcast itself, the station or broadcast organisation can achieve even more through extensive forward planning. The more people are involved, both within the organisation and the wider community, the better the chance of raising a spectacular amount of money. The broadcast charity event stands comparison with a major military operation. The characteristic spontaneity and immediacy of the output relies on weeks of preparation including the drawing up of complex staff rosters, the allocation of resources, the preparation of pre-recorded material, the booking of programme guests and a comprehensive range of contingency plans.

Elections

AS broadcasting events, elections also frequently give rise to special programming arrangements for many radio stations. General elections are called at least once every five years; councillors are elected every four years in most of England, Wales and Northern Ireland (with some districts electing a third of their councillors each year); regional councillors and district councillors in Scotland are elected every four years but on an alternating two-year cycle. European Parliament elections also take place every five years. And there are by-elections. Some years are fallow, but more years than not will include at least one election.

The public service role of the BBC involves extensive reporting of the democratic process, hence all BBC local radio stations are involved in election coverage. ILR stations decide at a local level on the extent of coverage they should give. Elections can have an impact on radio output in three ways. First, stations must decide on whether special programming is required in the period leading up to the election. The schedules are affected not only by the campaign itself but also by the Representation of the People Act 1983, a complicated piece of legislation which sets out broadcasting organisations' obligation to provide a balance of broadcast statements by candidates in any election. This obligation does not extend to two ways with political correspondents, interviews with candidates' agents or even comments by candidates themselves on issues not related to their own constituencies or wards.

The second impact of elections on radio output arises through the announcement of the results themselves. Local stations in particular must form a judgement on whether their audiences would expect comprehensive coverage of the count and results and whether the stations themselves are in a position to provide this service. There is even a principle at stake as to which station is the first to announce a key result, with BBC local radio, for example, vying with BBC television.

The third impact that elections have on programming is in the aftermath. Just as local radio audiences would expect a local orientation to the live coverage of the count – providing a depth and application of local knowledge that could not reasonably be expected on national coverage – so the principles of local democracy would be served by a subsequent analysis of the new political map and how that might affect the lives of people in the editorial area.

The campaign

A particular facet of radio's role and identity is highlighted as soon as an election campaign is under way. Like all mass media, radio is part of the democratic process and functions for many listeners as a reference point and source of information which may well determine their voting decisions. Much of the rationale behind programming and programme content of many stations during this period is based on notions of listeners' democratic interests, the accountability of political parties and the promises and perspectives of would-be councillors, MPs and MEPs. The station becomes not only the disseminator of news but also the forum for discussion.

The question of who sets the agenda for radio's election campaign coverage indicates a tension within the terms of reference that individual stations operate by. In their constant drive to connect with a targeted audience group, a station would presumably represent and discuss those election campaign issues that are most relevant to that group's needs and interests. But in the interest of dynamic, compelling and topical coverage of campaign events, a station could find itself inadvertently dancing to the tunes of the skilful campaign organisers of all parties involved – for example, through a perceived obligation on the newsroom to cover a visit to the area by a party grandee or a focus on a theme determined by one of the parties at their regular news conferences, such as law and order, transport or the economy.

This is a dilemma faced by all media organisations and for local radio is usually dealt with by concentrating on local issues. Thus an interview during a general election campaign with a leading government or opposition spokesperson on health or education would address the future of a *local* hospital or teaching resources available at a *local* school. Broad policy issues are presented and discussed in the more concrete and, for listeners, familiar terms relating to the institutions and life experiences in that editorial area. An even sharper focus is applied to tangible local issues in council election campaigns; the talk is not of political philosophy but roadworks, nursery provision, support for local arts, the quality of local sports centres, the frequency of refuse collections, and so on.

Local radio also provides an opportunity for voters to set their own agenda through the phone-in. Radio's democratic function is particularly visible when representatives of all parties are invited in turn to respond to listeners' questions. The incisiveness of some of these questions and the politicians' tactics in dealing with them can also produce engrossing and entertaining radio – some might say a worthwhile objective when dealing with the normally dry issues of policies and manifesto promises.

As far as broadcast media are concerned, the campaign finishes the moment the polls are open. From then on, reporters are restricted to comments on whether the poll is light or heavy, weather conditions and any other point that will not be construed as political propaganda. This restriction ends when the polls close (10pm for general elections; 9pm for local elections) although the challenge between this moment and the announcement of the first result is to provide an interesting build-up without rash speculation (that could be regretted later) or waffle.

The count

The main problem that local stations have in programming for the election night itself is a logistical one – do they have the people and equipment to cover the results of *all* the contested seats in the editorial area? BBC stations aim to have someone positioned to report back from every count in their area, but the resource implications of this vary across the country. Metropolitan district council elections may cover ten seats at one count, while county council elections in rural areas may have separate counts for individual seats. The counting of votes in general elections can also be widespread or involve several constituencies concentrated on one venue. In the 1992 general election, for example, results for all Birmingham seats were counted at the city's National Indoor Arena.

The turnout for council elections is usually lower than for general elections and fewer people feel the need to stay tuned in through the night for immediate news of the results. Instead, the biggest radio audience for council election results is usually during the morning after the count and the priority for all radio stations is to have the results ready by then. General election results, however, constitute a continuous series of major breaking news stories which reflect not only the political climate of the country but also the fortunes and misfortunes of many famous personalities – heroes *and* villains – plus a vast source of human-interest material on eccentric candidates, campaign events, family backgrounds and minority political parties. The professional priorities for every station in absorbing, processing and announcing this material are to be accurate, give a clear explanation and be the first to tell the story.

The returning officer's announcement of the results for a strongly contested constituency can form the basis for dramatic live radio, allowing listeners to share in the elation or disappointment of the outcome. Many BBC local radio stations have a permanent remote studio installed in their local town halls or civic centres, often the venues for counts. This enables stations to link directly to the event and carry interviews and commentary by a reporter with little difficulty. Alternatively, a station may set up an OB unit at the venue, or book a dedicated landline from, say, British Telecom, enabling them to carry studio-quality sound from the venue to the station. Live coverage of result announcements can be an expensive and labour-intensive matter, with each venue attended by a technician or engineer and an assistant acting as a 'gofor', rounding up candidates and bringing them to the interview microphone.

If counts are taking place in a number of venues spread across the editorial area, stations are unlikely to have the resources to give each one the same extent of coverage. Additional staff are brought in from the 'fringes' of a station's staff – students, trainees, part-time broadcasters, etc. – to support mainstream staff located at each of the local counts.

Back at the base studio, a team is busy poring over the results as they come in: a presenter, producer, technical director and results tabulator might make up the crew that provide the 'election special' broadcast. The presenter may be accompanied on air by a local independent political commentator, or even a panel of local political representatives, to discuss results and their implications. The station may also feed results into their own computer – or have access to a national computer network – to calculate swings or compare party performances in different areas.

The aftermath

The decision to be made by a local radio station for the period immediately following the election is whether different programming arrangements are required to analyse and comment on the results or whether this can be accomplished within the station's existing news and features provision. Continuing the point that local radio has a democratic function, it is clearly an appropriate medium for listeners to gain access to the issues and new personalities involved. Detailed statistical information, such as results, swings, majorities and turnout for every constituency or ward in the editorial area, makes poor listening and is therefore best left to the local press.

Among the points taken into account by stations for post-election coverage is whether results in the area give rise to new or important issues for that area – if, for example, there was a major swing from one party to another which will dramatically change the political complexion of the area, or if a particularly controversial candidate was elected. Against such considerations are questions of whether election fatigue has now established itself among listeners and the extent to which the audience of a particular station sees itself as politically active or orientated.

Stations covering widespread editorial areas may run the risk of losing their connection with a substantial part of their audience through concentrating on the result implications of individual constituencies. A partial remedy is to allocate a 'window' in the programme schedule for focused 'local analysis' programmes to be broadcast on split frequency – for example, covering the north and south of the region on different frequencies allocated to the station.

Outside broadcasts

LIVE OB programmes come under the heading of 'predictable special events' in that they create additional pressures for the production team but they are carefully planned in advance. The term 'outside broadcast' refers to programmes that are presented live from any location other than a normal studio. It does not normally apply to items inserted into a studio-based programme from, say, a radio car. Access to a more fully equipped radio vehicle (van, lorry, roadshow vehicle – see p. 110) enables the presenter to maintain reasonable control over the pace and style of the programme and address listeners via a high-quality line, although support from a silent technical operator is still needed in the main base studio to play CDs, jingles, trails and commercials.

Whether a station's product is music or talk output, OBs play an important part in branding strategy; they enhance the station's visibility within the editorial area and establish unequivocally the target audience which the station is setting out to address as well as the nature of the relationship between station and audience. A station that focuses on the community and the inherent interest in local people's lives and stories may include *vox pop* interviews in an OB to create – if the paraphrase may be used – a neighbourhood talking to itself.[4] Another station, with output more geared to pop music, fun and entertainment, may run challenges and competitions with members of a young audience at an OB roadshow or concert.

16 **_The outside broadcast_**: the presenter is using a backpack in a rucksack for greater comfort – it was necessary to climb a lot of stairs during the programme when this photo was taken. Here he takes an opportunity, while a record is being played at base, to confer with his producer on the running order for the next few minutes of this live programme.

The presenter wears a BBC and station logo on his sweater. Branding calls for visibility – the public can see the station team member at work and realise that an actual broadcast is taking place.

The presenter can hear cue through his headphones. Note that the producer also wears miniature headphones connected to a 'check-set' which enables her to hear the programme as it is going out.

17 **_Keeping the channels open_**: _out on location with the programme presenter, the producer quickly jots down up-to-date travel information received from base via a mobile telephone. This provides a line of communication for the programme team, alternative to talkback. The presenter is only given the information when it is needed and does not have the headphones filled with unnecessary and distracting talkback during the broadcast._
There are two basic but important points to note here. First, the producer is dressed to keep warm. Second, she has to write clearly as the presenter sometimes has to sight-read her notes on air. Often, students' and trainees' first taste of broadcasting involves helping out on OBs at the mercy of the elements and where there is no typewriter at hand.

More than this, however, OBs bring a distinctive sound into the radio experience. Birdsong, traffic or the cheering of fans of a visiting pop group – all are part of the 'real' outside world as opposed to the functional and comparatively clinical environment of the studio. Broadcasters coping with wind, rain, unexpected background noise, or revelling in sunshine, or being genuinely surprised by something they see or someone who turns up – these all form part of the essence of the live and often spontaneous radio event whereby listeners across the transmission 'footprint' can share in the immediacy of events at any single location within (or even beyond) that area.

18 ***Interviewing in transit****: the presenter here is live on air talking to a member of the public. The producer is in close attendance – not only keeping an eye on proceedings but also listening to ensure the interview sounds good. Often, in these circumstances, passing drivers with their car radios tuned in give a 'toot' on their horns – emphasising the genuine live and immediate quality of output in a way that cannot be achieved in a studio.*

The signal from the presenter's backpack is transmitted via a nearby radio van to base. In this programme, the presenter is covering the length of the street. Therefore, when the next record plays, the van will move to a new location, further down the street, to ensure the presenter remains within range of the receiver.

One of the main purposes of an OB, therefore, is to bring the personalities of the radio station away from the 'safe haven' of the studio and out among the people they are talking to. The OB enables the public to put a face to the voice and reduce the 'gap' between the participants in radio's discourse – speaker and listener. For a local radio station, the OB breaks down possible notions that the station's perspective of the area is restricted to that viewed from a particular town or city-centre location. For a national station, the OB helps to counter any 'London-centric' view of the United Kingdom and provides a variety of geographic and cultural focal points. It can also provide good public relations and opportunities for members of the public to be included in output as interviewees or competition contestants. Thus BBC Radio 1 tours British resorts and locations each summer with its Roadshow, whilst many specific BBC national radio programmes are broadcast from conferences, festivals, concert halls, sports venues, places of worship, factories, schools, prisons or any location that focuses listeners' attention on the heart of current events, issues and cultural activities wherever they may be taking place.

19 *A more leisurely OB vehicle?* *This shot was taken during a live programme, part of an extended series of OBs from a narrowboat touring the canal system in the editorial area. The aerial to the right sends a signal via a radio van (not in shot) to base. Here the boat was moored, but sometimes the van has to relocate while a record is being played, to keep within range if the boat is on the move during transmission.*

This OB proved anything but leisurely and very complex to organise. Staff travelling to and from base had to know exactly where the boat was located. Signals from every location needed to be 'site tested' in advance to ensure that they could be transmitted without interference. To make matters worse, the aerial had to be lowered at every bridge in between links!

This was nevertheless a successful two-week series and an investment of effort that paid off. Not only did it provide, for this station, an important opportunity to concentrate on rural issues, it also accessed an unusual audience and provided a focal point for marginalised communities. The series also enabled the station staff to meet more of their audience face-to-face.

In continuous flow programming, the presenter's location at a site away from the studio provides opportunities for a variety of links, 'slice of life' interviews with people who live or work nearby and commentary on events and scenery. Such output creates the impression of spontaneous broadcasting with passers-by stopping to chat with the presenter while the programme simply reflects a typical day at this location. Of course, nothing is further from the truth. The impact and interest value of OBs depend on advance preparation rather than a gamble that something or someone interesting will come along at the time of the broadcast. The location is researched for stories – from the topical to folklore – and people who can tell them effectively. It is worth mentioning at this point that broadcasters recognise, as an important benefit of OBs, their likelihood of providing a wealth of stories and contacts to be used in future programme items.

Ways of conveying the character and atmosphere of the location itself, whether a village green or a factory gate, are also considered. More pragmatic concerns in the research of a location are whether it is technically feasible in terms of signal strength, how much space there is to set up equipment and perform in, and whether there are any possible health and safety problems.[5] The station should also consider the inconvenience that may be caused to local residents or businesses by their turning up with a large vehicle, running cables everywhere, blocking off normal access routes and generally making a noise.

The essential quality of an OB presenter-led programme is that the presenter must *sound* as if he is interacting with the location and identifying its landmarks, views and overall atmosphere. In fact, technological developments make it more feasible for the presenter to be mobile and not tied to a studio desk. The radio microphone removes the need for a cable to act as an umbilical cord between the presenter and the radio vehicle. As alternatives to the talkback system – which may distract the presenter by filling the headphones with voices whilst he is talking on air – the cellphone and mobile fax machine offer excellent lines of communication between the OB team and the main base studio, enabling the producer, on location with the presenter, to receive last-minute cues or up-to-the-minute news and information that need to be incorporated in the programme.

One clear benefit of radio's ability to move out of the confines of the studio is the opportunity to broadcast (or at least record) live music. By turning up at a nearby music festival or concert and linking in directly with the sound system used in the venue, a radio station provides airtime to local bands, choirs and orchestras and reflects the specific regard that a listening community holds for its *own* musicians as opposed to international recording artists.

Local radio stations are particularly keen on broadcasting school music and this especially at Christmas. This is not just for its artistic merit (which could be considerable) but more cynically for the fact that for every child in a school concert, there is a potential group of proud listeners – parents, relatives, neighbours – who tune in and may just stay tuned in.

While OBs in general provide strong platforms for the immediacy and spontaneity of live programmes, they do not preclude the use of any of the production techniques that a programme maker may wish to incorporate in studio-based output, such as phone-ins, links with other locations or even packages previously recorded at the same location to maintain a continuity in overall sound and atmosphere. In programming terms, the OB represents another place for the presenter to work from, which for creative and strategic reasons presents itself as a more appropriate location than the studio for a particular programme covering a particular event or point of listener interest.

Programming for the unpredictable event

FINALLY in this chapter, we consider a situation that most tests the skills and adaptability of station staff – having to put together at the last moment a completely different programme from the one that was scheduled. This could happen for a wide range of reasons: a royal death, a major disaster or accident within – or involving people from – a station's editorial area, a bomb scare or bad weather. These represent the type of event that highlights radio's unique role as a medium: the consistent voice that keeps everybody in touch with reality at a time of crisis.

As far as a well-managed radio station is concerned, no event is really unpredictable. In principle, all scenarios that would call on the station to produce special programming have already been considered and plans for dealing with the situation are already in place, right down to the choice of solemn music to play if the Queen or Prime Minister were assassinated.

To illustrate the extent and detail of planning for the 'unpredictable' that a radio station undertakes – and the rationale behind it – we consider a situation that is often experienced in the UK: the sudden heavy snowfall that brings all transport grinding to a halt and always seems to take everyone else by surprise.

Dropping into 'snow mode'

As snow starts to fall, radio's audience goes up. Drivers want to know the chances of completing their journeys, parents want to find out if their children's schools are opening. Television covers too broad an area to give the level of detail that enables people to make individual travelling decisions. Furthermore, the structure and scheduling of many television programmes precludes the continuous flow of updated information of roads closed, events cancelled and trains delayed. Local radio, on the other hand, with its strip programming format and live presenter-led output, is the ideal medium to keep people informed of such developments.

The onset of heavy snow need not catch a station team unawares. Its weather forecasting arrangements will be based on a contract drawn up between that station and the regional meteorological office. If bad weather is on its way, the radio station will be forewarned. Satellite technology can give notice, sometimes up to twelve hours, that conditions such as heavy snow are likely. Once the information is passed on to the station, it immediately drops into 'snow mode' – the routine has been planned in detail and can now be put into practice.

An important practical consideration is ensuring that the station itself is staffed, even if every other institution and workplace in the area is closed down. Many radio stations are geared up for the hardest winter with a stock of food and drink, campbeds, sleeping bags and the 'snowfile' or 'snowbox', where all vital information that staff are likely to need is kept in one place. This includes all vital phone numbers (home and work) for contacts in the local electricity, gas and water companies, senior engineers for local authorities, all transport organisations, the police, fire brigade, ambulance and other emergency services plus all names and phone numbers of radio station staff members themselves.

Staff who happen to be in the station building when the blizzard starts may be well catered for but are expected to carry on working. Those who are at home at the time are also given no reprieve. They may be instructed to stay put but to keep the information coming in on the effects of the weather in their home area. Or they may be asked to demonstrate the intrepid spirit for which radio reporters are renowned and to try and reach the station somehow – if not by skiing then perhaps by hitching a lift off a snowplough!

Particular problem areas that radio stations deal with in bad weather conditions are schools, the elderly and hospitals. Local stations keep a list of head teachers' and senior staff names for every school in their editorial area. Not every school closes when the snow starts to fall; it is therefore important for the station to establish an agreed method of identification when school heads phone in to confirm that information they receive of a closure is genuine and not the ruse of a mischievous pupil.

Presenters have access to a stock of advice on care for – and self-help by – the elderly in cold weather. Frequent reminders are made for neighbours to check that elderly residents are keeping warm and fed. Radio stations are run by a high proportion of young staff who may themselves need reminding of the value of the service they are providing to older people and that radio can literally save lives. Information on hospitals and how their work is affected by the weather forms another important aspect of radio's emergency output. Poor weather may lead to cancellation of treatment for outpatients and even of certain acute operations.

Any information needed by station staff on these important services may be obtained by referring to details provided in the 'snowbox' or 'snowfile'. The contacts listed here are those in the best position, and with sufficient authority within their organisations, to keep the station updated. Nevertheless, the station cannot rely solely on their information to tell listeners everything they might need to know. Radio demonstrates its strength in bad weather and other unusual situations, not only through its capacity to relate to the 'here and now' of local conditions by providing the latest information in sufficient detail, but also through keeping the channels open for people to feed news in.

The best sources of information that a village has been cut off by a snowdrift are the villagers themselves. Apart from seeming to paralyse all vital services (with the exception of radio!), snow has an interesting effect on people – it evokes a national characteristic sometimes referred to as the spirit of the Blitz, a sense that 'we're all in this together'. As soon as a presenter asks listeners to phone in their news of cancellations, road blockages, and so on, the telephones in the station immediately light up and sufficent staff are needed to take the calls, verify them and pass on the information to the presenters.

An efficient system is needed to handle this flood of information. Again, this is planned in advance and normally involves a pro-forma in which details received from the public are set out, with all relevant questions asked when that information comes through. For example, if an event is cancelled, where was it to happen? at what time? are there alternative arrangements? who gave the information? what can people do to find out more or to check when the event will take place?

Programme presenters must not only provide this information clearly but also regularly. Audience turnover is high and key information has to be repeated. This gives rise to two presentation challenges.

First, there is the difficulty of confirming to listeners that emergency information announced earlier still applies. If listeners are told at 8.30am, for example, that a school is closed, do they assume that it is still closed at, say, 2.30pm? Information given over the air cannot be treated as standing until further notice, as many listeners will have missed the original announcement. Stations often deal with this by trailing set times when up-dates will be given on all schools in a particular area.

This, however, highlights a second challenge to the presenter's art. The fact that the radio station is providing reams of public service information should not negate its fundamental role to connect with listeners and construct a particular form of listening experience. Audiences expect to hear long lists of cancellation announcements at railway stations; radio stations on the other hand should be creating a link of shared experience between listeners and the rest of the stranded world. Announcements of closures and blocked roads should still form part of a fresh and exciting listening experience. Presenters seek unusual ways of reading out the same information plus material to 'humanise' this information – stories of stranded communities and how they are coping, babies born in front rooms, animals rescued, lambs born in the snow, appeals for help, unusual tips and recipes for keeping warm.

Programme makers may use adverse weather to their advantage by applying new and related ideas for features and programmes – challenges to children to build the biggest snowman in the area, tales of local heroes performing rescues or helping neighbours, stories of 'villain' organisations neglecting to grit roads or delaying claims for home insulation with red tape, and so on. Thus, in addition to providing an essential point of reference and source of information for its listeners, the voice of radio establishes itself as a focus for the 'Blitz' spirit, enabling the isolated (perhaps even stranded) listener to share in the listening community's response to the elements.

The art of the extemporary

A radio station's ability to react instantly to major changes in listeners' reality provides an effective illustration of an important quality intrinsic to the text of radio and the nature of the experience that it engenders. Perhaps the best way to emphasise this quality and its crucial role in the creation and structuring of the radio experience is to treat radio as an *organic* medium. In other words, its output is not just 'live' – it is 'living'.

This highlights the significance of the point where this book began – radio's intimate address to the *individual* listening experience of each member of its audience. Our characterisation of radio has reflected what could be construed as an anatomical model: building up the component parts, the items of communications technology, the individual production techniques, and discussing the different ways in which these are combined to create a particular form of programming. But this body has a 'lifeforce' – the pure moment of communication borne of one voice on the airwaves. It is this, rather than the technology or the 'rulebook' strategies, that underpins radio's *connection* with each of its listeners. In other words, that moment relates to the 'niche' in the listening 'market' and the particular and idiosyncratic forms of social and cultural experience that constitute listeners' lives and lifestyles.

The instant mobilisation of radio's resources and capacities as soon as the snow starts to fall is as clear an illustration as any of radio's ability to relate to the social environment in which it operates – as an organism. We have argued (pp. 186–9) that the 'edge' to radio's product is its point of contact with the listener at each unique 'here and now' point in that listener's ever-metamorphosing cultural experience. This edge would not be achievable if the business of making radio programmes were simply one of putting the resources and production techniques together in slightly different ways while conforming unflinchingly to formats and style policies. The essence of live – 'living' – radio lies in the responsiveness of its programming to the very conditions (weather conditions, traffic conditions, political conditions, cultural conditions) that prevail and that are experienced by listeners at the moment at which they interact with radio's text.

The radio experience therefore depends on the elements of spontaneity, immediacy and responsiveness in programmes and programming. Clearly, these elements can thrive in live broadcasts, particularly in interactive programme forms based on the phone-in, but their presence is intrinsic to all radio – even those stations whose output is based on sequence programming schedules or otherwise includes extended recorded items. The potential remains for the microphone fader and phone lines to be opened and contingency procedures to be followed whenever the need arises for a working information network to be activated instantly.

It is when this network operates to its fullest and most interactive extent, with equal participation from broadcasters and the listening body, that the listening experience is shown to transcend the mere act of consuming. Instead, it is shaped by radio's capacity to produce an instant web of communication channels between stations on a network, outside sources and listeners themselves playing a vital role as contributors to the radio experience in its ultimate form.

Activities and points for discussion

1 As a group, assume that you are a consortium planning to launch a new radio station in a busy metropolitan area and that you are preparing an application to the Radio Authority for a licence. The main purpose of the station is to keep travellers and commuters informed on the up-to-the-minute conditions on road, rail and air – in effect, an all-day travel bulletin with other travel-related programming scheduled for non-peak hours plus some music. You have been in consultation with all major transport organisations in that area – railway companies, bus companies, airlines and airports – as well as the major utilities (gas, water, electricity, telephone companies whose work involves occasionally digging up the roads), the AA, RAC and the Department of Transport itself.

First discuss how you would elevate the humble travel bulletin into a complete breakfast-time programme. What contacts and resources would you need and what forms and formats would you apply to transform a constant supply of travel information into an interesting and engaging listening experience? Agree on and draw up a sample programme plan for the hours of 6–10 am.

Then consider the station's overall programming policy. How would the rest of the day's schedule be organised? What would the station broadcast on Saturdays and Sundays? How would you characterise the station's overall style and sound? What music would it feature?

2 Obtain copies of newspapers, *Radio Times* or *TV Times* from the late 1960s, 1970s and 1980s and make a detailed comparison of weekday programme schedules for stations such as Radios 1 and 4, Capital or a local independent station. To what extent have schedules and programmes remained consistent over the years – if not in title and personality, then in style and format? Where there are significant differences, to what extent could these be explained in terms of changing lifestyles, male and female employment, availability of other media or other social, cultural and economic factors? (This may prove a useful discussion point with experienced broadcasters and experienced listeners.)

3 As a group, assume you work as a production team for a local talk and music station. Research of your audience's reaction to previous coverage indicates a positive response to the idea of basing a live, pre-senter-led programme on a single theme (for example, cars and taxis, as suggested in this chapter). Conduct a 'brainstorming' discussion to come up quickly with a list of at least twelve theme ideas. Choose three and work in sub-groups to explore how each one of these could be applied to a mid-morning programme. Draw up a list of possible features, live interviews, competitions and choices of music to reflect that theme. Form the main group again to compare and build on your ideas.

4 You represent a group of residents who have been awarded a temporary licence to run Friend FM, a community radio station to serve those living in a recently refurbished riverside area in the middle of a large city. Run-down old factories and characterless blocks of flats have been demolished to make room for an open plan, residential area with distinctive, high-quality housing, parks and all amenities. It is a new neighbourhood and people living here are only beginning to get to know each other. Therefore, the station provides a point of reference, informs them of local events, features local personalities and even carries advertising by local businesses.

Friend FM does not go for a 'glossy', heavily produced sound – just a simple format of people talking combined with a few choice CD tracks. It has proved very popular as a station that cares for and reflects the genuine concerns and interests of its audience. For this reason, it has been nominated for a national broadcasting award for this year's best new radio service and is widely tipped to win. In groups of three or four, script and record a typical Friend FM item (an extract of ninety seconds to two minutes) that could be played at the awards ceremony in the event that the station does win its category. Justify your approach in terms of how your idea best characterises and captures the essence of the station.

5 Select a local or national station and conduct an analysis of its content to compare its weekday and weekend programming. Your analysis should be based on a study of the station's programme schedule and listening to its actual output. It should be based on both *quantitative* and *qualitative* factors. Quantitative factors include: average length of programme, music-speech ratio, proportion of airtime given over to recorded and live output, maximum length of link, average length of individual programme item, etc. (you may identify your own categories for quantitative analysis). Qualitative factors include: style of address adopted by presenter, characterisation of overall sound (busy, up-tempo, steady, powerful, etc.) and strategies employed to relate to a particular target audience.

Present the findings of your analysis in a short talk supported by recordings of extracts to illustrate your points.

6 As a sports reporter for a radio station serving your area, you have been asked by your producer to record a weekly 4–5 minute feature on a sport that attracts a following in your editorial area but is not widely reported. Each feature will be broadcast during a regular slot on mid-Saturday morning. Conduct some research in your area to produce a list of at least five sports that you could cover and find out the name and telephone number of at least one contact for each sport.

Draw up a list of questions you would use in an interview recorded for each package.

If possible, select one of these contacts and record the interview. If you have access to editing facilities, produce the package.

8 Accountability

A RADIO station's *orientation* to its listeners involves elements of both constancy and change. Aspects that remain constant in the radio–listener relationship are the profile of that audience group or market segment and the style policy that the station adopts to maximise its appeal and relevance to that group. Aspects that change are contextual – the social and cultural climates in which listeners' interaction with radio takes place. The radio text both constructs and reflects each listener's life experience within these climates. It delineates a particular mode of experience that the listener must adopt in order to connect her personal, individual experience with the consensual terms of reference that underpin the text of radio and its forms of listener address. This text is itself integral to a changing cultural climate and it establishes its bond with listeners as a commodity that constantly renews itself to maintain its symbiosis with the consumer.

The relationship is admittedly complex (arguably like all human relationships), but there is a further dimension to be recognised and understood, one that provides an explanation and rationale for the bond between radio station and listener. This aspect of radio may be summed up as its *accountability* to its audience.

Accountability is apparent in the formal sense of laws and statutory obligations – issues that always feature highly in the training agenda for would-be broadcasters and journalists. It is further manifested in ways that are not so explicitly articulated but are of equal significance. These are to do with the discipline of broadcasting and the responsibility that each professional broadcaster recognises to produce the optimum radio experience. Radio cannot function effectively if broadcasters have to constantly 'refer upwards' in order to produce programmes. Neither can it allow space for broadcasters who select the easiest option – as opposed to the most interesting – in order to 'fill' as much airtime as possible with material that meets the minimum quality standards. The pressure to be accountable bears more heavily on those engaged in talk radio – there are fewer problems associated with playing a four-minute record than there are with conducting a four-minute live interview. Where talk does dominate a frequency, programme staff can call upon a support structure offering a wealth of printed and spoken advice, both on and away from the station premises.

All broadcasters work within a framework in which different and distinct bodies exist to whom media organisations are accountable in different ways. These bodies come under the broad headings of legislative, regulatory and responsive.

Legislative

Parliament drafts and implements laws determining the regulatory systems of broadcasting, how it is financed, the basis on which broadcasting organisations are themselves constituted, roles and responsibilities of statutory bodies overseeing broadcast practice, and specific constraints imposed by criminal and civil law on output ranging from defamatory material to the voices of members of proscribed organisations.

The extent to which the practices of radio broadcasting are shaped and determined by legislation imposed by parliament reflects wider issues about the type of society in which broadcast texts are circulated. Complex and specific legislation on what radio can and cannot broadcast would suggest government concern that radio is unable to make its own judgements on what should be broadcast without reference to an external guiding framework and that listeners' choices of what they want to hear should also be controlled.

The notion of deregulated radio seems to move away from this 'nanny knows best' model. The circumstances in which British independent radio has been given the 'freedom' to expand through deregulation reflected the emergent political philosophy of the late 1980s in which broadcast services are viewed as commodities and audiences as consumers. Within this model, programme makers' choices of what to broadcast are driven by the market and the existence of a sufficient demand for such choices to be viable. The reliance on market forces to function as the sole regulatory mechanism on broadcast practice is tempered by other social priorities and concerns also reflected by legislation. Thus there are legal mechanisms to ensure that broadcast material does not work against the interests of justice, unfairly represent a person or organisation, jeopardise national security, offend people's sense of decency, and so on, notwithstanding the potential existence of markets for such material.

The following is a summary of the main areas of law that impinge on the day-to-day routines of making radio programmes.

Defamation

This calls on the broadcaster's judgement whenever she passes comment on air about another person. The law does not provide a comprehensive definition of a defamatory statement, but the Broadcasting Act 1990 does specify that any such statement broadcast on radio or television is treated as libel. Guidelines on what constitutes a defamatory statement are: it unjustifiably exposes a person to public hatred or ridicule, causes a person to be shunned or avoided, lowers public estimation of a person, and/or disparages the business or professional capacity of a person (Greenwood and Welsh 1992: 120).

Reporting restrictions and contempt of court

Restrictions on the reporting of court cases are prescribed by law or ordered by judges of specific cases. Reporting restrictions may be imposed to prevent media coverage from adversely influencing the outcome of the cases; hence the Magistrates' Courts Act 1980 stipulates that media reports of preliminary hearings or committal proceedings in magistrates' courts are restricted to specified points of information – for example, names of people involved, bail arrangements, whether legal aid was granted – unless the defendant applies to have restrictions lifted or the court decides against committing the defendants for trial (Greenwood and Welsh 1992: 29–30). Restrictions are also designed to protect the identity of innocent parties involved in reported cases, such as victims of sexual attack, rape or attempted rape (Sexual Offences [Amendment] Acts 1976 and 1992), or to prevent the identification of juveniles (i.e. under eighteen years of age) accused or convicted of offences (Criminal Justice Act 1991). The identification of children involved in family proceedings is protected by the Children Act 1989.

Media organisations could be regarded as being in contempt of court if their reporting were likely to prejudice or give rise to serious impediment to the outcome of a pending or current court case. A radio station need not necessarily broadcast an item that could influence a jury to be in contempt – it would be enough for a reporter to attempt to obtain inside information on the jury's deliberations (Contempt of Court Act 1981).

Broadcasting voices of members of certain organisations

Since October 1988, British television and radio stations have been banned from broadcasting the voices of members of organisations such as Sinn Fein, the IRA, INLA and the UDA in circumstances where their words may be construed as supporting or encouraging support for any of these organisations. A reporter may record an interview, edit out the responses and replace them with the voice of an actor giving the same responses word for word.

Official Secrets

Section 2 of the original Official Secrets Act 1911 was replaced by the Official Secrets Act 1989. This dealt with earlier criticism of Section 2, that it could be applied to the disclosure of any trivial information obtained by a reporter from a crown servant, although the circumstances in which the receipt and reporting of various categories of information are in contravention of the new Act are very complex. Broadly, the 1989 Act is designed to prevent the publication or broadcasting of information that is regarded as a state secret, or where the act of publishing or broadcasting is in breach of official trust.

D-Notices

Radio newsrooms also hold copies of D-Notices which give guidance on how certain types of information related to national security should be (or not be) reported. There are currently eight D-Notices in operation covering topics ranging from defence plans and equipment to civil defence, cyphers and communication systems. Their status is advisory rather than legal. They are issued not by the Government but by the Defence Press and Broadcasting Committee which is made up of representatives of Government ministries (Defence, Home Office, Foreign Office) and the press and broadcast media.

Obscenity

It is possible for the Director of Public Prosecutions to agree to take action against a station for broadcasting material that may be considered obscene (Broadcasting Act 1990) or likely to incite racial hatred (Public Order Act 1986). Questions of what constitutes obscenity have formed the basis of some celebrated cases and illustrate the difficulties that a programme maker faces in judging whether an item broadcast at a particular point in time is acceptable within the terms of a developing and ever-changing cultural climate – and whether a member of the audience would make the decision to attempt to instigate a prosecution. The notion of inciting racial hatred may appear to be more absolute than the arguably personal judgement of what constitutes obscenity but still rests on a view of how a broadcast item may be reasonably interpreted. Similarly, blasphemy and sedition may also form the basis of prosecution, although judgement on these matters relates not to the content of the broadcast item but to whether it would create a breach of the peace through the manner in which that content is presented.

Election coverage

In the interests of fair and equal representation of candidates in elections, broadcasts in which candidates are involved or represented are governed by the Representation of the People Act 1983 (see p. 218).

The legal framework in which programme makers operate on a day-to-day basis provides a constant set of questions that beg to be answered throughout the preparation and presentation of broadcasts. From their point of view, these questions are motivated partly by a professional sense of self-preservation – can we be sued for this? Would people be justified in complaining? Are we unwittingly leading the station into a jungle of litigation? – and partly by a sense of responsibility.

Listeners and programme makers for the most part share and understand such principles as fairness and privacy which underpin many of the laws affecting broadcasts. Most listeners would accept, for example, that the identity of a rape victim should be protected. Consequently, skilled broadcasters can still communicate the sense and significance of a story of this nature without giving the impression that they are constrained. The station demonstrates its responsibility and accountability through the way in which it operates within the legal framework. The law need not be a straitjacket.

This is not to suggest that the law is unproblematic for broadcasters. Not only is there a complex and ever-increasing body of statutory knowledge that programme makers need to have, but some of it is highly contentious. Many would argue, for example, that the Home Secretary's ban on the broadcasting of voices of members of proscribed organisations runs contrary to the democratic principle of free speech.

Regulatory

The legislative framework in which broadcast organisations operate also establishes mechanisms which enable members of the public to take action other than going to court if they have complaints or grievances about programmes. These are the organisations empowered by parliament to take up and adjudicate on such complaints:

The Broadcasting Complaints Commission

An independent statutory body established in 1981, the BCC considers complaints by people who feel that they have suffered from unfair or unjust treatment in broadcast output or from unwarranted infringement of privacy by broadcasters obtaining material for programmes. The Commission's adjudication is normally published in the appropriate listings magazine (*Radio Times* or *TV Times*) and broadcast on the station at a similar time to the programme which was subject to the initial complaint. There are no sanctions requiring broadcasters to apologise, to broadcast a correction or pay compensation. Complainants wishing to sue have to take legal proceedings.

The Broadcasting Standards Council

Established in 1989, the BSC became a statutory organisation as a result of the Broadcasting Act 1990. The Council monitors radio and television programmes and researches public attitudes to representations of violence, sexual conduct, bad language, stereotyping, tasteless coverage of disasters or other issues that may be considered offensive or contrary to notions of decency in any aspect of broadcast output, including commercials. It also researches the effects of such broadcasts on the public, deals with complaints by members of the public or issues its own complaints where it feels particular broadcasts warrant them. The BSC can only act on complaints subsequent to the broadcast – it cannot preview recorded material and restrict the circumstances in which it may be transmitted, along the lines of the British Board of Film Censors. If it considers a complaint to be justified, the BSC may require the broadcaster to publish, or even broadcast its findings.

The Radio Authority

The Authority is empowered by the 1990 Act to license and oversee all local and national independent radio operations (see p. 9). It publishes codes to advise independent radio licence holders of their obligations under the law related to a range of issues. *Programme Code 1* (Radio Authority 1992) deals with radio news broadcasts, the coverage of political and industrial controversy, and coverage related to election campaigns and current public policy. This states the requirements of current legislation on such coverage – in particular the Broadcasting Act 1990 and the Representation of the People Act 1983 – and how this affects a wide range of programming practices including discussion programmes, phone-ins, interviews, editing of interviews, fiction, use of archive material and the representation of politicians on programmes.

Programme Code 2 (Radio Authority 1993d) specifies the requirements of the 1990 Act related to a wide range of issues including the portrayal of violence and sex, offence to good taste and decency, accuracy in news and advice programmes, privacy, coverage of crime and anti-social behaviour, religious programming, charity appeals and representations of royalty. The Authority also issues a code on advertising standards and programme sponsorship as required by the 1990 Act (Radio Authority 1993e).

The Radio Authority investigates public complaints on any aspect of independent radio output and is empowered to apply a wide range of sanctions if it concludes the complaint is justified – request a broadcast apology or correction, impose a fine or even shorten or revoke a licence to broadcast.

Responsive

In addition to the mechanisms so far covered, output is subject to reaction from formal and informal bodies. These may be quite specific in nature with clear channels through which they may communicate their responses to a station's performance – for example, shareholders and investors in an independent broadcasting group or non-statutory groups organised independently of broadcasting organisations such as the National Viewers and Listeners Association. Such bodies may constitute, in a general sense, the listeners; for BBC radio – the licence fee payers; for independent radio – the advertisers; for all radio – the market.

Members of the public with complaints or concerns on output may contact the broadcasting organisation itself, either by writing to the senior manager of the station, regional management, the managing director of an independent broadcasting group or the Board of Governors for the BBC, or by writing to a feedback channel made available by the broadcasting organisation itself – a programme that invites audience views on any issue ranging from allocation of wavelengths to content of specific programmes. Grievances about broadcast items, schedules or general comment on radio stations are sometimes expressed publicly through other media – for example, letters to a newspaper.

For BBC radio and television, a further option sometimes available is for the public to challenge the policies of the Corporation or complain about specific programmes at one of a series of public meetings organised across the country by the BBC itself. Radio station management may deal with complaints from listeners as and when they arise but attempt to measure overall response to output through an appointed advisory council – a cross-section of listeners who meet regularly and discuss the performance of individual BBC radio stations.

Within radio stations themselves, the organisational pattern of production staff is usually one of individual programme teams operating within a line management structure. This provides two internal mechanisms for programme makers to ensure that they are consistently working within the guidelines and style policy of that station which in turn is ultimately geared to providing an optimum service to its listeners. The programme team itself – even if this consists of just a presenter and assistant – reviews and evaluates its own output after every broadcast with the outcome of this process reported back to the line manager. If the programme is daily, so is the evaluation. Senior programme makers and members of management meet on a regular basis to discuss the station's overall output, review recent promotions, weigh up the implications of the latest audience statistics and agree on strategies that will drive the output forwards continuously to attract, engage and relate to audiences.

This ongoing process of internal evaluation is formally built into the station's routine. Within independent radio, the process works at all levels from the programme team to the board of directors for the station or group of companies. For BBC radio, there is a formal structure that connects the programme maker through all levels of the Corporation up to the Board of Governors. Local radio staff can refer to internally published documents and *The Producers' Guidelines* (1993),[2] which provide advice on the treatment of stories and issues. If need be, they can make use of the BBC's referral system which can instantly supply guidance on a problematic programme decision.

Output by its nature appears to be a spontaneous and ephemeral product, but its impact on listeners' lives and the relationship that it cements between station and audience is real and constant. The evaluation process is not confined to the presenter and producer but involves all team members who have a stake in the programme – researchers, reporters and assistants answering the telephones. Similarly, all programme teams have an interest in the total output of a station and can make worthwhile contributions in the ongoing review process. Not only is it important for the station team to talk about the output, they should do so in a structured and methodical way to ensure a useful and meaningful appraisal of their product. Thus three basic rules of feedback are applied: (a) make the obvious obvious, (b) make the obvious dubious, and (c) make the hidden obvious.

Making the obvious obvious means, quite simply, if an item works – a feature, a link, a format – say so. The technique can be used again. Other production teams in the station can try it out. A good idea could be wasted unless it is given recognition. Similarly, programme makers should not be squeamish about saying if a production idea is not working.

In making the obvious dubious, programme makers identify and challenge assumptions behind production ideas that may be in need of exposing to a critical light. The questions that this evaluation calls for are: why is this type of story always treated in this way? why do we always bring in this guest whenever that situation occurs? why do we always run this competition at this time? and why do we always play this jingle for that competition? The priority here is to prevent output from becoming stale or static from producing today's programmes according to yesterday's rationale. In order to engage and challenge the listener, the station constantly seeks areas of output that can be pushed a little further onwards.

Self-evaluation becomes self-analysis through making the hidden obvious. Behind the specific moments of broadcasting lies a continuously developing context of events, attitudes and values which, if tapped at the right source, can provide a wealth of ideas for programme content and approach relating directly with listeners' life experiences and attitudes. Thus part of the 'hidden' that can be made obvious is to be found in listeners' own responses to programming indicated, for example, by their comments and priorities in phone-ins. Or it can be apparent in analysis of trends occurring in news stories carried by the station itself or other media addressing that audience, or in the constant flow of news releases and information received by the station. Examples of issues that may become apparent through this analysis – and therefore should be reflected in output – include changing family structures and values, concerns that society is becoming more violent (nationally and locally), increased fears of unemployment or hopes of greater prosperity within the editorial area, increased health consciousness – the list goes on.

This form of evaluation has consequences not only for station output but also for the way in which the station as an organisation is perceived within its listening community. The danger exists in both national and local radio that those individuals engrossed in the professional working environment, making programmes according to their own production-orientated values, lose touch with their audience. It is easy for a presenter in the closeted environment of the studio to become isolated from the 'real world'. The gleaming technology, the red on-air light and the flashing lights of the telephone lines can dazzle the inexperienced presenter and prevent her from 'seeing' the listeners to whom she is accountable. The problem is often exacerbated in local radio where staff turnover can be high, with broadcasters using it as a stepping stone for their career development rather than a chance to relate to a community of which they feel part and to which they feel a personal commitment.

Reaching those parts of the audience . . .

Recognition by all members of the team that the station is accountable to its listeners is encouraged through its style of management and internal organisation. Stations build on their relationship with audiences through a holistic approach – their programmes, their publicity and their point of contact with the public. Even the voice answering the telephone has an impact on this relationship. It can work against the interests of the station for the least experienced members of the team – student helpers for example – to take calls without some formal telephone training. Similarly, details such as the reception area of station buildings, the condition of radio cars and of the studios themselves can provide an indication of how a station regards its public and values their contribution.

An indication of the extent to which stations are relating to their audience is gained through measurements provided by RAJAR[3] of audience weekly *reach* and audience *share*. Weekly reach is the number who listen to a station for at least five minutes in the course of an average week and is expressed either in thousands or as a percentage of the total adult population of an area (i.e. those aged 15 and over). The share is the total listening time for each radio station (i.e. the number of listeners multiplied by the number of hours they are tuned in to the station), expressed as a percentage of total listening time to all services in the area. Knowledge of the reach provides an indication of people's awareness and use of the station in the area, while the share indicates the station's competitiveness in that area.

RAJAR also provides a breakdown of reach and share for male and female listeners and within different age ranges and social classes. A further breakdown is given of audience figures in half-hour segments throughout the day, enabling station management to fine tune output and identify its least successful segments.

For independent stations, the need to relate successfully to audiences and to demonstrate a responsiveness to them is clearly driven by the need to attract advertisers. For the BBC, all aspects of its service are accountable to licence fee payers as 'customers' and to the public generally within the Corporation's public service remit. Audience figures provide the BBC with a scientific measure of the extent to which it is fulfilling its role as an integral part of public life, by *reaching* as many listeners as possible (hence, justifying the notion of a universal licence fee) as well as providing a quality and relevance of programming needed to produce a significant *share* of total listening activity.

For all stations, knowledge of reach and share provides a relative rather than absolute indication of their capacity to connect with listeners. Rather like the constantly moving needle on the volume meter, the figures indicate that people are listening but can offer little to characterise the nature of the radio experience that touches each listener individually. Instead the figures are interpreted. Assumptions are made, for example that a local radio station achieving a high reach *and* share is successful in its local branding and an accepted part of listeners' community experience, while a station that achieves a high reach but low share is listened to more selectively for specific programmed items rather than constituting background sound and companionship for a large number of listeners throughout the day.

Responsibility and trust

It is essential that broadcasters maintain an awareness of three areas of accountability: the legal responsibilities which affect their practice; the wider ethical issues which have a bearing on decisions about what to broadcast and how topics should be treated; and the ways in which the station relates to listeners on a day-to-day basis. The expansion of localised radio services under deregulation has highlighted a need for a sophisticated and workable mechanism to oversee broadcasting practice and to monitor output to the extent that laws governing the content of programmes are workable and that listeners do have a voice if they have cause for concern. Such a mechanism is based to a large extent on notions of broadcasters' self-regulation and professionalism. While any listener could report a station or instigate legal proceedings, it is the responsibility of – and in the interests of – broadcasting organisations to demonstrate their own accountability. Radio stations that are demonstrably capable of self-regulation – i.e. that do not face prosecutions – serve their own long-term interests. They maintain and reinforce a cultural climate in which broadcasters are treated as responsible, professional and serving the best interests of their audience by precluding any need for state intervention or control.

In professional terms, recognition by individual broadcasters of this responsibility arguably leads to 'better' radio. The need to check sources, to take care with phraseology and means of representing people and issues and to show sensitivity to likely listener responses and reactions encourages the extra care and attention to detail that provide a professional gloss to a broadcast item. A consumer programme, for example, that did not show this level of care in its research and preparation would quickly lose credibility as an outlet for genuine causes for public concern. The vital trust needed between broadcaster and listener to maintain the programme's integrity would be lost.

Activities and points for discussion

1 As a local radio news team, you receive a tip-off that somebody is buying cars that have been 'written off' after being involved in traffic accidents, performing inappropriate repairs, arranging for them to be given MOT certificates by an unscrupulous colleague working in a local garage and selling them privately to unsuspecting people. Several buyers have told you their cars have a twelve-month MOT but are unsafe to drive. As the cars are advertised in the classified section of the press for private sales, the seller may argue that he is not responsible for the condition of the vehicles under the Sale of Goods Act 1979. However, if it can be proved that he is in trade (and not disclosing this in the advertisements), he would be responsible for this and may also be prosecuted under the Fair Trading Act 1973. Based on the information you have, discuss whether the story should be covered and, if so, in what way. What action should you take as responsible broadcasters in preparing the coverage? What equipment would you use to record material for the programme and how would you use it?

2 It has been a bad day at the local radio station. In the course of five hours, the station has received as many complaints:

(a) A regular listener has telephoned the station manager to criticise the station's decision to axe a weekly half-hour programme on brass band music: 'It's bad enough that you only gave thirty minutes to something that's very popular round here. To get rid of it completely is a total insult as far as I'm concerned!'
(b) A sports teacher and member of a women's rugby football team has called into the station reception to comment on a recent bulletin report of the team's victory in a regional competition: 'I was just passing and thought I'd leave a message. I wasn't very happy about the report. I thought it was a bit childish and patronising to women playing rugby. No, I don't want to see the reporter – just ask him to be a bit less irresponsible in future.'
(c) A prominent local councillor has telephoned a senior member of the news team: 'I understand that you broadcast an interview last week with a local businessman about car parking and that he totally misrepresented my views on this issue. No, I didn't hear the broadcast. Somebody told me about it. It was a feature on your lunchtime programme last Wednesday.'
(d) The station manager has received a letter from a listener: 'I enjoy listening to your station but why do you have to read the news so quickly? I listen to local radio because I like to know what's happen-

244

ing in the area, but your newsreaders always seem to be in a hurry to make way for the next record. There's so much crammed into the news bulletins that it's hard to take it all in.'

(e) A letter has appeared in that day's edition of the local newspaper in which a war veteran criticises the station for not mentioning the anniversary of a significant allied bombing raid. 'Many of our young pilots didn't make it back that night. Some of them came from this area. They paid the ultimate sacrifice for our freedom. The least we can do is respect their memory.'

As members of the station team, you are conducting your weekly programme review meeting and considering how you should deal with each complaint. It is the policy of your station to offer at least a written reply to each complainant – how would you phrase the letters? Also, what other action would you take, if any, for each complaint?

3 Visit your local radio stations. The aim of your visits is to discover how closely each station relates to the community it serves. If possible, attend a station open day. Determine in advance a set of criteria against which you can measure each station's performance. For example, what information is available about each station in its visitors' reception area? Does the station publish a complaints procedure? What impression do you gain of each station's attitude to public enquiries and its listeners overall? Base your observations on evidence gained from reading station publicity and talking to members of the staff.

9 A speculative postscript

IF we were starting to write this book in ten years' time, much of the detail would quite probably be different. We would cite new, as yet unheard-of programmes to illustrate particular points on production technique. We would be referring to the output of stations not yet on the air, or the work of key broadcasters some of whom are currently in the middle of their studies of communications and media. We would probably be placing much greater emphasis on the use of solid-state circuitry in the newsroom and studio. 'Tools of broadcasting' such as reel-to-reel portable and studio tape recorders would be referred to (possibly) as museum pieces while our discussion on the studio itself would concentrate on the transfer and organisation of data on computer files as a basis for digital editing techniques with perhaps the touch of a key or a VDU screen rather than a fader to open up an audio circuit.

Hopefully – although we may be optimistic on this point – our discussion on radio in the curriculum would trace the development of well-funded research on radio's prominent position as a medium and the potential of radio text to relate, construct and feed off the living cultural experience of listeners more intimately and profoundly than any other mass communicated text. It would consider the findings of research related to listeners' choices and perspectives in applying RDS technology to construct their own programmes, their radios automatically searching the airwaves for the piece of music or the package that most closely relates to their priorities, lifestyles and propensities to consume specific types of audio product.

Such research would not only be of interest to communication and cultural studies theorists but would also become increasingly recognised within the broadcasting industry as a means of establishing a comprehensive understanding of the very fabric of listeners' life experience and the part that radio plays in providing structure and meaning to that experience. Reach and share figures offer a quantitive measurement of listening patterns but qualitative and interpretative analysis of how people relate to radio is needed to enable programme makers to build on radio's potential as a creative, living and responsive medium. There is scope for more focused research on how listeners interact with radio – for example, the prevalence and use of pre-set tuners or motivations for channel-hopping and planning of personal listening schedules – and on radio's role in the lives and lifestyles of different audience groups – as suggested, for example, by the number of radios in a household, the listening choices of different members of that household and whose choices take priority.

It is harder to predict what the significance of other themes and features of this book will be at the dawn of the twenty-first century. Not only are the structures of potential audiences evolving and opening up opportunities for creating new niches, but also behaviour patterns within society are changing. The growth in commercial activities on Sundays is one illustration of how new social and economic routines could have an increasingly dramatic effect on both the listeners' expectations of access to radio output and the style and tone of its content. Changes in working patterns generally, with more home-working and 'telecommuting', might allow greater choice for listeners' management of their own time and ability to organise work and leisure (and listening) routines more flexibly.

Social and cultural changes affecting the audience are matched by changes within the broadcasting industry. Over the last decade, both BBC and independent radio have undergone the considerable turmoil of reorganisation. Broadcasters could be forgiven for wondering if things will settle down to a 'new order' or whether the drive to restructure is to become a permanent aspect of the professional experience of making radio programmes. ILR has become more niche-orientated since deregulation and its prospects for growth reflect current priorities for increased consumer choice. INR has become a reality. The BBC has acquired a stronger consciousness of the internal market with 'Producer Choice' providing a more explicit formula for generating cost-effective programmes. It has made a commitment to speech-based and journalistically-led local radio. All of these changes are in the context of the inevitable uncertainties of the period leading up to Charter renewal.

The theme that we believe is most likely to remain central to our hypothetical future volume would be the notion of the radio experience. We introduced the concept here to emphasise radio's capacity to make a unique connection with listeners' perspectives of reality, using its own terms of reference and means of representation rather than borrowing from those of television and having to 'make up' for the lack of pictures. It provides a consistent basis for an understanding of radio's development both as a commodity and as a means of constructing a community of listeners, simultaneously driving and reflecting their participation in a culture of information, beliefs, values and consumption. While this development may be measured in terms of new forms of broadcasting technology and new systems of regulation, the core to the radio experience remains the immediate moment of interpersonal communication.

Advances in radio technology, developments in the management and organisation of the radio industry, applications of more sophisticated techniques in research and characterisation of niche audience profiles – all of these facets of radio as an industry call on specialist areas of knowledge and expertise, competences and skills that were not envisaged when the first strains of a distant human voice were identifiable through a crystal set. Through progress in these areas, the 'product' of radio is improved and its commodity value is enhanced. The presenter is able to say just the right thing and capture the most appropriate mood of a well-defined audience, tuned in on digital stereo sound systems that reproduce 'better than real' sound quality.

However, by focusing on the techniques of production and presentation and on the rationales of organisation within a radio station, one could believe that the business of learning about radio – and of becoming proficient as a radio broadcaster – is one of 'managed' communication. The voice of the presenter is the voice of the organisation, peopled by specialists who share the same corporate vision and embark on a strategic form of communication. They do this through clearly formulated policies on style, voice technique and music–talk ratios. They operate within a strategic plan, their route mapped out by performance indicators through a landscape of pre-determined values concerning professionalism, national and local interest and public service.

All of this seems a far cry from the basic spontaneity of interpersonal communication between a presenter who likes talking to people and an audience that likes listening to the presenter. The technology, the management techniques and the entire policy making mechanism that determines the direction of national, local and community radio are ultimately geared to the success of this seemingly simple one-to-one relationship. Formulae and formats carry authority on paper through their pseudo-scientific reductionism and their promise of a predicted outcome in terms of listener response to output. But models on paper are static. They are dated as soon as the ink is dry. Even the pre-recorded CD voice of the 'presenter' providing the 'ideal' links between computer-selected music tracks on the radio jukebox strives to become more 'realistic' and in tune with the rhythms and cycles of cultural consciousness, but never quite makes it.

As a *living* medium, radio can be capricious, growing organically and randomly. Its essence is that moment of one-to-one live communication between two human beings. Its material is the human imagination. Its venue is the mind.

Glossary

∙∙∙

act., actuality
Sound of an event or voice of an interviewee, either recorded at, or transmitted live from, a location outside the studio. The term is not used for a voice piece (qv) made on location.

AM – see frequency.

analogue signal – see digital signal.

AOR
Adult-orientated rock.

Assistant Editor
Member of a BBC local radio management team; in 1993, AEs replaced News Editors and Programme Organisers.

automatic level control
1. Device on a Uher (ALC) that keeps an audio signal at or near a particular level. 2. Circuit on a studio desk designed to prevent output level (qv) from exceeding a pre-determined peak.

back anno, back announcement, B/A
Announcement given by a presenter following the end of a (usually recorded) item; the back anno of a taped report is scripted by the reporter who prepared the item.

backpack
Portable device used by a reporter on location for receiving cue (qv) and talkback (qv) and may also be used for transmitting the reporter's voice to a nearby receiver.

band, banding – see leader.

base
Location of the on-air studio (qv); the point where input from all audio sources is channelled via the desk (qv) before it is relayed to the transmitter.

BASYS – see computerised newsroom.

bed, music bed
Recording, usually on cart (qv) of sound, usually music, providing a background for specific information given out by a presenter, e.g. 'what's on' information, travel bulletin, weather news.

bi-media
Describes any operation, e.g. a broadcast, campaign, that involves radio and television. In the BBC, the term is also applied to specialist correspondents serving both television and radio. A bi-media correspondent could be attached to a regional television newsroom and a cluster of local radio stations.

branding
Process of establishing the identity of a product, service, or provider of that product or service, that makes it distinctive from its competitors and suggests how it relates to the identity of the market at which it is targeted.

Broadcasting Complaints Commission
Statutory body that adjudicates on complaints of unfair or unjust treatment in an item on radio or television, or of unwarranted infringement of privacy by a broadcasting organisation.

Broadcasting Standards Council
Statutory body concerned with standards in taste and decency and the portrayal of sex and violence on radio and television; monitors programmes and acts on listeners' and viewers' complaints.

bulk eraser
Device for quickly erasing the entire contents of audio tape – mainly used for 'wiping' (or 'cleaning') carts (qv) and reels of quarter-inch tape.

bulletin
Broadcast functioning as a report, providing latest information on a topic, usually news, weather or travel, and delivered essentially as a series of announcements; may include newsclips (qv) and voice pieces (qv) but the central voice for any bulletin is that of a person announcing information rather than commenting on that information.

cans
Headphones; while they usually carry the left and right hand channel of a stereo audio signal, they may also be used as 'split cans' where each headphone carries a signal from a different source, enabling the presenter to monitor two different sound sources simultaneously.

capacitor mike – see condenser mike.

cardioid mike
Microphone most responsive to sound directly in front and to either side.

cart, cartridge
Plastic case containing a continuous loop of audio tape; used mainly for jingles (qv), trails (qv) and commercials although they may be suitable for any form of recorded output, with high-quality carts used by some radio stations for music. To 'cart' or 'cart up' recorded material is to make copies on cart of material originally recorded in another format, e.g. on reel-to-reel tape.

catchline – see slug.

CD
Compact disc; solid storage medium (qv) providing high-quality sound, usually for recorded music.

cellphone, cellular phone
Mobile telephone.

check-set
Lightweight radio receiver and headphones used by a programme team on location to monitor output (qv).

ciné reel
Reel of audio tape that can be fitted directly to the spindle of a tape recorder without the use of a NAB centre (qv).

circuit
1. Any line leased to a radio station by a telephone company for carrying broadcast-quality sound, and cue and talkback (qv). 2. Specifically, shorthand term for the system of lines that link newsrooms of all BBC radio stations to GNS (qv).

classic gold – see gold.

clean feed – see cue.

clip – see newsclip.

commentary
Report broadcast live in which the speaker describes an event – e.g. a sports match, a procession – as it is happening.

community radio station
Radio station serving a localised concentration of listeners, e.g. students

on a campus, residents of a housing estate.

computerised newsroom

A radio station's means of receiving and processing news stories in the form of computer files; each file represents one story that may be accessed on the computer – or any of a number of computers located at different radio stations and linked together – and edited or rewritten to suit the style of any particular station. The shorthand term used in BBC regional broadcasting for a computerised newsroom is ENS (electronic news system). The system used by the BBC is called BASYS while many ILR stations use Newstar.

condenser mike, capacitor mike

Versatile microphone that requires a small electrical charge from a battery.

copy

Words of a broadcast item prepared in written form.

copy story

Item in a news bulletin consisting solely of an account given by the newsreader.

cps

Centimetres per second; a measurement of tape speed – see ips.

cue, cue sheet

1. Generally – signal to start speaking, playing a record, running a tape, etc.; also used as a verb – to cue is to give such a signal, or to set up a recording such that it plays back at its precise starting point as soon as the fader (qv) is opened. 2. Specifically – introduction given by a presenter to a recorded item; the cue to a taped report is scripted by the reporter who prepared the tape and is provided to the presenter on a cue sheet. 3. Sound of output (qv) as heard through the headphones or over the telephone by a contributor to the programme who is not located in the on-air studio (qv); also sometimes referred to as feed or clean feed. Clean feed includes everything but the sound of the contributor's own voice.

cut – see newsclip.

DAB

Digital audio broadcasting; means of transmission which will dramatically enhance reception quality of radio broadcasts and enable a larger number of frequencies to be run from one transmitter.

DAT

Digital audio tape; considerably smaller than a standard audio cassette, a DAT cassette carries high-quality recorded sound suitable for broadcast.

delay system

Electronic device that delays transmission on air of a live signal for a few seconds, giving the presenter time to press the obscenity or prof(anity) button if a programme guest makes a comment that is obscene, defamatory, etc. The listener instead hears something innocuous such as a jingle (qv). When the system is in operation, a programme is sometimes referred to as being 'in profanity' or 'in prof'.

desk

Control panel in a studio, operated or 'driven' by a presenter or technical operator (qv) during a broadcast or recording. Comprises faders (qv) which open up channels for audio sources; meters (qv) which indicate sound level (qv); and off-air communication systems referred to as talkback (qv). The desk is the principal means of bringing together all components of a programme – the presenter's voice, music, recorded items, voices of contributors at other locations, etc. – and selecting or mixing them for transmission.

digital recording, digital signal, digital sound, digital editing

The term digital refers to a high quality sound signal which is made up of discrete electronic units as opposed to an analogue signal which is a continuous waveform. Digital recordings can be stored compactly, for example on CD (qv) or DAT (qv). When stored on computer disk, the recording can be edited at a workstation.

double-heading

Co-presenting; use of two presenters' or newsreaders' voices to provide greater texture and variety to a programme or bulletin.

drive (as in drive a desk or programme) – see desk.

drive time

Time of day when a relatively high proportion of listeners are driving to or from work; for many radio stations, peak listening times.

dub

To make a copy of an audio recording, sometimes on another format, e.g. recording on cart (qv) material stored on quarter-inch audio tape.

duration (dur.)

Length of time to the nearest second of a programme item. The duration of a recorded item is provided on a label and where appropriate a cue sheet; the latter may also give the 'total duration' which also includes the time it takes to read the cue (qv) and back anno (qv).

dynamic mike
Hardwearing microphone that contains a coil attached to a diaphragm which moves within a magnetic field as the diaphragm vibrates.

editorial area
Geographical area served by a radio station, as reflected in that station's output (qv); need not be the same as the station's footprint which refers to the area that the station is technically capable of reaching.

embargo
Request, normally stated on a news release (qv) that an item of news is not to be made public until a specified date and time.

ENS – see computerised newsroom.

fader, pot
Control on a desk (qv) that opens up an audio channel and regulates the volume of that audio material. Each studio microphone, for example, is controlled by a separate fader and a speaker's voice is only clearly heard if that fader is fully open. Some audio sources – e.g. CD players, grams (qv) or studio tape recorders – are fader activated, i.e. they only start working when the appropriate fader is opened.

feature, item
Any prepared component of a radio programme other than a link (qv). An item that has been recorded may be referred to in general terms as a production piece.

feed – see cue.

feedback, howl, howlround
Effect produced when a signal from a microphone is transmitted through a nearby loudspeaker, is picked up again by the microphone and keeps going round in circles to produce a high-pitched 'howling' tone. Can be produced if a phone-in (qv) contributor has a radio tuned into the programme located near the telephone. When opened, microphone faders (qv) automatically cut off loudspeakers in the studio to prevent feedback.

flow programming – see strip programming.

FM – see frequency.

footprint – see editorial area.

format
1. Set of rules drawn up by the management of a radio station on the structure and presentation of that station's programmes; may specify the maximum duration of a link (qv), that every link must refer to one town in the station's editorial area (qv), or the frequency of timechecks and station idents (qv). A programme that is subject to such rules is said to be formatted. 2. Means of storing audio material, e.g. tape, vinyl (qv), CD (qv), DAT (qv).

frequency
Measurement of radio waves denoting the number of cycles per second, expressed in units called Hertz (Hz). A station's frequency denotes its position on the dial although this may be calibrated by wavelength. Frequency is converted to wavelength by dividing 300,000 by the frequency in kilohertz (kHz). Thus a frequency of 1152 kHz is 300,000 ÷ 1152 = 260 metres. Frequencies on the AM (amplitude modulation) waveband (including medium and long wave transmissions) are expressed as kHz and on the FM (frequency modulation) waveband as MHz (megahertz).

generic skills – see transferable skills.

gold, classic gold
Describes a station broadcasting mainly popular music and chart hits of the past, e.g. music first listened to by thirty- or forty-year-olds when they were in their teens.

GNS
General News Service; BBC's main newsroom which acts as collection and distribution point for stories to all its radio and television operations.

gram library
Location at radio station traditionally for storing vinyl (qv) records although used for storing music on all formats (qv).

grams
Turntables for playing vinyl (qv) records.

GTS, Greenwich Time Signal
Now no longer from Greenwich but generated by the BBC, refers to the six pips broadcast at the top-of-the-hour and providing the most accurate timecheck possible.

handling noise, mike rattle
Noises produced by some microphones when hand-held or moved about.

hot seat change

One presenter handing over control to another who is broadcasting a live programme from the same studio; literally the new presenter takes over the control seat at the desk (qv), usually while a recorded item is on air.

howl, howlround – see feedback.

IBA

Independent Broadcasting Authority; body that regulated all non-BBC broadcasting before the Broadcasting Act 1990 set the terms for a 'lighter touch' in regulation, an increase in listening choices and a mechanism for maintaining programme standards. All non-BBC radio is now regulated by the Radio Authority (qv).

ident, ID

Any means of informing or reminding listeners of the name of the station, programme or presenter; may take the form of an ident jingle (qv) or a simple statement by the presenter included in a link (qv).

ILR

Independent Local Radio; all non-BBC local radio, now regulated by the Radio Authority (qv). The first ILR stations began broadcasting in 1973.

incremental radio station

Independent station operating within the same editorial area (qv) as a major ILR operation but targeting specific audiences not addressed by that operation.

induction loop system

Means of transmitting a radio signal within a small, clearly defined area such as a campus or a single building. The signal is restricted to an area surrounded by a length of cable that carries and transmits that signal to radios tuned in on an appropriate AM frequency (qv).

INR

Independent National Radio. The first INR station (INR1) was Classic FM, followed by Virgin 1215. An independent national talk station, currently referred to as INR3, should be on the air by Spring 1995.

insert – see newsclip.

in-words, in-cue

The first few words of a recorded item.

ips

Inches per second – recording or playback speed of audio tape; speech is usually recorded at 7.5ips and music at 15ips.

ISDN
Integrated Services Digital Network; system of telephone lines capable
of carrying high-quality audio signals and may be used as cheaper
alternative to specially laid landlines (qv).

item – see feature.

jingle
Musical piece, usually only a few seconds long, providing an ident (qv)
or reinforcing a theme or idea. May specify the station's name, for
example, while indicating the 'mood' of the time of day, or may
identify an ongoing charity campaign. Jingles are recorded on cart (qv)
and are often used to signpost (qv) or punctuate a programme.

jukebox
Programmable device for storing CDs (qv) and lining up CD tracks for
broadcast, removing the need for a presenter to set up individual CDs
in the studio.

kHz – see frequency.

landline
Length of cable leased to a broadcasting organisation by a telephone
company, capable of carrying a high-quality signal, e.g. from a remote
studio (qv) to base (qv).

lavalier mike
Small microphone attached to lavalier (cord) that hangs round speaker's
neck.

lead body
Group of employing organisations which agrees on training standards
for NVQs/SVQs (qv). The lead body representing the interests of
broadcast, film and video industries is Skillset.

leader
Colour coded non-magnetic tape attached to beginning and end of audio
tape or used to 'band' or separate out recorded sections of audio tape.

level
Volume of recorded or broadcast sound as registered on a meter (qv).
To take or set a level is to adjust the volume of any audio source to
ensure consistency in a station's overall levels of output (qv).

link
Any device in a programme that takes the listener from one item (qv)
and onto the next; usually, but not always, spoken by a presenter.

lip mike
Version of ribbon mike (qv) favoured by sports commentators; held directly against the speaker's lips when in use.

log
1. Recording of all a station's output (qv), usually on slow-speed audio or video tape; stations are required to maintain an audio record of output for a minimum period. 2. Record of all music broadcast by a station, usually held on computer, for notification to PRS (qv) for royalties.

long wave – see frequency.

magazine format
Common programme structure for talk radio – a presenter-led show covering a range of different topics from serious to light-hearted and may include music items.

Managing Director
In radio terms, person responsible for day-to-day running of an ILR (qv) station, appointed by representives of the shareholders in that station.

Managing Editor
In radio terms, person responsible for day-to-day running of a BBC local radio station, appointed by the appropriate regional management.

media release – see news release.

medium wave – see frequency.

meter
Device for monitoring audio level (qv); a VU (volume unit) meter provides an approximate continuous reading while a PPM (peak programme meter) gives a steadier measurement emphasising whenever the signal peaks.

MHz – see frequency.

mike rattle, mike 'rack' – see handling noise.

mixing
Combining two or more audio sources, often when making up a package (qv) or production item (qv) – e.g. speech against background music.

music bed – see bed.

NAB reel
10.5 in. reel of audio tape which fits onto removable NAB centre – a block attached to the spindle of a studio tape recorder. NAB stands for the US National Association of Broadcasters.

name check
Giving out the name of a person or organisation in a broadcast; presenting technique that highlights radio's direct connection with people but also promotes awareness of businesses or voluntary organisations mentioned in listeners' messages, phone-ins (qv), etc.

NCA
1. News Contribution Area; a form of remote studio (qv) located in all BBC local radio stations, normally used for direct links to network (qv) programmes from Broadcasting House, but can be linked with any other BBC radio station. 2. Abbreviation for news and current affairs.

needletime
Total amount of airtime that a station may use to broadcast commercial records as agreed with the PRS (qv) and PPL (qv).

network
1. Radio station broadcasting nationally. 2. Large broadcasting operation on a regional or national level, characterised by links between individual radio stations capable of sharing source material and output (qv).

newsclip, clip, insert, cut
Brief extract from longer recording of an interview or speech related to a story in a news bulletin (qv).

News Editor
Person in charge of ILR (qv) newsroom. See also Assistant Editor.

news release, media release, press release
Document circulated to newsrooms by any organisation carrying a potential news story about itself; usually a means of obtaining publicity although news releases can also provide the organisation's official position on any current issue, or a public statement if the organisation is already the subject of a current news story.

Newstar – see computerised newsroom.

niche
Clearly defined section of the public which may constitute a targeted market for the producer of any goods or services. For radio, a group of listeners sharing a specific characteristic – e.g. interest, taste in music, membership of ethnic group – which is addressed by a programme or service.

NVQs
National Vocational Qualifications (SVQs in Scotland) awarded by National Council for Vocational Qualifications (NCVQ) to those who meet national standards in specified vocational skills. Standards for skills related to radio broadcasting are drawn up by Skillset (qv).

OB, outside broadcast
Programme, or substantial part of a programme, broadcast from a location other than a studio.

obscenity button – see delay system.

on-air studio
Main studio for live broadcasts and location of the desk (qv). In stations equipped with two main studios, when one is on air, the other may be used for recording programme items.

out-cue, out-point, out-words, out time
Indication of how or when a recorded item ends; expressed as the last few words spoken, a description of the final sound, and/or the precise time when the recording finishes. See also standard out-cue.

output
The product of a radio station; its sound as heard by the listener.

outside studio – see remote studio.

PA, programme assistant
BBC local radio position; responsible to a producer (qv) and undertaking basic presentation or reporting tasks.

package, wrap
Recorded item combining links (qv) by a reporter with interview material, actuality (qv) and sometimes sound effects or music; prepared for broadcast with cue sheet (qv).

phone-in
Part of a live broadcast in which listeners are invited to telephone the radio station and make a contribution to the programme. Usually, callers are selected to talk on air, for example to discuss an issue or take part in a competition.

pips – see GTS.

pirate radio
Unregulated and unlicensed radio broadcasting. A pirate radio station in 1990s Britain is one that has not been licensed to broadcast by the

Radio Authority and is thus operating illegally. The pirate radio stations of the 1960s proved to be the starting point for the careers of many successful and established presenters of later years.

playlist
List drawn up and regularly updated by radio stations of key records or music tracks to receive the most frequent airplay and hence reinforce the station's branding (qv).

pot – see fader.

pot chop
Premature ending of an item (qv) forced on the presenter by the pressure of time or an important breaking news story.

pot point
Optional out-point (qv) for a recorded item as indicated by its reporter.

PPL
Phonographic Performance Ltd; represents record companies, regulates and receives payment from radio stations for broadcasting material on records.

PPM – see meter.

pre-fade
Facility on desk (qv) that enables a presenter to listen to part of an audio source and adjust the level (qv), before the fader (qv) is opened to put it on air.

pre-set tuning
Facility that programmes a radio to receive the listener's choice of station at the touch of a button.

press release – see news release.

producer
In radio, person in charge of a production team responsible for a particular segment of output (qv) such as a programme, bulletin or social action (qv) campaign.

Producer Choice
BBC management strategy based on the concept of an 'internal market'. Each service required by producers to make a programme has a price. The producer may choose to 'buy' that service, or a similar one from outside the Corporation if that is seen as more appropriate. This

assumes that each operation within the BBC functions as an autonomous business unit.

production item, production piece – see feature.

prof, profanity – see delay.

Programme Controller
An ILR (qv) position denoting responsibility for the station's programming activities.

PRS
Performing Right Society; represents interests of musicians, singers, composers and publishers and acts as a clearing house for royalties from broadcast organisations for the use of their material, both live and on record.

PSA – see public service announcement.

public service
Function of broadcasting to provide output of practical or useful value to audiences in the form of news, travel reports, helplines, weather reports, advice, emergency information during bad weather, 'what's on' information, etc.

public service announcement, PSA
Brief item (qv) or link (qv) that performs a public service function. A PSA campaign may comprise a series of items on cart (qv) each providing information or advice on a specific topic or theme.

Q and A – see two way.

Radio Authority
Statutory body that licenses and regulates the Independent Radio industry and supports the development of an independent radio network (qv) in the UK to offer a wide listening choice.

Radio Data System, RDS
Means whereby a station transmits a signal that instructs programmed car radios automatically to tune to that station's frequency (qv). This facility may be selected at particular times – e.g. when the station is broadcasting a travel bulletin – or the radio may be programmed such that it is always tuned to whichever frequency of a station provides the strongest signal.

radio mike, wireless mike
Microphone that sends signal to nearby receiver via radio waves rather than cable.

reach
In radio terms, the number of people, aged 15 or over, who listen to a station for at least five minutes during an average week.

remote studio
Small studio linked to a main studio, usually by landline (qv) or ISDN (qv), normally self-operating and located at key population centres within the editorial area (qv); similar to but smaller than a satellite studio (qv).

ribbon mike
High-quality microphone suitable for studio work, usually on a fixed stand or suspended from the ceiling to pick up the voices of two or more speakers; not suitable for outdoors.

ROT, record of transmission
The practice of radio stations recording sections of their own output (qv) on quarter-inch tape for possible later use as newsclips (qv) or repeat programming.

royalties – see PRS.

RPA, radio production assistant
In BBC local radio, the RPA is responsible to a producer (qv) and carries out basic research, administrative and editing tasks.

running order
Planned order of items (qv) in a programme.

SAB – see social action broadcasting.

satellite studio
Similar to a remote studio (qv), i.e. linked to a main studio, usually by landline (qv) or ISDN (qv), but with playback equipment such as grams (qv), CD player, cart machines (qv) such that it can be used as a location to present a programme. May or may not be permanently staffed.

schedule
Planned sequence of programmes throughout a week.

segue, seg
A sequence of two or more tracks of music broadcast without interruption by a presenter.

sequence programming
A schedule (qv) comprising a number of distinct and discrete programmes, many recorded, and linked by a continuity announcer.

SFX
Indication on script of special or sound effects.

share
In radio terms, the total listening time achieved by a station expressed as a percentage of the total amount of time spent by people listening to all radio services covering the same transmission area (qv).

sig
Signature tune of a programme or presenter.

signposting – see trailing.

simulcasting
Practice of broadcasting the same output (qv) on different frequencies (qv).

Skillset – see lead body.

slash tape
Audio tape discarded through editing.

slug, catchline
Brief identification of a news story, e.g. 'Skateboarding duck'.

social action broadcasting, SAB
Any broadcast that is practical or useful to listeners, involves audience interaction and/or is backed up by documents or factsheets available from the radio station.

sound-bite
Brief but significant or memorable extract of audio.

special events station
Radio station granted a temporary licence to provide an exclusive service for people involved in a particular event such as a conference, or to run for a short period during a celebration, anniversary, campaign, etc.

splicing tape
Sticky tape use for holding together edited audio tape.

split cans – see cans.

splitting
Practice of one station to broadcast two different outputs simultaneously on different frequencies.

stab, sting
Very brief chord or burst of music on cart (qv) used by the presenter to punctuate output (qv).

standard out-cue, SOC
An agreed form of words for a reporter to use at the end of an item (qv), e.g. 'Mike Rack at the Heritage Centre for Muse AM'.

station ident – see ident.

storage medium
Material capable of holding audio information, such as magnetic tape, vinyl (qv), CD (qv) or computer disk.

strip programming, flow programming
Schedule (qv) comprising long, presenter-led programmes to maintain a continuous flow of music and/or speech.

SVQ – see NVQ.

talkback
Off-air communications system between members of a radio station or programme team, either in the building or on location.

technical operator
Person other than a presenter who drives a desk (qv) during a broadcast or recording.

Telecaster
Telephone switchboard capable of connecting any incoming or outgoing call to a studio desk (qv).

telephone balance unit, TBU
Device that matches signal of studio presenter with that of a speaker phoning in to the studio.

teletext
Printed or graphic data and images transmitted via the airwaves onto a television screen, as provided by CEEFAX and Teletext UK.

timeshift viewing, timeshift listening
Watching or listening to a broadcast at a time later than when it was actually transmitted, i.e. on video or audio tape.

topping and tailing
Attaching leader (qv) at the beginning and end of a length of audio tape containing a recorded item.

traffic
To timetable a week's broadcasts of commercials or trails (qv).

trail, trailer
Announcement on air to promote forthcoming programme or item (qv); may be recorded on cart (qv) or spoken live by a presenter.

trailing, signposting
Means of providing structure to a programme by announcing forthcoming items at key points.

transferable skills
Skills with a wide range of applications, e.g. communication, decision making, problem solving.

transmission area – see editorial area.

trim control
Control for adjusting level (qv) of an audio source.

two way, Q and A
Staged 'interview' of correspondent by presenter as a device for providing details and analysis of a news story.

Uher
A German make of portable reel-to-reel tape recorder.

variable tuner – see pre-set tuning.

VCR
Video cassette recorder.

VDU
Visual display unit; monitor or television screen.

vinyl
A collective term for any form of gramophone record – single, EP or LP.

visual talkback
Communications system enabling producer to transmit visual data to presenter via a keyboard linked to a screen in the studio.

voice piece, voice report, voicer
Scripted background and further detail to a news item provided by the voice of a correspondent or reporter in a news bulletin.

vox pop
'Voice of the people'; a clip (qv) solely comprising recorded responses by members of the public, who have been asked by a reporter about a given topic or issue.

VU meter – see meter.

waveband, wavelength – see frequency.

wildtrack
Recording of background noise or ambient sound which may be edited or mixed in (qv) to a recorded item to provide atmosphere.

wire service
News agency that transmits text of stories via lines linked to tele-printers or computers in newsrooms.

wireless mike – see radio mike.

wrap – see package.

zoo format
Programme production technique involving several voices in addition to that of the main presenter, suggesting a lively studio full of people and creating a busy and sometimes noisy effect.

Notes

....

Introduction

1 These are the five BBC services, Classic FM, Virgin 1215 and Atlantic 252 which broadcasts from Ireland but effectively competes with other British stations.

2 Scotland, Ulster, Wales and Cymru.

3 Independent Local Radio groups often 'split' wavelengths such that different station identities are given to FM and AM outputs.

4 Paul Donovan, 'LBC may be switching off – but radio is making waves', *The Times*, 8 September 1993, p. 21.

1 Learning about radio

1 H. Purdey, 'Training for broadcasters', *Radio*, Issue 1, October 1989, p. 30.

2 The Radio Authority sets out its role in *The Radio Authority Pocket Book* (1993a) and on a video, *The Radio Authority: What It Is, What It Does*. Both are available from the Radio Authority, Holbrook House, 14 Great Queen Street, London WC2B 5DG.

3 A stereo signal can be received from Virgin 1215 by linking a radio to the Sky satellite television system and selecting the appropriate audio channel.

AM (amplitude modulation) and FM (frequency modulation) refer to different methods of linking the output of a radio station to a carrier signal. On AM signals, it is the difference in height of each radio wave that re-creates the sound of the station's output. With FM, the radio waves are of the same height but it is the variation of distance between each wave that carries the sound. Medium or long wave stations use AM while those broadcasting on VHF use FM. The quality of AM signals has improved in recent years and can be used for stereo broadcasting. However, music-based radio output sounds better on the superior quality signal of FM. The 'behaviour' of medium wave signals is affected by climatic conditions and they tend to travel further in cooler air with no sunlight – hence they are more subject to interference from other AM stations at night.

The Radio Authority is critical of the fact that FM is available to four national BBC services (including the talk-based Radio 4) and only one independent station (Classic FM). They also argue that the move to more talk output on local BBC stations should lead to a redistribution of FM frequencies to the mainly music-based ILR stations (Radio Authority 1993c: 6).

4 The *Radio Authority Pocket Book* (1993a: 4) sets out its expectations for new local and national independent licences in the UK for 1994. The aim is for the new national service, currently referred to as INR3, to be on air by Spring 1995 (Radio Authority 1993b: 9).

5 Lewis and Booth (1989: 20) refer to a growth in the use of car radios in their summary of radio's historical development: 'by 1979 95 per cent of American cars were fitted with radio.'

6 Barnett 1993, Chapter 12 – Radio. Cited here with kind permission of the Henley Centre for Forecasting.

7 Barnett 1993, Chapter 9 – The Future of Television. Cited here with kind permission of the Henley Centre for Forecasting.

8 Desmond Bell 'On the box, on the course . . . and on the case', *The Times Higher Education Supplement*, 6 July 1990.

9 NCTBJ leaflet: 'A Future in Broadcast Journalism? Your Questions Answered.'

10 New standards in several areas, including sound, are being drawn up by Skillset at the time of writing. Copies of standards and further information on NVQs in broadcasting, film and video can be obtained from Skillset, 60 Charlotte Street, London W1 2AX.

11 These BBC training schemes are in operation at the time of writing. Details of training courses in broadcast news for BBC employees or external applicants are available from BBC News and Current Affairs Department, Room 128, Broadcasting House, London W1A 1AA.

12 Analytical studies of radio texts and practices do exist (e.g. Crisell 1986, 1994), but compared with studies of visual media these are few and far between.

13 The BBC has since transformed Radio 5 into a 'rolling' news and sports channel on medium wave – Radio 5 Live.

14 For technical advice and details on how to obtain a licence, contact the Information Office of the Radio Authority (see note 2).

15 Second and third year undergraduates on the Communication Studies course at the University of Central England, Birmingham, have taken part in a 'Radio Day' and a 'Radio Week' through this arrangement and precisely for the purpose of assessment. The FM service was publicised locally and could be heard clearly within areas of the city surrounding the campus. The station was called Heart FM in 1992 and Sonic FM in 1993. Output was broadcast for twelve hours a day and consisted mainly of music with the inclusion of regular news items, interviews, studio discussions and public service announcements.

16 O'Sullivan *et al.* offer a useful explanation of the concepts of paradigm and syntagm: 'The paradigmatic dimension of language is that of choice, the syntagmatic that of combination . . . the alphabet is a paradigm, and letters chosen from it may be combined to form written words (syntagms). A man's wardrobe holds a number of paradigms for instance – one each for shirts, ties, socks – which are combined into a syntagm (his dress for the day) . . . A paradigm, then, is a set of units which have an overall generic similarity' (1994: 216). Thus, in radio, the 'set of units' for the paradigm of the human voice comprises the individual presenters, announcers, interviewees, etc. whose voices are heard on the air; the 'set of units' for the paradigm of music comprises each record, CD or album track available to the station, etc. It is the combination of such paradigms that produces the syntagm of a radio broadcast.

2 Radio style

1 Murdock *et al.* 1986, Hartmann *et al.* 1987 and Murdock *et al.* 1992.

2 Neither the FM and AM franchises for LBC, which was Britain's first commercial radio station, have been renewed by the Radio Authority. These have been awarded to London News Radio (LNR), which takes over in October 1994 with a rolling news service on FM, and London Forum Radio, a talk and phone-in service, on AM. Ex-LBC Managing Director and now LNR Managing Director Peter Thornton describes the proposed FM service as "clock" radio with everything at a fixed point' while the AM service will be '"companionship" radio' (*Daily Telegraph*, 4 September 1993).

3 Classic FM came on air on 7 September 1992. Almost 4.5 million people were listening to its output during the second quarter of 1993, building up from 4.2 million at the end of 1992; 2.5 million people listened to Radio 3 during the final quarter of 1992, the figure rising to almost 2.74 million for the second quarter of 1993, although Radio 3's share of the total number of listeners remained the same at 1.3 per cent for both quarters (*Source*: RAJAR/RSL).

4 *Source*: RAJAR/RSL. The BBC's Media Correspondent Nick Higham points out that this is still lower than Classic FM and Atlantic 252 and comments 'One problem for all three networks is that their listeners tune in for much shorter periods every week – between five and 6.5 hours – than do listeners to established services. Compare Radio 1's 11 hours and independent local radio's 13.7' (Higham 1993: 4). These figures are for the second quarter of 1993.

5 CWR, GLR, GMR and WM refer respectively to Coventry and Warwickshire Radio, Greater London Radio, Greater Manchester Radio and (BBC Radio) West Midlands. BBC Radio Bedfordshire is now Three Counties Radio.

6 *Ariel*, 10 August 1993, p. 2.

7 In the final quarter of 1992, 16.5 million people listened to Radio 1 during an average week. Of these, 4.91 million were aged 25–34, a slightly higher figure than the 15–24 age group – 4.87 million. A significant 3.23 million aged 35–44 also tuned in while listeners aged 45 or more totalled 3.53 million.

Average half-hour audience figures for Radio 1 for the period 22 March–20 June 1993 indicate a 6pm weekday and 5pm Saturday watershed for listener age groups. Up to those times, numbers of 25–34-year-old listeners are consistently higher than 15–24-year-olds. After those times the situation reverses (*Source*: RAJAR/RSL).

8 The 1988 White Paper, *Broadcasting in the 90s – Competition, Choice, Quality* (Cm 517), sees the BBC as maintaining the position of 'the cornerstone of British broadcasting' (para.3.2) but states that the government 'looks forward to the eventual replacement of the licence fee' and – following the Peacock Committee's conclusion on financing the BBC – 'intends to encourage the progressive introduction of subscription' on BBC television, adding that 'Account will need to be taken in due course of the implications for financing BBC radio services' (para.3.10). In its comments on the 1992 Green Paper on *The Future of the BBC*, the Radio Authority highlights the risk of a Radio 1 type of commercial service driving down advertising rates to threaten the viability of other services (Radio Authority, 1993c: 28–40).

9 'Now for the Programmes' – transcript of John Birt's 1993 Fleming Memorial Lecture in *Television – The Journal of the Royal Television Society*, April/May 1993, v.30/2, pp. 8–13.

10 Andrew Culf, 'Musical chairs at Radio 1', *The Media Guardian*, 27 September 1993, p. 14.

11 *Ariel*, 28 September 1993, p. 3.

12 A comment in the Pilkington Report flies in the face of today's market-led rationale for media provision: 'if people do not know what they are missing, they cannot be said not to want it' (Pilkington 1962, para.811).

13 Abolition of BBC Regions was proposed in the BBC document *Broadcasting in the Seventies* (1969).

14 This coincided with the Conservative Government's decision to disband the initial Annan Committee on the Future of Broadcasting.

15 Some studies of local radio during its early years were critical that the concept of locality was promised but not adequately delivered. The Local Radio Workshop, which monitored London's two independent services, Capital and LBC, plus the BBC service, then called BBC Radio London, suggested that local listeners were not being as well informed as they might be. They argued that the BBC's 'implicit' promise to involve listeners more actively in their communities was not met in London because of competition from independent radio and cuts on the BBC's local radio budget. The same promise by ILR also had little credibility in the view of the LRW, as the provision of in-depth news was not a commercially viable proposition. (Local Radio Workshop 1983: 59–60).

16 In its response to the 1992 Green Paper *The Future of the BBC*, the Radio Authority argues that the 'public service tradition of Independent Radio lives on' and states that 'Though no longer

required to provide news and information about and support for local events, most stations do these things, partly, no doubt, out of enlightened self-interest . . . Independent Radio needs to provide social action programmes, accessibility, news and information to enable it to maximise its audience and thereby its advertising revenue. BBC services do the same to justify the licence fee' (Radio Authority 1993c: 3–4).

17 Ronald Neil quoted in *Ariel*, 26 January 1993, p. 8.

18 ibid.

19 ibid.

20 ibid.

21 ibid.

22 Barnard (1989: 79) refers to the IBA's call for 'flow programming' in ILR output and cities Bill MacDonald, Managing Director for Radio Hallam on his station's programming – 'like a tapestry which weaves in non-antagonistic but not bland music, news and information' – quoted in David Berry, 'Complementary rivals conflict – but only over survey figures', *Broadcast*, 21 June 1985.

23 BBC stations use a computer system called SABLE/PLG to catalogue and select music. SABLE (Studio Automated Barcoding Logging Equipment) maintains a record of music played on air for royalties payment. PLG (Playlist Guide) is the system for selecting music running orders for programmes. Information on music tracks held by the system includes 'start pace' and 'end pace' plus 'start density' and 'end density'. Density refers to the fullness of sound. A quiet, tinkly piano is entered as density 1; a 'headbanging' Bon Jovi sound is density 5. With this information in the system, it is possible to programme in limits to ensure a smooth musical flow without drastic jumps in style and tempo from one record to the next. Information on tracks also includes 'image'. This determines how frequently a track is chosen. Image A are the tracks to be selected most frequently. Images B and C may be novelty tracks or pieces of music that would lose impact or prove too tiresome if selected too frequently.

24 Recorded by Brass Incorporated and no longer commercially available.

3 Getting organised

1 Technically, 'radio' refers to signals transmitted in the form of electromagnetic waves. The sound to be transmitted is converted into an electrical current (audio current) which modulates (i.e. influences the shape of) the carrier wave generated by a transmitter at a fixed frequency, or number of cycles per second. A medium wave transmission may generate a carrier wave at a frequency of 1,359,000 cycles per second. This is expressed as 1359 kilocycles per second or 1359 kilohertz (kHz). The carrier wave, modulated by the audio current and referred to as RF (radio frequency), is radiated through the air in all directions by the transmitter. A receiver which is tuned in to the frequency picks up the signal and the carrier wave is filtered out, leaving the audio current. This is amplified and fed through a loudspeaker, converted back to sound acceptable to the human ear.

2   Sir William Haley, Director General of the BBC when the new regional structure of broadcasting was established in 1945, was a strong advocate of regional services as means of promoting creative broadcasting and healthy competition within the BBC, and of avoiding a solely London-orientated, metropolitan service. However, insufficient wavelengths were available to achieve the full potential of regional broadcasting – see Briggs 1979: 84–117.

3   Further frequencies up to 108 MHz will become available in 1996.

4   The sub-bands for FM are organised (with some exceptions) as follows: 87.6–88 MHz – short-term 'restricted services'; 88–94.6 MHz – BBC National and Regional Radio; 94.6–96.1 MHz – BBC Local Radio (and Radio 4 in places); 96.1–97.6 MHz – ILR; 97.6–99.8 MHz – BBC Radio 1; 99.8–102 MHz – Independent National Radio (Classic FM) and ILR; 102–103.5 MHz – ILR; 103.5–105 MHz – BBC Local Radio (Radio Authority 1993a: 5). The new 105–108 MHz range will be made available to ILR (Radio Authority 1993b: 16).

5   There are in fact two lines that come into the station: one carrying news and the other carrying other operational information. These lines are known as LDS1 and LDS2 (line distribution system).

6   See Chantler and Harris 1992: 66. BASYS was not originally designed for BBC local radio and was first used by ITN.

7   Vinyl is still played – specialist, novelty or limited edition recordings are regularly borrowed from the BBC's central record library and many of these are only available on vinyl. Also, BBC CWR often broadcasts from its West Orchards studio based in a shopping centre in Coventry and not linked to the station's jukebox system. Here, the presenter may play 7in. singles kept as duplicate copies of tracks held on CD in the jukebox.

8   Although one of the support studios is referred to as the phone-in area for historical reasons, both support areas are used in the same way during live broadcasts.

9   This point is illustrated by BBC CWR's decision to be the first BBC local radio station to install jukebox technology. The station went ahead with this, despite the cautious view that it could wait for another to take the first step and then learn from their difficulties. Now that the system is established and running successfully, the station's case is vindicated. As one senior member of staff told us, it is much more fun to learn from your own difficulties.

4 The tools of radio broadcasting

1 The classic textbook for describing radio equipment and techniques in using it has been *The Technique of Radio Production* by Robert McLeish. Although published in 1978, the book offers sound advice on dos and don'ts that are as relevant as ever, while much of the technology described is still in widespread use. A more succinct but nevertheless useful guide on ground rules for equipment usage is provided in Chapters 1 and 2 of *Guide to Independent Radio Journalism* by Linda Gage (1990), while the most up-to-date detailed text on equipment and techniques that is accessible to non-specialist readers is the second edition of *Broadcast Journalism: Techniques of Radio and TV News* by Andrew Boyd (1993).

2 On some tape recorders, one head is used for both record and playback.

3 For a step-by-step explanation of how to edit tape, see Boyd 1993: 224–30, or Chantler and Harris 1992: 58–60.

4 Best practice is never to load tape containing old splices onto a portable recording machine, in case one of the splices snags in the recording mechanism. Some stations have a policy on the minimum length of unspliced tape that can be reused. However, drives towards cost-effectiveness and tighter budgets put pressure on reporters to reuse old tape whenever possible.

5 One of the conditions that the Radio Authority makes when licensing independent stations is that the stations make a copy of all output and retain it for at least forty-two days. This enables the Radio Authority to investigate any complaints by listeners on issues of, say, taste and decency or fair practice in advertising.

6 The practice of 'croc-clipping' involved unscrewing the mouthpiece of a telephone handset and using crocodile clips to connect a tape recorder to the wires to feed audio directly to the newsroom (see Boyd 1993: 238–9). As most telephones today are fitted with removable plugs, it is now possible to connect tape recorders directly to telephone wall sockets with a coupling device.

7 As illustrated dramatically by Boyd in his description of how a live voice report from the scene of a train crash is incorporated into a mid-afternoon news bulletin (1993: 190–204).

8 The standard advice for checking audio levels for speech was to ask studio guests to relate what they had for breakfast. This gave them something to say and helped inexperienced guests acclimatise themselves to the strange experience of taking on radio – guests have been known to 'dry up' through nerves or self-consciousness. Today many professional broadcasters regard the 'what did you have for breakfast' line as adding to the artificiality of the situation and prefer to relax their guests by gently chatting to them whilst unobtrusively tweaking the pre-fade controls.

9 Stations establish peak levels that reflect their branding. For example, a station may stipulate slightly different levels for speech and music, either to give the presenters a 'stronger' voice or to emphasise the presence of the music.

10 Terminology varies slightly from station to station when it comes to describing recorded items on tape ready for broadcast. Short recordings used in news bulletins of somebody's response to an interview question or an extract from a public statement are referred to as newsclips, clips, cuts or inserts. These are recorded on carts which are 'fired' by the newsreader at appropriate points in the bulletin. Longer recorded reports which contain some actuality, such as an extract of an interview, plus narratives by the reporter are referred to as packages, wraps or featurettes. Chantler and Harris (1992: 147–8) indicate that 'package' is a BBC term while IR stations refer to 'wraps'. In some stations, longer and relatively complex reports are referred to as packages while shorter punchier ones are referred to as wraps.

11 The dynamic or moving coil microphone is best suited for unidirectional or cardioid pick-up patterns. It responds to noise through the vibration of a diaphragm which in turn moves a coil within a magnetic field to produce an electric signal or audio current. This signal is converted back to sound by the loudspeaker.

12 This is so-called because its diaphragm comprises a thin ribbon of aluminium foil. This produces audio current through its own vibration within the poles of a horseshoe magnet. It is also referred to as a velocity microphone because the diaphragm responds to the velocity of the sound that it picks up.

13 Omnidirectional mikes can also be dynamic – see note 11. While some types of field mike or remote mike are omnidirectional, others are designed to respond to a cardioid pick-up pattern.

14 These are technically referred to as capacitor or condenser mikes. They respond to the air movement of sound which vibrates a delicate film to vary the distance between that film and a backplate. Capacitor mikes need a power source; a small battery is fitted and needs checking periodically.

5 The voice of the station

1 The preferred BBC term is 'voice piece'. A term more widely used in independent radio is 'voicer' (Chantler and Harris 1992: 147).
2 Package formats are discussed in greater detail on pp. 166–70.
3 An example of a cue sheet is given on pp. 168–9.
4 Interview techniques are discussed in greater detail on pp. 156–65.
5 Fiske refers to the process of maintaining the authenticity of outside sources while presenting these sources within the terms of the dominant value system as 'clawback' (Fiske 1987: 289; see also

Fiske and Hartley 1978: 87).

6 If a broadcast is 'in profanity' or on 'delay', it is possible to prevent certain statements by studio or phone-in guests from getting on air. A delay system, sometimes referred to simply as 'prof', prevents live output from being fed to the transmitter for up to ten seconds; 'if anyone swears, libels someone, commits contempt, or whatever, the producer or presenter in the live studio can press the prof button' (sometimes referred to as the obscenity button), 'and a jingle will be played to air instead of the offending remark' (Gage 1990: 46).

7 cf. Boyd 1993: 56.

8 Both Chantler and Harris (1992: 30) and Boyd (1993: 62–4) exhort their readers to avoid clichés, providing many painful examples. Common to the lists of *bêtes noires* included in both texts are

> at this moment/point in time
> bid (as in attempt)
> boss
> chief
> got/get under way
> grim/painted a grim picture
> mercy dash
> probe
> rushed to hospital/to the scene
> up in arms

There are many, many more.

9 Professional opinions differ on how statements in radio reports should be attributed. Chantler and Harris advise would-be radio journalists:

> Never start your story with an unattributed statement. It could sound like the opinion of the radio station . . . For example, 'Most managers are mean. That's the finding of a new survey out today' becomes 'A new survey out today claims that most managers are mean'.
>
> *Chantler and Harris 1992: 33*

Nevertheless, this technique is sometimes used on BBC Radio 4 news programmes when introducing a new item to capture listeners' attention – stating something controversial, then qualifying it with an attribution. This illustrates that 'rules' for broadcasting technique need not be 'inscribed in stone' but often reflect specific house styles.

6 Production techniques

1 Hartley draws on structural semiotics and the writings of Ferdinand de Saussure (1974) and Jonathan Culler (1976) to discuss how news as a sign-system provides a representation of the world it reports, and indeed of itself as a concept referring to a particular form of information as opposed to, say, fiction, gossip or analysis (Hartley 1982: 11–37).

2 Chantler and Harris (1992: 147) identify 'two way' as a BBC term, and 'Q and A' as an IR term, although this is becoming more interchangeable as staff move from one work area to the other.

3 Boyd provides a set of detailed guidelines for good practice in interviewing on radio and television; researching the background of the story and the interviewee, sorting out arrangements for the interview itself, preparing the interviewee before going on air, phrasing the questions and winding up (1993: 87–101).

4 Sometimes referred to as 'tradio', these invite callers to advertise items for sale on air.

5 Gage (1990: 117–18) provides a checklist of considerations for whether a caller should be allowed on air: is the caller coherent? Is the point relevant? Is there sufficient time to deal with the point? And is the caller able to hang on until the presenter is ready? In phone-in discussions on sensitive or controversial topics, callers may also be asked to confirm that they are qualified to speak on a particular point, especially if they claim to represent an organisation or be experts with specific advice for listeners. Furthermore, judgement is needed on whether callers are genuine. Apart from spotting the made-up names (Mr L. Viss from Gracelands Road, Sally Mander from the local zoo), experienced producers can detect possible hoaxes when callers are asked to give a summary of what they want to say on air.

6 Listen, for example, to the difference between the newsreaders' and presenters' style of talking on Radio 4's *Today* and *PM* programmes. Note also that newsreaders do not normally conduct interviews or engage in extended dialogue with presenters.

7 Crisell describes one famous American radio production, the 1938 adaptation of H.G. Wells's *The War of the Worlds*, which confused the codes of radio fact and fiction with dramatic effect:

> The mock news bulletin with which it began announced an invasion by creatures from Mars and caused widespread panic. According to some accounts, over a quarter of the estimated six million listeners believed what they heard, and a number of those living near the supposed invasion site got into their cars and fled.
>
> *Crisell 1994: 206*

8 Lewis (1991: 15) cites this figure, given in a Radio Academy seminar by Richard Imison, Queen Elizabeth Hall, 24 March 1986 (op. cit., p. 29). Lewis draws further on this source to state that of the five hundred original plays broadcast each year, between seventy and eighty are by new writers.

7 The programme

1 In 1985/6, sport accounted for 1026 hours or 3.3 per cent of total output for BBC network radio. The figures for 1989/90 were 1195 hours (3.8 per cent). This was a similar proportion to drama (3.3 and 3.2 per cent respectively), whilst news accounted for 6.1 and 5.9 per cent during those periods. With the appearance of Radio 5 in 1990, sport increased its share of total output to 4.7 per cent (1632 hours) in 1990/1 and to 5 per cent (1944 hours) in 1991/2. Figures for drama were respectively 3 per cent and 2.9 per cent. Figures for news were respectively 7.1 per cent and 5.5 per cent (Policy Studies Institute 1993: 48).

2 Research conducted in 1993 by Coventry University student Judith Habib led to a report entitled 'Equal Opportunities for Women in Radio?', which included a range of views from women broadcasters on their roles and opportunities within the industry. Among the issues covered were the areas deemed appropriate for female and male presenters to address, and the roles that they occupy within the structure of a radio text. It is not always a question of whether women's voices are heard in sports programming, rather the priority and status given to women's voices on the radio generally.

3 It is sometimes the practice for cue sheet information prepared with packages to identify a 'pot point' – a precise point where the playback of the recording could be halted early if necessary without losing its overall meaning. This is identified to the nearest second and requires the presenter to close the fader abruptly rather than fade out slowly. Presenters may also identify a point in a piece of music where it can be slowly faded out before the end of the track – for example, the beginning of a long instrumental ending – or quickly faded before the singer launches into the next verse.

4 cf. Arthur Miller, 'A good newspaper, I suppose, is a nation talking to itself', *The Observer*, 26 November 1961.

5 Any BBC station proposing to set up an OB is required to complete a hazard assessment form for the location. All OB planning involves checking for permission to park vehicles, whether consultation is needed with the police on potential traffic obstructions and whether local authorities need to be consulted if the OB is located in a public space.

8 Accountability

1 The Advertising Standards Authority only deals with complaints about published as opposed to broadcast advertisements.

2 An internal BBC document which offers guidance on how various topics may be treated on all BBC radio and television programming.

3 Radio Joint Audience Research Limited, owned jointly by the AIRC (Association of Independent Radio Companies) and the BBC. The research itself is currently conducted on RAJAR's behalf by RSL (Research Services Ltd) and is based on a diary completed by a sample of listeners.

Bibliography

Baehr, H. and Ryan, M. (1984) *Shut Up and Listen! Women and Local Radio: A View from the Inside*, London: Comedia.

Barnard, S. (1989) *On the Radio: Music Radio in Britain*, Milton Keynes: Open University Press.

Barnett, S. (ed.) (1993) *Media Futures*, London: The Henley Centre for Forecasting.

BBC (1993) *The Producers' Guidelines*, second edition, London: British Broadcasting Corporation.

Bell, D. (1990) 'On the box, on the course . . . and on the case', *The Times Higher Education Supplement*, 6 July 1990.

Berry, D. (1985) 'Complementary rivals conflict – but only over survey figures', *Broadcast*, 21 June 1985.

Boyd, A. (1993) *Broadcast Journalism: Techniques of Radio and TV News*, second edition, Oxford: Focal Press.

Briggs, A. (1961) *The History of Broadcasting in the United Kingdom: Volume I – The Birth of Broadcasting*, Oxford: Oxford University Press.

Briggs, A. (1979) *The History of Broadcasting in the United Kingdom: Volume IV – Sound and Vision*, Oxford: Oxford University Press.

Broadcasting in the Seventies: The BBC's Plan for Network Radio and Non-metropolitan Broadcasting (1969), London: British Broadcasting Corporation.

Broadcasting in the 90s: Competition, Choice and Quality (1988), London: HMSO (Cm 517).

Brown, G. (1991) 'Enterprise learning: an introduction' in *Competence and Assessment*, 17 Sheffield: Training Enterprise and Education Directorate of the Employment Department.

Chantler, P. and Harris, S. (1992) *Local Radio Journalism*, Oxford: Focal Press.

Crisell, A. (1986) *Understanding Radio*, London: Methuen.

Crisell, A. (1994) *Understanding Radio*, second edition, London: Routledge.

Culf, A. (1993) 'Musical chairs at Radio 1', *The Media Guardian*, 27 September 1993, p. 14.

Donovan, P. (1993) 'LBC may be switching off – but radio is making waves', *The Times*, 8 September 1993, p. 21.

Extending Choice: The BBC's Role in the New Broadcasting Age (1992), London: British Broadcasting Corporation.

Fiske, J. (1987) *Television Culture*, London: Methuen.

Fiske, J. and Hartley, J. (1978) *Reading Television*, London: Methuen.

The Future of the BBC: A Consultation Document: (1992), London: HMSO (Cm 2098).

Gage, L. (1990) *Guide to Independent Radio Journalism*, London: Duckworth.

Goffman, E. (1980) 'The radio drama frame', in Corner, J. and Hawthorn, J. (eds) *Communication Studies*, London: Arnold.

Goffman, E. (1981) *Forms of Talk*, Oxford: Blackwell.

Greenwood, W. and Welsh, T. (1992) *McNae's Essential Law for Journalists*, twelfth edition, London: Butterworth.

Hartley, J. (1982) *Understanding News*, London: Methuen.

Hartmann, P., Murdock, G. and Gray, M. (1987) 'Family failing', *The Times Educational Supplement*, 19 June 1987.

Hartmann, P. (1992) 'New technologies, new possibilities: for whom?', in French, D. and Richards, M. (eds) *Anatomy of British Television*, Communication Studies Centre, Coventry University and Worcester College of Higher Education.

Higham, N. (1993) 'Virgin audience quick on the dial', *Ariel*, 10 August 1993, p. 4.

Hilliard, R.L. (1985) 'Writing', in Hilliard (ed.) *Radio Broadcasting: An Introduction to the Sound Medium*, New York: Longman.

Horstmann, R. (1991) *Writing for Radio*, second edition, London: Black.

Hutchby, I. (1991) 'The organization of talk on talk radio', in Scannell, P. (ed.) *Broadcast Talk*, London: Sage.

Kumar, K. (1977) 'Holding the middle ground: the BBC, the public and the professional broadcaster', in Curran, J., Gurevitch, M. and Woollacott, J. (eds) *Mass Communication and Society*, London: Arnold.

Lewis, P.M. (1991) 'Referable words in radio drama', in Scannell, P. (ed.) *Broadcast Talk*, London: Sage.

Lewis, P.M. and Booth, J. (1989) *The Invisible Medium: Public, Commercial and Community Radio*, Basingstoke: Macmillan.

Local Radio Workshop (1983) *Nothing Local about it: London's Local Radio*, London: Comedia.

McLeish, R. (1978) *The Technique of Radio Production*, London: Focal Press.

Murdock, G., Hartmann, P. and Gray, M. (1986) 'Home truths', *The Times Educational Supplement*, 7 March 1986.

Murdock, G., Hartmann, P. and Gray, M. (1992) 'Contextualising home computing: resources and practices', in Silverstone, R. and Hirsch, E. (eds) *Consuming Technologies: Media and Information in Domestic Spaces*, London: Routledge.

O'Sullivan, T., Hartley, J., Saunders, D., Montgomery, M. and Fiske, J. (1994) *Key Concepts in Communication and Cultural Studies*, second edition, London: Routledge.

Peacock (1986) *Report* of *the Committee on Financing the BBC* (Chairman: Professor Sir A. Peacock), London: HMSO (Cmnd 9824).

Pilkington (1962) *Report of the Committee on Broadcasting 1960*,

London: HMSO. (Cmnd 1753)

Policy Studies Institute (1993) *Cultural Trends*, Issue 17, Volume 5, No. 1.

Purdey, H. (1989) 'Training for broadcasters', *Radio*, Issue 1, October 1989, p. 30.

Radio Authority (1992) *Programme Code 1: News Programmes and Coverage of Matters of Political or Industrial Controversy or Relating to Current Public Policy*, September 1992.

Radio Authority (1993a) *The Radio Authority Pocket Book*, June 1993.

Radio Authority (1993b) *Annual Report and Financial Statements: For the Year Ended 31 December 1992*.

Radio Authority (1993c) *The Radio Authority's Comments on 'The Future of the BBC'*, April 1993.

Radio Authority (1993d) *Programme Code 2: Violence, Sex, Taste and Decency, Children and Young People, Appeals for Donations, Religion and Other Matters*, May 1993.

Radio Authority (1993e) *Radio Authority Code of Advertising Standards and Practice and Programme Sponsorship*, February 1993.

Radio Choices and Opportunities: A Consultative Document (1987), London: HMSO (Cm 92).

Smith, A. (1990) 'Introduction', in Mulgan, G. (ed.) *The Question of Quality*, London: BFI.

Index